Sādhan Samar:

Battles in a Sacred Quest

Devī Māhātmya: Glory of the Goddess

A spiritual Commentary on *Śri Śri Candī* or *Dūrgā Saptaśati* by

Brahmarṣi Satyadeva

Sādhan Samar:

Battles in a Sacred Quest

Devī Māhātmya: Glory of the Goddess

A Spiritual Commentary on *Śri Śri Caṇḍī* or *Dūrgā Saptaśati* by

Brahmarṣi Satyadeva

Volume Two

Unraveling the knot of *Viṣṇu*: Destruction of *Mahiṣāsura*

Translated by Narendra Bhadra

2023

MLBD PUBLICATIONS

Motilal Banarsidass Publications

MOTILAL BANARSIDASS
PUBLICATIONS
4741/23, Ansari Road, Daryaganj, New Delhi - 110002 (India)
Email: mlbd@mlbd.com | sales@mlbd.com | exports@mlbd.com
Website: www.mlbd.com

Sādhan Samar: Vol. II
by
Narendra Bhadra
(Translator)

First Edition Published in 2023

Published in India by Motilal Banarsidass Publications

ISBN : 978-93-91759-74-2 (HB)

Printed and bound in India

This volume is dedicated to
Daṇḍisvāmi Dāmodar Āśram,
of Dakṣineswar Ramkṛṣṇa Sangha
Ādyāpeath

Table of Contents

Foreword to Volume Two

This is the Second Volume of an English translation of *Sādhan Samar*, the commentary on *Devī Māhātmya* by Brahmarṣi Satyadeva (1883-1932). The original Bengali edition was first published from Kolkata in the 1920s.

Volume Two of *Sādhan Samar* is a commentary on chapters two to four of *Devī Māhātmya.* It is the second character (*madhyam carit*) of the text. Brahmarṣi designates it as the piercing of the knot of *Viṣṇu*, from the destruction of *Mahiṣāsura* by the Goddess. A spiritual seeker would reach this state by the establishment of life force (*prāṇa*).

This translation had been proposed by Sri Saumyendranāth Brahmacāri (1946-2012), late Ācārya of Dev Sangha Aśram, who was in the lineage of Brahmarṣi Satyadeva. The translation follows the words, construction and verse numbers of the mantras from the Bengali text by Brahmarṣi. Textual quotes and verses of *Devī Māhātmya* have been transliterated following IAST (International Alphabet of Sanskrit Transliteration). The choice of English words for much of the terminology used by Brahmarṣi follows Śri Aurobindo's Glossary to the Records of Yoga (2005). Footnotes were added by the translator to give sources of many of the scriptural texts quoted by Brahmarṣi Satyadeva and some occasional English explanations.

Unraveling the knot of *Viṣṇu*[1]

Destruction of *Mahiṣāsura*

Ascension: Love of Mother

'Discover knowledge, all you immortal souls in this world.'[2]

Beloved children! Has the blessed call of truth reached your ears? Opening your sleep-glazed eyes, do you see a line of the light of truth in the distance? Is your deluded sleep of many lifetimes ready to be removed by the cool, loving hands of my Mother? You are awake, but cannot get up yet? The lethargy of sleep has not passed? Let it be, my child. Stay at this juncture of sleep and wakefulness and remain attentive. Listen to the constant call of Mother. That attractive call will surely make you rise and run towards its source. The inertness of eternity will be removed. Keep your ears open eagerly. The one who has awakened you will give you the energy to arise and will bring ardor to your heart. By the great attraction of that ardor, you will leave the shore of material things and move rapidly towards me, towards Mother.

Alas! All you children are engrossed by self-imagined delusion. You are absorbed with a tinge of joy that you find from contact with material things. If you sit on the lap of Mother and look at her divine play, you will find a million-fold of joy, a sense of supreme bliss. You will be showered by the ambrosial love of Mother. You will be overcome by her affection.

This is why I call you repeatedly. Come all you children, come immortal children. If you are awake, if you have learned that this universe is truth, if you treasure what is inert to be sentient, if you are used to seeing the divine spirit in all beings, then come and stand here. Look at me. See that the innumerable host of stars worships me at all times. Innumerable worlds adorn me for ages. Innumerable beings carry offerings for me on their heads and run

---

1 *Viṣṇu granthi veda*

2 *jñānāntu viśve amṛtasya sattāḥ, Svetaśvatara Upanisad*

towards me. Look at the ceremonial house of this universe, every atom is offering its life force to me. The goal is to offer oneself, to see me once and be me.

O my drops of life! How much longer will you stay separated and be torn apart by joy and sorrow, life and death? Come, run towards the ocean of supreme life. Fear not, you will not be lost. You will find yourself. What you are absorbed with now is very inconsequential, mixed with sorrow. It has the touch of desire, it has the reception of the undesired, it has the torment of life and death, the torture of disease and sorrow. Here, there is nothing, yet everything is present, complete bliss, immortality, affection, unending flow of the love of Mother and inexhaustible, stable life, supreme truth.

Children! You are established in truth, now be established in consciousness, in life force (*prāṇa*). May the blessings of the *guru* be showered on you.

Madhyam carit: Middle Character

ṛṣicchanda – upodghāt sutra[1]

madhyamcaritasya viṣṇurṛṣi mahālakṣī devatā uṣṅikchandaḥ śākambharī śaktiḥ durgā bījaṁ vāyustattvam yajurvedah svarūpaṁ mahākakṣmīprītyarthaṁ jape viniyogaḥ|

Translation:

In this middle character, the sage is *Viṣṇu*, the goddess is *Mahālakṣmī*, the rhythm is *Uṣñik*, power is *Śākambharī*, the seed mantra is *Durgā*, the principle is *vāyu* (air), nature is of the *Yajur Veda*, for the pleasure of *Mahālakṣmī*, it is for chanting her rosary.

Explanation:

Middle character, the destruction of *Mahiṣāsura*. The sage (*ṛsi*) here is *Viṣṇu*. The composite life force (*prāṇa*), by which this universe is supported is *Viṣṇu*. The outer face of disturbance by the active attribute (*rājasa*) is *Mahiṣāsura*. It disappears into the heart of this great life force, so *Viṣṇu* is the seer or sage of this middle character. The goddess is *Mahālakṣmī*. *Lakṣmī* is another name for the power of the life force. As long as this power of life remains in the body, so long we apply the word '*srī*', another name for *Lakṣmī*, before our names[2]. The individual life force is named *Lakṣmī* and the universal life force is called *Mahālakṣmī*. She is supreme energy with active attribute of the lower nature (*parā prakṛti*). This is the action of the active attribute toward the Self. The disturbance due to attraction to worldly things is destroyed by *Mahālakṣmī*, so she is the goddess of the middle character.

The rhythm is *Uṣñik*. The life force of the spiritual seeker entering into this character acquires the vibration similar to the

1 verses by the seers- Introductory lines

2 *Srī* and *Srīmati* are used as titles like Mr. and Ms.

Vedic rhythm *Uṣñik*. The force is *Śākambharī*. The mystery of *Śākambharī* will be discussed in Volume Three. The seed is *Durgā*. Adding the destructive suffix '*ā*' to the root '*durg*' gives the word '*durgā*.' The one who removes all misfortune (*durgati*) is *Durgā*. When *Mahiṣāsura* is destroyed, the sorrows of human beings are relieved. The removal of sorrow is the seed of this middle character.

The principle is air. When life force materially shows itself, it appears as air. Breathing is the outward sign of life. So, air is its principle.

Its nature is of the *Yajur Veda*. From perception of the principle of air, appears the flow of words of the *Yajur Veda*. So, the *Yajur Veda* begins with mantras to the god of air. This is used for the pleasure of *Mahālakṣmī*, that is, finding the great affection of Mother in the form of supreme life force.

Chapter 2

Destruction of the Army of *Mahiṣāsura*

Verse 1.

ṛṣiruvāca|
devāsuramabhūdyuddhaṁ pūrṇamabdaśataṁ purā|
mahiṣehsurāṇāmadhipe devānāñca purandare||

Translation:

The sage said, in ancient times, when *Mahiṣāsura* was king of the demons and *Puraṇdara* king of the gods, a battle raged between the gods and demons for a full one hundred years.

Explanation:

The demons[1] *Madhu* and *Kaiṭabha* have been destroyed. The seeds of future actions have been removed. Spiritual seekers *(sādhakas)* are no longer involved in actions, with any continuation of new hopes and desires in their hearts. Residing in the body, in the arena of work, they have to act. So, they try to carry out present actions without any involvement, as far as possible. They are not thrilled by success in action, nor are they sorrowful with failure. Such a condition is very desirable for a seeker and is the result of good fortune. But, the hopes of eternal residence in the folds of Mother, of complete dissolution of the state as a worldly person, that made King Suratha seek the grace of the intellectual formed *guru* Medhasa, with the help of Samādhi, have not been fulfilled. Because, as the eye of intellect opens, as the darkness of ignorance is removed, a seeker can see unnoticed faults in one's self. Just as one does not notice any special marks on a dirty piece of cloth, but as it is cleaned, marks formerly not noticed appear, in the same manner, as long as beings are in blind ignorance, they do not notice their faults. Then, by the grace of the *guru*, as the eye of knowledge opens, one can see the expression of nonmanifest errors.

1 *asuras*- those opposed to the gods (they are *suras* with demonic natures)

Worldly persons turning towards supreme Self, to the folds of Mother, in the beginning, think that spouse, children and family are the chief obstacles to discovering Self. Without leaving domestic life, one cannot be free of these obstacles. But then the *guru* points out that spouse and children are not obstacles. The true obstacles are the multitude of internal past tendencies. Worldly life (*saṁsāra*) resides inside. However, remote a place, to mountain caves, we might go, *saṁsāra* will not leave us. When a seeker realizes this in the heart and takes care to remove the root of worldly life, then, by the establishment of truth in the world, by the arousal of sleeping life force by the grace of the *guru*, one can destroy this demon of the seeds of future actions, *Mahiṣāsura*. One of the stems of the great tree of worldly life has been uprooted. But at first, two others, being deeply rooted are not noticed.

As you call for Mother and go forward with a keen heart, wishing to climb into her folds, playful Mother moves away a little. One cannot merge with her. One cannot offer all of life force at the feet of the great life form of Mother and have eternal rest from the disturbance of multiplicity. Mother also seems not to bind the children forever in her loving embrace. She picks them up and then lets them down. Mother does not seem to merge her eye of intellect with the eyes of beings. Why does this happen? The indomitable demons *Madhu* and *Kaiṭabha* have been killed. The roots of new desires have been removed. Why then can we not find eternal rest in the heart of Mother? When a seeker is disturbed by such thoughts, unable to find its cause, and seeks the help of a *guru*, then the intellectual *guru* reveals a scene to their eyes. This will be described as the slaying of *Mahiṣāsura* or the piercing of the knot of *Viṣṇu*.

After the destruction of *Madhu* and *Kaiṭabha*, the great sage Medhasa had told Suratha, 'I will tell you again about the glory of the Goddess.' He knew, that what had been said up to then, the glory of the Goddess that had been seen in the destruction of *Madhu* and *Kaiṭabha*, would not be enough to satisfy the hopes of Suratha. As long as a small fragment of existence as a worldly person remains, expectations do not end. As long as one does not alight on *Brahmaṇ*, as long as one does not realize non-difference with *Brahmaṇ*, expectations do not end. Understanding this, the intellectual formed, insightful *guru*, without giving the disciple a chance to ask, begins to speak. So, this chapter begins with, 'the sage said.'

Suratha, my child! The seeds of your future actions have been destroyed, but your stored actions have not been wiped out. That they can still produce fruits of multiplicity, have not been taken care of. You may not be asking for anything new, you may not be acquiring new things, the enchanting form of new hope may not overcome you, but, the multiplicity you had asked for, the innumerable hopes that you had fostered for many lifetimes, these collections of tendencies of multiplicity are established in your spirit. Look and see. Your stored tendencies, even now, wield boundless power. Until they are destroyed, you cannot have unlimited bliss. But do not fear, I am your Mother. I have appeared as your *guru*. Now I will appear on the battlefield, sword in hand, and dissolve all your past tendencies. You have only to reside in my folds and with attention, look at my actions, my incredible divine play. My engrossed child! My fearful children! When you have called me Mother, when you know me to be your only shelter, when you wait to merge your life into my great one, then you need not be afraid. I will rend all your bonds apart and make you one with me. You will be honored.

Do not think this to be just an overflow of feeling, a music of words. Just once, truly, with simplicity, call for Mother. Truly, in your heart feel me to be your only refuge. You will see that you have to do nothing else. I will complete all your spiritual effort, all your purification. In joy or sorrow, you will be in my folds like an indifferent, happy, naked child, only as an onlooker or in the spirit of a witness. I will cleanse the imagined impurity of your container. Your birth and life will become hallowed.

In this second character, the stored tendencies of action (*karma saṁskāra*) will be described as demons. By conducting prescribed actions for many lifetimes, or by yoga and austerities, or by pursuing knowledge or devotion, worldly persons collect stores of past tendencies of *paramātmā.* These are the gods, that is, the movements or wishes for confluence of mind, intelligence and senses towards *paramātmā* are called divine forces. The movement of mind, intelligence and senses for the desire for material things are those opposed to the gods (*suras*) and are named demons (*asuras*).

We need to briefly mention here, the division between gods and demons that was given by the Lord in the sixteenth chapter of the *Bhāgavat Gitā*. The wealths of the gods or the actions of divine force are mentioned to be, dedication, donation, sense-control, sacrifice, scriptural study, austerities, simplicity, non-violence, truthfulness, lack of anger, renunciation, peace, lack of longing, gentleness, bashfulness, strength, forgiveness, steadfastness and humility. The opposites, that is, fear, impurity, etc. and arrogance, pride, anger, cruelty, ignorance and the like, are the characteristics of demons, or demonic actions.

In the second chapter of the first part of the *Chāndogya Upaniṣad*, it is said that 'gods and demons … fought with each other.' The implication of the commentary on this by Lord Śankarācāryā was that 'the battle between gods and demons is waged eternally in the bodies of worldly persons.' The scriptural sense tendencies are gods and tendencies towards external things are demons. Both sides are in eternal conflict, ready to steal the riches of the other. Both tendencies reside in the body of living things, the tendencies for scriptural knowledge about *paramātmā* and the sense tendencies for the enjoyment of desire for worldly things. The opposition between these two natures is eternal. In this manner, we will learn about the mystery of the battle between gods and demons from the *Gitā*, the *Upaniṣads* and Śankarācāryā, to bathe in the 'Glory of the Goddess.' On the other hand, we have to also consider that although in the *Vedas* and other literature, such spiritual explanations of gods and demons have been given, there is no reason to believe that such beings cannot exist. The material, subtle and causal are all three equally true. These things have been discussed in detail in Volume One.

This battle between gods and demons took place when an *asura* named *Mahiṣa* was the king of the demons, and *Puraṇdara*, that is *Indra*, was the king of the gods.

Mahiṣāsura is the active attribute (*rājas guṇa*). The *Gitā* says that lust and anger arise from this active attribute. Elsewhere, in the directions for internal worship, it has been said one should imagine anger as a buffalo (*mahiṣa*) and sacrifice it to the Goddess. Although only anger is mentioned here as a buffalo, we will understand the active attribute as *mahiṣa* and not only its expression as anger. The three mysteries of *Caṇḍī* are analyses of the three attributes (*guṇas*). In the first character, the external manifestations of the right attribute (*sattva*) are described as the tendencies of *Madhu* and *Kaiṭabha*. In this second character, the tendencies for being many, for the external expression of the active attribute (*rājasa*), will be described as a host of demons. The feeling, 'the one I will be expressed as many' is gone; but the tendencies of multiplicity that are stored from eternity inside the spirit, have not been removed. These are the demons of the second character. All desires, and demonic tendencies of pride and arrogance, etc. described in the *Bhāgavat Gitā*, are expressions of the active attribute. So *Mahiṣāsura*, the form of the active attribute is their king.

On the other hand, the inward expressions of the active principle are gods. Their king is *Puraṇdara*. The one who destroys the house (*pura*) is called *Puraṇdara*. The effort to destroy this nine-doored body house, that is, ending the sense of body and merging into the folds of the supreme Self of Mother, beyond body conditions and *guṇas*, is named *Puraṇdara*. He is the king of the gods. All divine forces, that is fearlessness, purity, compassion, restraint, etc. follow him. All divine percepts follow his orders.

We have to discuss a little about the principle of the three *guṇas* here. Assume that in pure consciousness, that is, in the nondual, solitary, supreme spirit, there is an eternal lack of knowledge. The nature of that is, 'I do not know myself.' This ignorance exists in the field of knowledge because the ignorance of 'do not know' is a piece of knowledge. This eternal, wonderful meeting of knowledge and ignorance is called the *māyā* or divine play, or the union between *puruṣa* and *prakṛti*. If one whose characteristic is knowledge, thinks 'I do not know', then we need to call it divine play. This is like a grown-up father, who without forgetting the status of his knowledge, enjoys playing with his young son, acting like a child. *Paramātmā*, the sentient Mother, becomes vibrant, saying 'I do not know myself.' There is a self-willed desire in pure consciousness, to know oneself. This disturbance is the active attribute (*rājasa*). Together with this, two other vibrations appear on the sides. One of them is a presence, the other is stationary. The first vibration, the special perception, the wish to know oneself is the right attribute (*sattva*). The other vibration is the stationary attribute or *tāmasa*. They appear together. One does not remain without the others. But they attempt to overcome the each other. Just as these three attributes (*guṇas*) have the characteristic of external vibration, they are also turned inwards. It has been said, that these threefold attributes occur over the combined nature of knowledge and ignorance. Therefore just as they have an expression towards ignorance, they have one towards knowledge. The vibrations that are ignorance, that particularly express not knowing 'I' are called demons (*asuras*). Those vibrations that are knowledge, that is, those that arouse the nature of Self are gods (*suras*).

This is not an easy topic. Those not used to thoughts about philosophical principles may feel this to be indigestible. So, let us briefly and simply state the previous theme. The effort or attempt to know, saying 'I do not know' is the active attribute, *rājasa*. The perception or knowledge that slowly appears because of this attempt, is the right attribute, *sattva*. The part holding on to the sense of 'me' is the static attribute *tāmasa*. These are the states of *prakhyā*, *pravṛtti* and *sthiti* in the literature on yoga. In the *Gitā* these are called expression, tendency and delusion (*prakāś, pravṛtti, moha*). Without taking time to appreciate the nature of the three *guṇas*, one cannot understand the battle between gods and demons. Let me repeat. The right attribute, *sattva*, is the expressive percept. *Rājas* is the active attribute. *Tāmas* is the static attribute that holds the two. They are mutable, always changing. The material universe is a result of these three *guṇas*. From *Brahmaṇ* to an atom, everything is a result of the interaction of these three *guṇas*, and nothing else.

Happiness and sorrow are also of the nature of the three *guṇas*. People call it sorrow, whenever even with much effort, only a small sense of Self is expressed, because it is more active but less expressive. Where the expression of the right attribute, *sattva*, is greater, and the action of *rājasa* is lower is called happiness. When the action of *tāmasa* is strong, and there is no expressive percept, there is no feeling of joy or sorrow, it is delusion (*moha*).

The final result of the right attribute is undivided expression, that is, the manifestation of Self, the pure expression of Self. Arriving here, the active attribute, *rājasa*, reaches its final result. This is high renunciation, that is, even the lack of effort to know 'who am I.' Similarly, the final result of *tāmasa* is obstructive, that is, the end of any effort to arouse *rājasa* again.

In this manner, two aspects of these three attributes are seen. On one hand, in the world of beings, creation-maintenance–dissolution, birth and death, joy and sorrow. On the other hand, undivided expression, superior renunciation, and cessation. To state it more simply, on one side satisfaction of desire and on the other, freedom or liberation. The movement of the three *guṇas* toward worldly desire is the demonic nature. The movement towards liberation is divine. This battle between gods and demons is occurring in all worldly persons for eternity. When this battle ends, one will move beyond the three attributes. Desire or renunciation, bondage or freedom, these puzzles will end forever.

A brief indication is being given here of the various names of the demons in this middle character. The *asura* king is *Mahiṣāsura*. The names of sixteen main demons are *Cikṣura, Cāmara, Udagra, Karāl, Uddhta, Bāskala, Andhak, Ugrāsya, Ugravirya, Mahāhanu, Virāla, Durddhara, Durmmukha and Asilomā*. They will be explained respectively as, the active attribute (*rājasa*), distraction, concealment, pride, fear, arrogance, worldly desire, covetousness, delusion, anger, physical strength, false prestige (*abhimāna*), censure, lack of forgiveness, cruelty and hatred. These will be discussed in detail in the appropriate place.

Let us now face the central concept. We have explained the words *Mahiṣa* and *Puraṇdara*. When we have them on opposite sides, as kings of the demons and the gods, they are prepared to drain the energy of each other. There is a battle between gods and demons. This battle is acted out in every being at all times, with worldly desire on one side and the lure of freedom on the other. This mutual collision is occurring in every molecule at all times. Even then, until one becomes human and withdraws Self into the intellectual sheath (*vijñānamaya koṣa*), one cannot perceive it. By good fortune stored over many lifetimes, by the immense grace of Mother, by the unconditional encouragement of the *guru*, this battle is perceived by a spiritual seeker in the heart. Then one understands that one's life is glorified. This battle will soon end.

Look! On one side, your stored tendencies (*saṁskāra*) apply demonic forces to weaken you, to repress your thirst for finding Mother. You understand that the divine forces, courage, purity, knowledge, those that are of help in gaining Mother, your incomparable companions for entering the ambrosial golden temple, these divine forces are at this moment, tormented and abused by the demons of pride, hatred and others. Seeing this, be sorrowful, be pitiful, seek refuge, fall on the ground and cry for Mother. With tears, pray for strength from the supreme force. With simplicity, feel yourself to be tormented. You will see that Mother will appear on the field of battle and destroy these demonic forces, bring joy to the gods, and find you a place in the immutable nectar of her fold. Come, let us like simple children, call Mother, and offer ourselves at her feet, be carefree and cease action.

The battle between gods and demons took place for a full one hundred years (*pūrṇamabdaśataṁ purā*). The span of human life is one hundred years. The significance of the statement that lifespan was a hundred thousand years in the time of *Satya yuga* is different. In all ages, the general human life span is one hundred years. By the power of yoga or such things, some may be able to increase it by a little. The two methods of calculation used by our astrological systems also account for the human life span to be about a hundred years. By these methods, the life span is found to be one hundred and eight to one hundred and twenty. It may be seen that humans may live a few years beyond one hundred. This does not destroy the truth of the *śrutis*. There are also some differences in the calculation of months and years between then and the present. So, there is no need for controversy on this point.

The significance of a full one hundred years is the full life span of a human being. That is, the battle between gods and demons is felt for a full human life. 'After many lifetimes, the wise ones take refuge in me.'[2] Then they know their selves, Mother. Slowly learning to know Mother, they find out about this battle. To perceive this battle between gods and demons for a full lifetime, one has to pass many lives and deaths. In general, our present life span is about sixty years. Of that, thirty years are spent in daily acts like eating and sleeping. Of the rest thirty years, deducting the time for youth, old age, sorrow and sickness, very little is left over. Even that is spent on earning a livelihood and thinking about material things. So, in a lifetime, how many moments can we spend perceiving the battle between gods and demons?

Our present life cannot be called a proper life, because life means something with movement. Think of a steam engine. Every day it produces steam from coal, water and fire, but, the engine does not move at all. It stands where it was built, and for sixty years, wastes coal, water and steam. Are we not the same, wasting our lifetime? Every day, food and water are being given to this body. The purpose is to go forward, the purpose is to perceive the battle between gods and demons and to view the angry form of my *asura*-destroying Mother. But does that take place? We are born and we die. In this manner, not only one but a hundred lifetimes

---

2 *bahunām janmanāmante, Bhāgabata Gitā,* 7:19

pass and we do not perceive the battle between gods and demons even for one complete life.

Some will say that we do not need to view such a battle in our hearts. Why should we dig a channel and invite crocodiles into our homes? Why would we want to intentionally go through such trouble? This spiritual battle is not for them. Those who have become Suratha, those who understand that they have been banished from the kingdom of Self, only they will find great joy in viewing this battle.

Whatever that be, the battle between gods and demons took place for many years, so taking the meaning of '*śatavarṣa*' to be a long time does no harm. The word '*purā*' is used to signify that this battle began in past lifetimes. Remember that the intellect to understand the *Caṇḍī* that has emerged today is not the right action of just one or two lifetimes. After proper action for many lives, one perceives such a thing as 'the grace of Mother.' From it, one begins to have the ability to understand these principles. But if someone perceives in oneself this battle between gods and demons, then one is honored. Their lives are glorified, meeting them brings good fortune to others and their blessings are always active. They are jewels on this earth, they sanctify the air and the touch of their feet purifies the earth. Can you see this battle by Mother in your heart? If not, then address Mother as *guru* and fall at her feet, she will open your eyes to knowledge. Then you will see that the land in your heart has turned into a great battlefield.

Verse 2.

tatrāsurairmahāvīryairdevasainyaṁ parājitam|
jitvā ca sakalān devānindrohabhūnmahiṣāsuraḥ||

Translation:

In the battle, the warriors of the gods were defeated by the powerful demons. Having conquered the gods, *Mahiṣāsura* became king.

Explanation:

The demons were very powerful. Because of the externally oriented tendencies of action practiced for many lives, we come to a condition where the spirit is comfortable to be always satisfied with the form and flavor of material things. It does not want to face inside, towards Mother. It does not even for a moment want to reside in the wide, sentient arena. This is a sign of the intense power of the demons. On the other hand, the warrior gods, the intelligence oriented to the divine, are weak, because they have only appeared recently. The good tendencies have not as yet developed well. Under these conditions, the gods are defeated by the demons.

Think of a large steel spring. Even if you turn and compress it, by its natural tendency for stability, it will always apply a force towards expansion. But, if you place a very large stone on top of it, then, the natural tendency of the spring to expand, even though it is active at all moments, will be stilled. This is similar to the suppression of the gods by the demons.

You tell your eyes 'give me beauty'[3] and try to engage them in looking at the beauty of Mother that fills this universe. You apply all your forces to engage it with the beauty of Mother. But the eyes bring the forms of the world to you. Similarly, you engage the ears with the sound of the internal sacred *Oṁ*, or some self-pronounced special mantra. Within moments it brings back failed sounds from the world. You center your mind and move forward to engage it with *sadcidānanda paramātmā.* But, within moments it regains its former nature and delves into material resolutions. In this way, the battle rages between gods and demons. Those who are truly fortunate, who are close to finding divine nectar, only they can realize this battle.

Whatever that be, in the beginning, the gods are defeated in this battle. Inner facing, attractive force is disempowered. Although, an attraction towards Mother always remains, even then, as long as the downward force is greater, this battle is not

3 *rupaṁ dehi*

realized. Then, by the grace of Mother, attractive force increases. Then the conflict with opposing forces begins. The first result of this conflict is defeat. We have explained before why it is so.

When the gods are powerless, *Mahiṣa* (the external expression of the active attribute, *rājasa*) becomes king. He acquires the power to rule over all the divine forces. Until now, *Mahiṣa* was the ruler of the demons. Now the divine forces also fall under his rule.

Try to understand. The final result of the inner facing active attribute is high renunciation. Complete withholding of the flow of all energy is the action of the inner-facing *rājasa*. This is named *Puraṇdara*. When this *Puraṇdara* (one who destroys the city or *pura*), is the king of the gods, then the flow of all externally faced tendencies is withheld. As a result, there is high renunciation (*para vairāgya*). But now *Mahiṣa* is the king of the divine world. His nature is external activity. So, he turns the divine forces outward. When divine tendencies like sympathy, mercy, tolerance, etc. are disempowered, there is no chance for higher renunciation. In practice, as long as the seeds of all actions are not destroyed, higher renunciation cannot take place.

More clearly, the active attribute has two sides, higher renunciation on one and desire for material things on the other. They are respectively *Puraṇdara* and *Mahiṣāsura*. The nature of higher renunciation is leaving everything, even the body, mind and senses. The nature of desire for things is taking everything. *Puraṇdara* wants liberation and *Mahiṣa* wants material desire. As long as the wish for liberation is not strong enough, *Puraṇdara* is disempowered by *Mahiṣa* and *Mahiṣa* will be *Indra* the king.

Verse 3.

tataḥ parājitā devāḥ padmayoniṁ prajāpatim|
puraskṛtya gatāstatra yatreśa garuḍadhvajou||

Translation:

After this, the defeated gods, with *Prajāpati* in front, went to meet *Śiva* and *Viṣṇu*.

Explanation:

Brahmā is born within a lotus (*Padmayoni*). He is the ruler of all perceptions (*bhāva*). He is also called *Prajāpati*. We have mentioned in Volume One that perceptions and the subjects (*prajā*) are the same thing. It is said in the *Upaniṣad* that both gods and demons came from *Prajāpati*. The power of both gods and demons are perceptions of the mind. The part of the mind that is ruled by demons, although coming from *Prajāpati*, is not *Padmayoni*. The area below the umbilicus or the *Maṇipura* lotus is the arena of the demons, above it is the arena of the gods. *Brahmā* develops in the umbilical lotus. The part of the mind that is truly turned towards *paramātmā*, that truly forms the desire to find Mother, is *Padmayoni*. Keeping him in front, awareness residing in the senses, arrived in front of *Viṣṇu* and *Śiva*. *Viṣṇu* is the power of life force (*prāṇa*) and *Śiva* is the power of knowledge (*jñāna*). The site for *Viṣṇu* is the heart lotus or *Anāhata*. The site of *Śiva* is the center of the brow, the *Ājñā cakra*. So, the defeated gods approached *Śiva* and *Viṣṇu* with *Padmayoni*. The significance of this is that the forces of the senses and mind, which face *paramātmā*, being tormented by demonic perceptions, arrive in front of life force and knowledge.

Spiritual seekers may realize that one cannot use all of the mind to seek Mother. On the other hand, one cannot even use all of the mind to enjoy worldly things. Just as the wish for viewing Mother and hearing her glory rises on one side, desires for family and other things continue. On one side of mind, we see the rule by the king of gods, *Puraṇdara*. On the other side, we see the torment by the rule of *Mahiṣa*, king of the demons. Because of this, at first, the power of the gods is taken away. When the power of life force and knowledge are not fully turned towards Mother, mind cannot find its complete strength. So, it has to seek help. One knows that before this, by seeking the refuge of life force, it had been aroused and destroyed *Madhu* and *Kaiṭabha*. The intellectual *guru*, who emerged as Medhasa, is slowly removing the darkness of ignorance. This attack by the demons will be removed. This is the hope of *Prajāpati*.

How will mind seek refuge in life force and knowledge? The realization, that the mind does not have any separate spirit other than that of life force and knowledge, that it is powered by its spirit, is the seeking of refuge by the mind. As long as a worldly person holds on to their 'I'-ness tightly, so long ego does not want to lower its head. This seeking for refuge does not take place. This feeling of seeking shelter and offering of Self is the same thing. One has to say, "I do not know anything, I am powerless, I am weak, I am an ignorant child." Saying this, one has to hold oneself like a tuft of grass and offer oneself at the feet of the *guru*. This is called offering of oneself. One has to understand that those who have carried out severe spiritual enterprise for a long time and not found divine nectar, have not based their quest on self-surrender. A spiritual quest cannot begin without this self-surrender, without giving away Self. One cannot find Self without surrendering Self. O children of divine Mother! Bow your heads, and you will find Self. Remember, one finds life by giving life. Without analyzing sentient or insentient, learned or ignorant, offer your life. You will see that you are eternally in the heart of the great, life-giving Mother. It is the conclusion of the scriptures that this sense of surrender is the goal of spiritual enterprise and also its means. So, we see that even *Prajāpati* seeks refuge from *Iśa* (*Śiva*) and *Viṣṇu*. The Lord said to *Arjuna*, 'seek refuge in me'[4].

Verse 4.

yathāvṛttaṁ tayostadvanmahiṣāsuraceṣṭitam|
tridaśāḥ kathayāmāsurdevābhibhavavistaram||

Translation:

The gods described to them (*Śiva* and *Viṣṇu*) the actions of *Mahiṣāsura* and the defeat of the gods.

---

4 *māmeka śaraṇam vraja, Bhāgavat Gitā,* 18:66

Explanation:

Mind, tormented by the attack from demons, seeks the help of life force and knowledge. It presents to them the attacks by externally facing tendencies of desires and the miserable condition of internally facing tendencies of renunciation. It is from the mind that life force and knowledge, learn about the actions of these disrupting forces. *Prāṇa* is the enjoyer and knowledge is the expresser. The mind finds worldly things through the senses and presents them to *prāṇa*. Illuminated by the light of knowledge, *prāṇa* enjoys things. It is the function of knowledge to express the material gathered by the mind. The joy or sorrow that is experienced from these materials is the function of life force. In other words, the mind is the collector or creator, *prāṇa* is the master or enjoyer and knowledge is the expresser or destroyer. The knowledge we are talking about here is the knowledge of intelligence. In simple terms, it is better called intelligence (*buddhi*). Matters expressed by the senses are completed in this intelligent principle. There is no expression of material things beyond intelligence. That is why intelligence or intelligent knowledge is called the god of destruction.

Mind unfolds the tales of torment by demons to life force and knowledge. Until this time, it has not described them as torment. Whatever has come, whatever tendency has appeared, was illuminated by the light of knowledge and presented to *prāṇa*. Until this time, *Prajāpati* was carrying out his usual activities. So, life force and knowledge did not take this to be torment. But, today, mind is describing material expression as an attack by demons. Therefore, they are taken to be torments by life force and knowledge. Other than this, *prāṇa* has been awakened from the sleep of yoga (during the destruction of *Madhu* and *Kaiṭabha*), and the force of knowledge has expressed itself as the intellectual formed *guru*. Therefore, although they had not taken these material vibrations as torment, they now well understand that these are nothing else but attacks by demons.

More clearly, as long as matters of form and delight or wealth and desire are felt to be the ultimate goal, mind, life force and knowledge are completely engrossed by them. Then, as the eye of intellect opens, they understand that these things are demonic vibrations.

When you are tormented by the attack of natural desires, do not run about here and there. Do not take the help of difficult and severe, physical yoga or other things to suppress these desires or take this to be the goal. Like *Prajāpati*, you too should seek help from the awareness in your heart, life force. Seek refuge at the feet of the *guru* of knowledge in your heart. Weep and say, *guru* of my heart, save me from this attack by these demons. I have tried and failed. I have not been able to get rid of this attack by the demons and remain near you. I have not been able to accept you as a close relative. Whenever I come towards you, the demons pull me away. I become attracted again to the things of sound, touch, form, taste and smell. How long do I have to tolerate these attacks by demons? How many more days will I have to accept the orders of demons and count my days of sorrow? By kind and save me from this opposing attraction of stored tendencies. Lord! Who else will we seek shelter with? You are our 'sole goal, lord, witness, home, refuge and friend.' Weep in this manner. If you weep, the attack by demons will be calmed. But be careful, do not weep for the sake of weeping. Weeping for itself is a weakness. It is against the establishment of truth.

Verse 5.

sūryendrāgnyanilendūnāṁ yamasya varuṇasya ca|
anyeṣāṁ cādhikārān sa svayamevādhitiṣṭhati||

Translation:

The privileges of *Sūrya*, *Indra*, *Agṇi*, *Anil*, *Indu*, *Yama*, *Varuṇa* and the other gods have been taken over by *Mahiṣāsura*.

Explanation:

This extraordinary story of the gods is described in two mantras. *Sūrya*, the Sun, is the reigning deity of the eyes, *Indra* the ruling deity of the hands, *Agṇi* (fire) the one of speech, *Anil* (air) the one of touch, *Indu* (Moon) the one of mind, *Yama*, one of the excretory organs and *Varuṇa* of the sense of taste. Apart from this, the privileges of the other gods, that is, the reigning deities of all the senses, have been taken over by *Mahiṣāsura*.

We should discuss here the principles of divinities. Then, it will be easier to understand the mystery about this taking over of privileges. Particular or special states of awareness are gods, meaning that special awareness is a god. When awareness is without attributes, it is called pure, unstained (*nirañjana*) or featureless. When it expresses itself as a special perception, it is a god. Think of a tree. The part of special consciousness in which this perception 'I am a tree' arises, that part is called consciousness expressed as a tree or a god. The consciousness that is expressed as the Sun is the Sun god. That expressed as 'my intelligence' is the god of intelligence, *Acyuta*. The consciousness that feels its ego in creation is *Brahmā*. Similarly, in other cases. In general, the number of gods is three hundred or three hundred, thirty million. It is described as such in the ancient scriptures. Our ten or eleven sense organs (mind being one too), multiplied by the three attributes, *sattva*, *rājasa* and *tāmasa*, become the number thirty or thirty-three. As innumerable things, it becomes very large. The millions, stand for these innumerable numbers. In this view, the three or three hundred and thirty million is not illogical. The expression of separate awareness that is sensed by our eyes and other senses are the presiding gods of those senses. We have to understand this about all the senses. When we concentrate on forms in the meditation hymns described for the Sun, *Indra*, *Agṇi* and other gods, the nature and power that is experienced in them, makes it evident that they reside in our hearts. Those who understand the heart to be a little organ inside their chest can never share this experience. There is no outside, only 'inside', but that is another matter.

We can arrive at this truth in another way. If we are united with the flows of spirit that are expressed as the senses of the eyes and other organs, we can experience the nature and power of the

Sun and the others. So, a spiritual seeker has to remember that to directly experience the Sun and other gods, or to indirectly find their grace, one has to take the power of the senses as symbols and meditate on them as the Supreme being (*Brahmaṇ*). By only focusing on an individual sense, and meditating on it, one will not be able to realize or find the grace of that divinity. However small maybe one's focus of worship, one has to take it to be *Brahmaṇ*, otherwise, one cannot have expected results. This is a secret in a spiritual quest. This advice is also seen in the words of the *Chāndogya Upaniṣad* and other texts. One has to seek the support of fire, air, water, the Sun, food, mind and life force and view them as Supreme being. Do not understand *Brahmaṇ* to be an unknown, peculiar thing. 'From what this universe is born and so forth.'[5] That from which this universe is born, is maintained and destroyed, that which is the greatest, that is *Brahmaṇ*. It is evident in front of me as a symbol. From this symbol, the entire universe is created, maintained and destroyed. It exists as an envelope for the universe. It resides in the heart of all beings. Holding on to this flow of perception is the worship of symbols as *Brahmaṇ*.

Say you seek the blessing or wish to see the god *Indra*. Then, you have to take the seed mantra of *Indra*, (it is best to receive this from a powerful teacher), and taking the work sense (*indriya*) of one's hands as a symbol, meditate on or worship them. Holding on to the right perception of the focus of one's devotion is called worship (*upāsanā*). When by doing this, the organ of the hands becomes well perceptible to you, then one should take that perception as *Brahmaṇ*, that is, concentrate on it as the universal great hand or receiving force. Soon this concentration (*dhāraṇā*) will condense into meditation and *samādhi*. In this condition, whatever tendencies (*saṁskāra*) you have about *Indra* will be perceptible as a form (*mūrtti*). Or, if you do not have inclinations to any special form, you will rise and see that you have been blessed by the fortune you wished for. This is a brief account of the mystery of divinities.

---

5 *janmadāsya yatah, Brahma Sutra*, 1.1.2

In general, by not worshipping these special gods, if one worships the 'source of it all', supreme energy, that is experienced as creation-maintenance–dissolution of the visible universe, then all gods are satisfied and one receives blessings from all. This is just as when the upper body is cooled, the whole body feels cool. That is why it is said in a mantra, 'when you are satisfied, so is the world.' When *paramātmā*, my Mother is pleased, then this universe is pleased. When Mother is satisfied, all the worlds are too. Because all is Mother. There is nothing else but her. Instead of trying to please this or that, try to please Mother, then all will be satisfied.

Let no one argue as to what is satisfaction, for one who is eternally satisfied? Is she fond of flattery? Will she be pleased by our words of praise and flattered, like a wealthy person, to satisfy our desires? Those that still have these questions after reading the first volume of *Sādhan Samar*, have to read over again. As long as you do not understand that she is completely satisfied, you only mouth the words 'what is her satisfaction or dissatisfaction?' As long as you see that the wish to satisfy her arises in you whenever you are in trouble, so long, night and day, in every action be engaged in satisfying her. This is your humanity, and may this be the sacrament of your life. By doing this, you will realize that you are satisfying yourself because she is your soul.

We have moved far away, let us get back to our topic. The basic meaning of the mantra is that *Mahiṣāsura* has usurped the rights of the Sun and other gods. The presiding deities of the senses, have lost their perception of awareness (*cit*), their union with *paramātmā*, and are now in love with the inert material world. They are reflected as inert forces. The expression of the senses has forsaken their movement towards *paramātmā* and is now attracted to material things. Whose influence is this? It is that of *Mahiṣāsura*, the active attribute (*rājasa*).

Think of an undivided ocean of awareness. Some red dye is poured into it. As long as the portion of the ocean that is colored red does not think itself to be different from the ocean of awareness, it retains its sense of divinity. But as soon as by seeing its red color, it forgets its true nature, it loses its rights. The reason for the fall from its rights is its tendencies (*saṁskāra*). These tendencies are demons, and the active attribute is their conductor, their king. So, we see that *Mahiṣāsura* has removed the gods from their positions and taken over their rights. Meaning that the senses have discarded their perceptive awareness and been taken over by inertness.

You will also see that your eyes and other senses prefer inertness and are attracted and conducted by it. This is persecution by *Mahiṣāsura*. You tell your eyes a thousand times that all beauty is that of Mother. Yet it always takes it in as that of material things. You tell your ears that all sounds are the voice of Mother, her call or waves of primal sound (*Praṇava*). Yet, night and day it acquires the language of humans. You let the skin know that all touch is nothing but the embrace of Mother. But every day it brings the touch of the world. So, it is everywhere. Do you understand why this takes place? It is because of *Mahiṣāsura*, the rights of inertness, of the disturbances of activity. That is why they cheat you in this manner. Alas! If they were not tormented by demons, if they were not ruled by inertness, then these awareness-based senses would have found undivided consciousness, would express the perception of Mother everywhere and would remove the puzzle of inertness forever.

When by the grace of Mother, one approaches this perception of Self, then one understands this persecution by the senses. The perception of consciousness arises for a moment, then quickly, demonic perception or inertness covers it. Under these conditions, both these perceptions are seen in the senses. On one side, fond of consciousness, on the other bemused by inertness. In other words, this war between consciousness and inertness is the battle between gods and demons. In general, worldly persons do not realize this battle until they are human. Before that, the presiding deities of the senses are inert. When one arrives at the level of humans, this inert nature dissipates. Remember, consciousness is tormented by inertness. This is the real mystery of the battle between gods and demons. In reality, there is nothing inert, only a feeling of inertness. This perception of inertness is bondage. This is of the nature of demons. The realization of consciousness is liberation. That is the feeling of divinity. One should also know here the meaning that scriptural authors have given to inertness and consciousness. One who knows oneself and can know others is conscious. Anything that does not know itself and cannot know others is inert. In this sense, the three attributes, intelligence, mind, the senses and all visible things are inert. The one who is the viewer or expresser of all this is conscious. These principles will be expounded later.

Whatever it is, as long as you have even a sliver of liking for inertness, you must realize that you are under attack by the demons. So, you have to get rid of them in whatever manner possible. The knowledge of inertness is ignorance. There was nothing perceptible as inert, there never was, can never be. Coming to this realization, one truly finds conscious spirit and ends ignorance.

Verse 6.

svargānnirākṛtāḥ sarve tena devagaṇā bhuvi|
vicaranti yathā martyā mahiṣeṇa durātmanā||

Translation:

Having been driven out from heaven by the wicked-natured *Mahiṣāsura*, the gods roamed the earth like mortal beings.

Explanation:

Mahiṣāsura is of wicked nature (*durātmanā*). It was said in Volume One that when existence (*sat*) natured *paramātmā*, because of its divine play (*lilā*) is expressed in a limited form, it is called untruth (*asat*). When nature is driven towards this untruth or limited direction, it is of wicked nature. In everyday terms, it is to be understood that when the nature of Self appears to be the enjoyment of divided forms and senses, it is a sorrowful condition of Self. The seeds of prior actions are always ready to express Self in this divided or untruthful manner. The active attribute, *rājasa*, is their center, therefore wicked. Because of its attacks, the deities residing in the senses, have been driven out from heaven, from the arena of consciousness. Coming under the rule of inertness, they have been driven out from their residence in the awareness-natured heart of Mother. Even though immortal, they are now forced to roam the earth, that is, live as earthly figures like mortal beings.

Look. Consciousness is the true nature of worldly persons. Your senses are flows of consciousness. Where there is consciousness, there is divine nectar. Eternal bliss resides there. But you have been robbed by the demons, so even after a serious search, you cannot find a sliver of bliss. You reside eternally in an ocean of nectar, in the heart of Mother. Yet, with every breath, you advance from death to death. In this manner, not just for a day or two, your sorrow lasts many ages. These are gods roaming on earth like mortals. Steadlily watch these attacks by the demons.

If you think calmly, you will understand that even those, who in this world think themselves to be happy with worldly things, are short of true happiness. The happiness from the enjoyment of wealth and desires are so transient and mixed with sorrow that they are better not called happiness. Despite that, those that are bemused by thinking it to be happiness are like camels chewing on thorns. Camels like to feed on thorny grass. It is not that they do not get some pleasure out of it, but their mouth and tongue injured by thorns, bleed and hurt. Worldly pleasures are like this. Remember, there is no bliss in inert things. Bliss is the nature of awareness (*cit*). Until the sense of inertness is removed, one cannot find true happiness. The *Upaniṣad* says, 'that which is infinite, that which is great, that is happiness'[6]. There is no bliss in that which is limited, that which is not '*sat*.' Heaven is another name for happiness. What is obtained by right action is heaven (*svarga*). The gods are connected to this infinite happiness. That is why

6 *yovai bhumā tat sukham, nālpe sukhamasti*, *Chāndogya Upaniṣad* 7:24:1

their world is called heaven. Because of the strong attraction of inertness, the gods are now unable to arouse their consciousness. That is why it is said in the mantra that they are banished from heaven.

More clearly, the gods, that is, consciousness residing in the senses, are special arrays of ego. By taking the sense of Self into the intellectual sheath (*vijñānamaya koṣa*), one can perceive this ego. This is heaven. When earthly vibrations of the senses arise, one is removed from heaven.

Verse 7.

etadvaḥ kathitaṁ sarvamamarāri viceṣṭitam|
śaraṇañcaḥ prapannāḥ smo vadhastasya vicintyatām||

Translation:

The activities of these demons have been described to you. We seek your protection. You have to devise a way to destroy him.

Explanation:

Mahiṣa is an enemy of the immortals and is opposed to immortality. The story of his attacks and the description of his torment of the gods have been described. The gods now wish to be free from the hands of inertness, of the fondness for untruth. They seek the sanctuary of *Viṣṇu* and *Śiva*. This feeling of seeking sanctuary (*śaraṇāgati*) is the path in a spiritual quest. One in whom this characteristic is expressed is sure to succeed in spiritual effort. Without it, carrying out yoga and austerities do not bring complete results. Any temple to a spiritual quest is firmly built on this feeling of *śaraṇāgati*. We have to understand that those who have not found the expected results, even after a long time practicing many methods of spiritual search, have discarded seeking sanctuary, or carried it out incompletely in their quest. It is one's duty to accept the divine as the only shelter, whether in worldly activity or the kingdom of the spirit. By this, the power of our acts is enhanced.

Although they are being repeated, these words are worthy of discussion over and over again. It is by repeated blows that an iron nail can be placed well into a piece of wood. I do not know about the success of those who do not first seek the refuge of Mother but seek the help of yogic methods to remove disturbances of their spirit. We can see even here that the gods, saying 'we seek your refuge', come to *Viṣṇu* and *Śiva* for help. If you can hold on to this feeling of seeking sanctuary without artificiality, if you can let yourself go with a simplicity, then you will be worthy of enjoying uninterrupted peace and be saved from all danger. Remember, all your spiritual effort is to bring this sense of *śaraṇāgati.* The day you see that having got rid of shrewdness in your heart, you seek refuge at the feet of Mother, that day, your spiritual quest will end and your life will become precious.

When beings wish to be free from their sorry condition, the smallness and inertness of that which destroys immortality, they also have to seek the help of knowledge and life force. It has been said before, that which outside is *Viṣṇu* is the life force inside. He who is *Śiva* outside is knowledge inside. As long as one does not find this knowledge and life force, as long as one does not understand knowledge to be *Śiva* and life force to be *Viṣṇu*, as long as the inner center of knowledge and life is not touched by uttering the words *Śiva* and *Viṣṇu*, how can one seek support from them? Without this support, one cannot defeat *Mahiṣāsura*. So, I say again, wherever you reside, do so relying on God. Even if your shelter is inert, it will not hinder your spiritual quest. An inert form of a deity or an inert body will not obstruct your knowledge of God. The son of a hunter, *Ekalavya*, learned the incredible art of weaponry from a clay image of *Droṇācārya*[7]. An infinite store of knowledge is in your heart. The outside object, outside shelter is just an instrument for arousing that knowledge.

---

7 episode in the *Mahābhārata*

Verse 8.

ittham niśamya devānāṁ vacāṁsi madhusūdanaḥ|
cakāra kopaṁ śambhuśca bhrūkuṭīkuṭilānanau||

Translation:

Hearing about this appalling torment of the host of gods, *Madhusudana* (*Viṣṇu*) and *Śambhu* (*Śiva*) were angered. With furrowed brows, their faces looked furious.

Explanation:

The children are in torment. How long will Mother tolerate this imaginary covering of consciousness by what is inert? Life force has been awakened. The god of dissolution, the *guru Śambhu* is angry. The time has come for the warrior form of Mother to appear. The destruction of *Mahiṣāsura* is inevitable.

The moment at which you think yourself to be tormented, the moment at which you weep and say "Mother! I am under attack. I cannot tolerate this torment by the demons, cannot carry the weight of this world. Give me a place on your peaceful lap." At that moment, you will see that *prāṇa*, who had in the past, destroyed *Madhu* and *Kaiṭabha*, has become angry. He who is *Śambhu*, who determines the good of this universe, the chief priest of the universal ceremony of Mother, is also angered. His brows are furrowed.

As long as life force and knowledge forget their self-power, the spirit of Self, and are bemused by the play of multiplicity of this universe, this feeling of anger is not noticed. But now, hearing of the attacks by the demons from mind, they are moved. In the battle of Kurukṣetra, the installer of the kingdom of *dharma*, *Śri Kṛṣṇa* saw that even after hearing the unparalleled principles of *Gitā*, the great *Arjuna* was not ready to fight with full effort, and was only protecting his compatriots. He arranged for the death of his son *Abhimaṇyu*, to bring pain to *Arjuna* and arouse his anger[8]. In the same manner, as long as the spiritual aspirant does

8 episode in the *Mahābhārata*

not enter the sacred quest with complete effort, Mother raises the power of the demons and brings great torment to the divine forces. Without great force, a great attack, our power of Self is not truly aroused. To make us understand well that we are all-powerful, that the energy of creation-maintenance–dissolution is resident in us, the grace of Mother flows as attacks by demons. The sole reason to nurture the materially faced nature of the senses is to arouse the force of the Self. In the beginning, this is neglected. When the degree of torment crosses the limit of toleration, then one can no longer be silent. Life force and knowledge are moved. Spiritual aspirants can feel it in their lives. All this is divine play, the incredible, blissful luxury of my *Mahāmāyā* Mother.

Verse 9.

tatoḥatikopapūrṇasya cakriṇo vadanāttataḥ|
niścakrāma mahattejo brahmaṇaḥ śaṅkarasya ca||

Translation:

After this, great energy radiated from the faces of the very enraged, discus holding *Viṣṇu* and that of *Śiva.*

Explanation:

In this mantra, the word '*tataḥ*' is used twice. The first means, after this. The second means 'famous', used as an adjective for their faces. *Viṣṇu*, *Brahmā* and *Śiva* were very angered. Their energies could not find space within their bodies and came out. This is just as when much heat is applied to a container full of water. Heat comes out of it. There is a special mystery in the meaning of this mantra. Let us salute the feet of Mother and progress slowly. Let Mother appear in her intellectual form in our hearts and honor us by lighting up the very deep, mysterious principles of *Caṇḍī.*

What is anger or energy? Anger to the demons, the externally oriented natures. is the special movement of mind, life force and knowledge towards *paramātmā.* When anger appears, energy is expressed. When a person is angry with someone, the face turns red and sparks fly from the eyes. These are external manifestations of anger. In this case, the movement of the active attribute (*rājasa*) of the three deities towards *paramātmā* is anger. Before, we had understood *Mahiṣāsura* to be the root of desire and anger of *rājasa*. Now we see here that the anger of the gods is also an expression of *rājasa*.

This is what happens. Just as one needs to remove a thorn with a thorn, anger has to be brought down by anger. This is a beautiful mystery of psychology. Some say that one has to conquer anger by peacefulness, desire by non-desire, and violence by non-violence. That is, one has to arouse opposing natures to conquer the other. We however see that it requires much effort and maybe repeatedly unsuccessful. With long practice, a patient seeker might achieve some success. This is not what the sage of *Devī Māhātmya* is saying. His intention is that to conquer anger show anger towards anger. Similarly, to conquer desire, show desire for desire. (You will see this in the episode of the destruction of *Śumbha*.) For persons who are of angry nature, anger is easily aroused. If they are shown how to focus anger towards their anger, then they easily find success. But success in the practice of pacification is difficult for those who are easily angered.

Similarly, to remove envy, show envy towards envy. In connection with this, let me say something here. Among spiritual seekers, the strongest tendency is the one by which one should try to embrace Mother. Mother does not say that one has to unite with her only with proper attributes like respect and devotion. Sinful tendencies like desire, anger, envy and hatred can also be used to achieve union. The *gopis* in Vṛndāvana by desire, *Kaṁsa* in Mathurā by fear, the king of giants *Hiraṇyakaśipu* by envy, *Cedirāj Siśupāl* by jealousy, were all united with divinity[9]. The lord also did not show any reservation in giving them a place in his folds. Mother does not say to pick our attributes and come to her. She says, 'seek refuge with all percepts'[10]. Good or bad,

---

9 episodes from the life of *Kṛṣṇa* described in the *Bhāgavat Purāna*

10 *tameva śaraṇaṃ gaccha sarvabhāvena, Bhāgavat Gitā*, 18:62

right or wrong, praised or disapproved, seek my shelter with any tendency that you have. Try to unite with me by any attribute you have. Try to come near me in whatever way you can. I will grant you union. I am Mother, you are my children. Do I not have eyes to see what is good or bad for you? I only see if you have turned your faces towards me. My goal is that you turn away from the world towards me. I do not have the leisure to judge what attribute you use to turn towards me. I am your Mother.

I know Mother, that you are blinded by love. You do not have the eyes to see my good or bad. But we are not able to find eternal union with you with any of our attributes. Whether good or bad, we cannot use any faculty to become engrossed in you. One who was able to do so was *Hiraṇyakaśipu*. He was so united with you by his propensity for hatred, that all daily activities, were conducted with hatred towards God. He nurtured such hatred towards you, that he tried many times to send his dear son to death. That kind of hatred for the divine, that is ready to destroy a God-loving son is beyond our understanding. Mother, because of that hatred, you appeared from a crystal pillar in the form of *Nṛsiṁha*, uniting every fiber of the physical body of *Hiraṇyakaśipu* into yourself. What is the level of such hatred? The son of this God-hating man was *Prahlāda*. Can we imagine what the degree of hatred is in such a person? We are your weak children. We do not have such power in our minds. If we had such power, you would be attracted and honor us. Would that be a special manifestation of your nature as Mother? One who is strong will find Self. But, if you draw us to your heart and hold us forever in your embrace, those who are weak like us, whose spirits are torn by doubt, colored by distrust, tormented by desire and anger, then will the nature of your Motherhood be completely expressed. If the distrustful call of our weak voices like those of lambs, can raise even a faint disturbance in your great heart, you can be expressed in the world as Mother of the weak. Mother of this universe, then are you worthy of the name of Mother. We too will be honored.

You should strongly hold Mother with the trait that is expressed relatively well in you. With this method, the natural traits are subdued with ease. We also see here that to subdue the anger-natured *Mahiṣāsura*, anger is aroused. How does it work? The same active attribute (*rājasa*) has two-fold expression. The external, whose manifest expression is desire, anger, etc. The other is internal. Its manifestation is higher renunciation, restraint, withdrawal, detachment and forgiveness. *Rājas* that as *Mahiṣa*, flowing as desire and anger, is keen to embrace as precious, the repeated earthly movements of birth and death, as higher renunciation works towards a path of liberation. This is the battle of *Mahiṣāsura* with the gods. Whatever external trait is aroused, the same trait raised internally can reach a solution. 'The same controls the same' is valuable advice. Spiritual seekers should consider this. The Yoga literature that advises suppression of anger etc. by the opposing traits, should be taken to be the result of spiritual enterprise. To suppress anger, show anger towards anger; the result is pacification. Similarly, violence to violence will bring non-violence. Similarly, in the other cases.

Here too we see the anger of *Brahmā* and others against the demons. When your mind, life force and knowledge become angry and say 'we will not tolerate the torment of the demons anymore', that day you will understand that the time has come for the suppression of these demons.

niścakrāma mahattejo- the word '*teja*' means illumination or expression. The light from mind, knowledge and life force are moved and come outside, that is, they are perceived in the physical world. Truly one can see this light. The mental light is red-hued, life force dark-hued and the one of knowledge is white. Those who have established truth, that is, have practiced the establishment of truth in the world and discovered the peaceful, wide, great space of the spirit, those that have mastered it, can perceive and maintain it at will, can see the red-hued light of *Brahmaṇ*, whenever they focus on this mental space. Similarly, they can perceive in the focus of life force the dark hue, and in that of knowledge a snowy white color. Normally this energy is radiated from the *cakra* between the eyebrows (*Ājñā*). That is why the mantra uses the word 'from the face' (*vadanāt*).

In the view of *Sānkhya* yoga, this great energy is perceived as the great principle (*mahat tattva*). Until one meets this great principle, the disturbances due to the connection of material things with the senses and the torment of joy and sorrow from the knowledge of ownership and sufferance are not removed. But, if the sense of Self can be once withdrawn into the great principle, the perception of ownership and sufferance are uprooted. This great principle is God (*Īsvara*). That is why it has been named the energy of *Brahmā*, *Viṣṇu* and *Śiva*. Creation, maintenance and dissolution take place in this great principle. It has been called *Hiraṇyagarbha* in the *puruṣa sukta* of the *Ṛk Veda*. We will clarify these things later.

Verse 10.

anyeṣāṁ caiva devānāṁ śakrādīnāṁ śarīrataḥ|
nirgataṁ sumahattejastaccaikyaṁ samagacchata||

Translation:

In the same manner, great energies emerged from the bodies of *Indra* and all the other gods and condensed together.

Explanation:

Before this, we have discussed the principle of divinities. Each of the divinities residing in the senses was moved. As a result, great energies emerged from each of their bodies. All this energy condensed into one. It has been said before that each sense has the percepts of both gods and demons. Think of the eyes. On one hand, it is attracted by material things, on the other, it is keen to perceive things beyond form. As long as this feeling does not appear, that is, the senses are only drawn to material things and do not want to turn to God for a moment, one is to understand that the time has not come to understand the principles of *Caṇḍī*. When the gods, tormented by demons, saw that their source of shelter, their very spirits were under attack, they were inevitably angered. When mind, life force and knowledge are angry, that the senses sheltered by them are also moved is not surprising. When the tide comes from the seas, it also runs up into rivers and streams. Mind is the center, life force the holder and knowledge the expresser of the senses. When energy flows from the former, it comes out from the senses too.

What is the energy of the senses? Each sense has its own force. The eyes and ears or hands and feet, each have their expressions of energy. They are expressed by knowledge. Even though all water comes from the ocean, water from a river is called river water. Similarly, although everything is expressed by knowledge, each has its nature of expression. Until now, they were working individually. They were each trying to conquer the demons separately. So, their attempts were not successful. Today, all the individual forces have come together. The forces of the gods are united, so, conquering the demons is inevitable. Even in worldly matters, we see that when a nation needs to rise, then its forces need to be united, then its goal is achieved. It is the same in spiritual effort.

The various senses have discarded their individuality and united their forces for the same purpose. That is why the mantra says 'it all united together' (*taccaikyaṁ samagacchata*). Being united is an inevitable way to achieve success in action. What is the union of the senses or their separation? Think of this. As long as the eyes are no longer attracted by the material world, and try to focus on the form of Mother everywhere, but, the ears and nose do not help, then even with all its effort, it is not completely successful. But, when the senses unite with mind, life force and knowledge, then they have unlimited energy and can achieve their aims. Other than this, they also help each other. Every spiritual seeker will realize this in their own life if they pay attention to it.

The way to look at the force of individual senses is to focus on each of them. We have to remember that king Suratha is going forward in this battle of the spiritual quest with the help of Samādhi. When one can enter *samādhi*, these things begin to be lit up. When one is focused on the unique, undivided, dense awareness that is inserted in the process of the senses, is expressed as the senses, one can observe the different expressions of the different senses. When one can do this, one can change the nature and condition of the senses at will. This is the conquering of the senses. These different expressions or lights are observed to be of different colors. The colors are also different according to the nature of the seeker. Whatever attribute (*guṇa*) is more strongly expressed by one, the forces of their senses are also the same color. The right attribute is white, the active one red and the inactive one dark. These are the basic colors of the attributes. By changes in their mix, the different colors of the senses are observed.

Here too, one has to understand supreme principle (*mahat*) by the word '*mahat teja.*' Because of its expressiveness, in this verse, it has been called an energy instead of a principle. As long as the senses are expressed independently, a spiritual seeker cannot find any trace of this energy. When all the individual expressions of the senses, come to a united expression, then one can understand that it is the supreme principle. It is intellect or *Gāyatri*, the empress of creation-maintenance-dissolution. When one arrives here, 'unity' or one-ness is especially expressed. It is a beautiful place. Seekers can understand after arriving here, how unity and multiplicity can be expressed together. They are enthralled by wonder and joy. Arriving here, Ācārya Śankara loudly sang, 'the world envisioned inside, like a city reflected in a mirror'[11].

Verse 11.

atīva tejasaḥ kūṭaṁ jvalantamiva parvvatam|
dadṛśuste surāstatra jvālāvyāptadigantaram||

Translation:

The gods saw the flares from this cluster of energy spreading to the horizons like a fiery mountain.

11 *viśvaṃ darpaṇadṛśyam . . . nijāntargataṃ, Dakṣināmurti Stotram*

Explanation:

All the individual forces are united. That is why they have condensed and fill the horizons. The gods can observe them. As long as this vision does not appear on a spiritual path, the movement of a seeker does not increase. How long can one stay on a spiritual quest just by guesswork? Even steady and forbearing persons will have doubts appear. The Yoga scriptures also say that such unreachable situations are obstacles to progress. Therefore, direct perception is very necessary. By the grace of Mother, when spirit and senses are turned inward and steadied, one can see this light spreading to the horizons. It cannot be compared to any other object in the world. The Yoga literature has termed it '*viśokā*' or '*jyotiṣmati*.' By the rise of this, all sorrows of a seeker end. Its expression makes a seeker speed in the direction of the divine like an arrow. It is what seekers call divine light or the glow of the body of Mother. When it falls on the eyes of spiritual seekers, they are enthralled by it. That is why the mantra uses the word 'viewed' (*dadṛśuḥ*).

Here I will speak a bit about spiritual effort. One has to assign the four aspects of *Brahmaṇ*, to the space of awareness (*cidākāś*) mentioned before. The *śrutis*[12] mention these four aspects of the nature of *Brahmaṇ*, directional, infinite, illuminated and mind-life. When one assigns the directional and infinite natures to the inner space of awareness and becomes used to the third aspect of illumination, this space or sky becomes evident as 'lit up to the horizons.' The Sun, Moon, fire and lightning are the illuminated aspects of *Brahmaṇ*. By this, the 'illumination to the horizons' may be seen. This is one way to envision illuminated *Brahmaṇ*. Other than this, by the establishment of truth in each sense function, when one arrives at mind, life force and knowledge, at the identity of Self, an undivided, sentient light appears. This is the 'great cluster of energy' (*atīva tejasaḥ kūṭam*).

---

12 revealed scriptural texts

Verse 12.

atulaṁ tatra tattejaḥ sarvadevaśarīrajam|
ekasthaṁ tadabhūnnārī vyāptalokatrayaṁ tviṣā||

Translation:

When these energies from all the gods united or became one, they turned into the figure of a woman. Her beauty filled the three worlds.

Explanation:

The light that has been previously mentioned, is not just a principle of energy. It is not just an illuminated state. It is 'someone', it has character. All personal characteristics were fully expressed in it. The powers of sight, hearing, smell, movement, receiving, confrontation and forbearance are all evident in that mass of light. It says 'united into … a woman' (*ekasthaṁ tadabhūnnārī*) to explain this. This mantra says that the light was a woman or special energy. The word '*nārī*' does not just mean a female. The word also means 'energy.' This is the chosen deity (*iṣṭa*) of a spiritual seeker. In this place, the word should be understood as *Kṛṣṇa*, *Kāli*, *Śiva* or any other form (*murtti*). Each form is a special energy. When this energy condenses and is moved by the pitiful prayers of a spiritual seeker, it is expressed as a special form. Here the meaning of the term '*nārī*' is *murtti*. Because the word '*murtti*' is feminine, the mantra uses the word '*nārī*.' How such special forms are envisioned is expressed by the words '*ekasthaṁ tadabhūnnārī*.' All spiritual seekers envision their chosen deities in this manner. This is the mystery of the appearance of the figures of *Kṛṣṇa*, *Viṣṇu*, *Śiva* and others. At first, a dense, sentient, light or expressed spirit is experienced. Then by the chill of devotion of the seeker, it condenses into a form according to their tendencies (*saṁskāra*). Other than this, one may view forms condensed from the imaginations of the mind. But these cannot grant liberation or satisfy the goals of the seeker.

Do you want to be honored with a direct perception of the form of your chosen deity? Even though a little difficult, it is not impossible or rare. However disturbed your spirit may be, whatever inattention you may have, carefully advance on the path of establishment of truth. Let a space of awareness appear. Assign the spirit of illumination to it and patiently wait to view the appearance of your chosen form. Weep like a simple-hearted child so you may see. Soon, your wishes will be fulfilled and the form of your chosen deity will appear like a material body. These are not just a web of words. One can truly perceive this. But do not think that your life will be honored by just seeing such a form. As long as this form is not united with supreme principle, as long as you do not envision a form with life force, so long, it cannot fulfill you.

Those who from the beginning, are used to spiritual practice with a special form, should try to concentrate on the universal supreme energy around that special form. Just as the Sun, from one location, covers the world by its expressive and attractive force, your chosen form exists eternally with the universal supreme principle. Try to perceive this. Seeing such a form with the supreme principle is proper vision. After this kind of view, one has to practice establishing this in Self. The one who resides inside as Self is expressed outside as your chosen form covered by supreme principle (*mahat*). One has to understand it in this manner. The *Gitā* says, 'out of compassion, abiding in their hearts, I destroy the darkness of ignorance with the light of knowledge.'[13] As long as this form is not perceived as Self, that is, as long as a chosen deity does not appear by its grace to the seeker as Self, darkness of ignorance is not removed. Therefore, not only the chosen form, but all forms in the world have to be envisioned as Self. Only by perceiving Self everywhere, can all doubt and ignorance of a spiritual seeker be removed. Then one can taste divine nectar and become immortal, understand oneself to be an eternal, pure and free spirit.

How is the form perceived as Self? First, the chosen form has to become like a close friend. A close relationship (*ātmiyatā*) is

---

13 *ahaṁ ajñāna jaṁ tama ... jñānadīpena bhāsvatā, Bhāgavat Gitā*, 10:11

the nature of Self (*ātmā*). One has to understand that it is a close relation. Just as in this world, you love your close relatives, give this the same degree of love. If once, even if a drop of your impure love touches its sentient form, then it will with purity, transform a thousand-fold. Then you will be overwhelmed by love. As soon as this happens, the chosen form will become perceived as Self. Remember, you have to be overwhelmed by it, to arouse a perception of Self.

The *Śrimat Bhāgavat* says that the *gopis* participated in the *rāsa lilā* with *Kṛṣṇa*. But, as long as they did not find supreme knowledge that *Kṛṣṇa* was Self, the higher devotion, that he was the monarch of all creation-maintenance–dissolution, they could not find him. That is why he advised them to meditate on Self and stayed away for a long time. That is why I said that just by viewing a form, one does not find God. One has to perceive its eminence. The degree of eminence that is perceived, that is, the amount of greatness that is expressed by a single viewing, a spiritual seeker will acquire the same amount of greatness. Whatever measure of Mother you perceive, that measure of her characteristics will be expressed by you. It cannot be that you have seen Mother, but your attraction to worldly things has not diminished, that conflict of happiness, sorrow, joy or grief is not gone, your spirit is not calmed and your fear of death is not removed. My Mother is without desire, Mother is unmoved. Mother is the nature of divine nectar. Even though she is always involved in the creation-maintenance–dissolution of this entire universe, she is unhurried, deliberate and without parallel. Oh! After seeing such a Mother, even once, can you, like common beings, be disturbed by joy and sorrow, be fearful of death, attracted to worldly life? Can it be? Never. But that is something else.

Whatever it is, the expression of divinities in the eyes and other senses is energy. They have become one. This great expression covers the world. Yes, such expression has this kind of power. The whole world disappears. I will explain this a little. You all know about a discovery of modern science called x-rays. With this instrument, physicians examine the bones inside the body.

The rays of this instrument have the remarkable ability to travel through skin, muscle, blood and soft parts. In the same manner, when the light of intellect is lit, it can travel through all objects in this world. Therefore, the spirit of the world vanishes. Even space and time are not perceived. X-rays can be stopped by bones and other hard objects. The light of intellect is not stopped by anything.

Let us try to understand how this takes place. Wherever light or expression is obstructed or blocked, an object is revealed. This is the secret of perception of form by light from the Sun and others. We can see objects that obstruct light, that is, cannot penetrate them. The light of the Sun penetrates the sky and air, so we cannot see them. But it is obstructed by things on the earth, so they are visible. You see a wall built of brick. This means that the expressive power from your eyes can go up to the wall and no further. It is obstructed there and comes back, so you see the wall. Your power of expression cannot show you what is on the other side of the wall. In the same manner, when we see something, hear, smell, taste, touch or in other words know, it also means 'we do not know' many parts of it. 'Knowing' means that only a portion is known. My knowledge is so narrow that it cannot reveal the complete knowledge of the object known to me. That is why worldly knowledge is called 'ignorance' or partial knowledge. If you think about it, the moment you say "I know the tree", at that moment there is a very large 'unknown' next to the known. As "I know the tree" is said, an ignorance saying "I do not know anything other than tree" stands next to this knowledge. All matter in this world is based on such known and unknown. Knowledge lets us know that there is ignorance. *Vedānta* says that this knowledge is *Brahmaṇ* and the ignorance is *māyā*. Whatever that be, when we say expression, only knowledge is implied. What is knowledge internally, is energy externally. What is ignorance inside, is darkness outside. Knowledge is '*cit*', that is awareness. By realizing this knowledge or awareness, a self-revealed object can be found. This self-revealed thing now expands to the horizons. There is nothing that can obstruct it. This all-penetrating expression, goes through the nature of all things, unaccountably invades all atoms and finds supreme expansiveness. So, the nature of the world disappears. No object can obstruct the self-expression of this knowledge.

Under this condition, there is no existence of space and time. We perceive space by the interference of material things. When no material object can be perceived, we cannot have the knowledge of space. Then, time; what is time? By the occurrence of events, we perceive a thing called time. Some say that the container of actions is time. Some say that actions are time. These differences of opinion cause no harm to the special knowledge of the nature of things. All these opinions are right. Whatever it is, we understand time by the occurrence of actions. We see a sunrise, then another one, and say that a day has passed. In reality, time is undivided and unmoving. Time does not pass. We are unstable and mobile, so we see that 'time moves.' In reality that is not so. This is the same as someone in a fast-moving vehicle seeing the land on the sides move. We were saying that with the rise of self-expressed knowledge, the sense of time vanishes. It has been said before that knowledge appears with the removal of the sense of material objects. Without objects, there can be no sense of action. When the sense of action is removed, knowledge of time is gone. Let me mention here that arriving at this self-revealed spirit of awareness beyond space and time, Ācārya Śankara declared the world to be false or ascribed truth. The world does not exist there, never did and never will.

We have digressed into other things. Let us discuss the meaning of the mantra briefly. When the individual expressions of the gods came together, it was perceived as a light filling the horizons. At first, it is seen as a principle of space. But it is not just a principle. This horizon-filling spirit of light has the properties of all the senses. Although it has no specific senses, it has the characteristics of all the senses. In other words, it has character. To explain this character, it is said, 'it united into the figure of a woman' (*ekasthaṁ tadabhūnnārī*). It was not just a light, it was someone. This is the import of the mantra. Other than this, that the chosen form of a spiritual aspirant is expressed in that horizon-filling light, has been already mentioned.

Verse 13.

yadabhūcchāmbhavaṁ tejastenājāyata tanmukham|
yāmyena cābhavan keśā bāhavo viṣṇutejasā||

Translation:

Her face was composed by the energy of *Śambhu* (*Śiva*). Her hair was formed by the energy of *Yama* and her arms by that of *Viṣṇu*.

Explanation:

Serially in five mantras, the parts of this figure are described. Although the collection of the flow of energies from all the gods unites to be seen as an expressed form (*murtti*), in the finer view of truth realized sages, the individual portions have not been discarded. So, the energy of the deity from which each part of Mother was formed is described. '*shāmbhava teja*'- the energy of *Śambhu* or *Śiva*, which is the expressive power of knowledge. It formed the face of Mother. The five sense organs are present in the face. Although, the sense of touch in the skin, is present all over the body, even then, it is especially present on the lips. So, the knowledge formed god *Śiva* formed the face.

'*yāmya*'- the energy of *Yama*. He is called '*Yama*' because he is the lord of concurrence and restraint of divided piece-wise expression or uncontrolled movements, immersing them into the united ocean of great time. The scriptures describe him as black or dark. Where multiplicity or all colors disappear, is for the world very dark. Truly, in that place, all perceptions are dissolved. So, when it is perceived, it has to be called dark. The dark locks of the hair of Mother were formed by the energy of *Yama*. The flowing dark locks of hair behind Mother seem to tell her children that they cannot see what is beyond her. What is beyond the force of supreme time (*mahākāl*) is beyond word and mind. My Mother covers the expression of supreme time that is behind her.

Her arms came from the energy of *Viṣṇu*. The power to hold is expressed by the arms. The arms of Mother are formed from the energy of *Viṣṇu*, who holds this world. One has to remember that the mantra uses the plural '*bāhavaḥ*.' So, her form (*murtti*) may have four, ten, eighteen or a thousand arms. The *Vaikṛtik Rahasya*[14] says that she can be worshipped in forms with eighteen or a thousand arms. So, the *murtti* of *Mahālakṣmī* can have either eighteen or a thousand arms. The appearance of this form is according to the tendencies (*saṁskāra*) of a spiritual aspirant. So, there is no reason to argue about it. Mother has no defined form. All these forms are of her. With whatever *saṁskāra* a spiritual aspirant thinks of her, my Mother appears in that form.

The important thing is that she 'appears as supreme energy' (*nirgataṁ sumahattejaḥ*). Supreme energy emerges as the *murtti* for the satisfaction of the wishes of spiritual seekers. If one discovers the substance that this form is made of, then with resolve, at any time, any form can be envisioned. Just as a sculptor who has mastered the art of clay can make statuary at all times of the year to earn money, a spiritual seeker who has mastered supreme energy can envision it at will, find satisfaction in envisioning any form and have special joy in worshipping it. That is why in the Hindu texts there are instructions for making different figures of deities and worshipping them all twelve months of the year. This is why the worship of many gods and goddesses is prevalent in India. This may not be seen in most other lands. In the view of those with little knowledge, it might seem divisive. But remember, in a land blessed by the dust of the feet of a host of sages, you will seldom see an injunction that does not inside, have a deep sense of spirituality and expression of scientific logic (*vijñān*). Because of our present education, there is wild behavior even in the arena of spiritual enterprise. That is why, those with limited knowledge, seeing the worship of many gods and goddesses,

14 a subsidiary text to the *Devī Māhātmya*

without hesitation, deride Hindus as polytheists. Alas! We can now hear such criticism even from some people in this land. Blessed is the unconquerable power of time. Words like these are truly painful, for people who are monotheist, whose message is 'I who am One, will become many', who see this monotheism undistorted in themselves, in the world, in each atom. But that is something else.

Today, in this land, divisive knowledge about deities is becoming so ingrained that even those who profess to be religious, who carry out spiritual practice and worship, and say that all various gods are one, only different in name and form, hold in their heart great divisiveness. One does feel that any form other than a special form one is especially attracted to, is the same as 'my chosen deity.' Why does this happen? Only because of the lack of knowledge. The cause is the lack of pursuing knowledge that removes divisiveness, which uproots its tendencies. So, I have said, that if one focuses on the substance that a form is made from, and loves it, then one cannot feel divisiveness with other forms.

If even now you have the unfortunate tendency of seeing polytheism in the many deities, focus on what substance is expressed as a *murtti*. If you turn your gaze to equality, the bliss-filled oneness that exists undivided in this infinite variety, your divisiveness will disappear. One has to advance by noticing where the faults are in spiritual practice. You have to understand that divisiveness, multiplicity and derision of other views, are not the right paths. At the beginning of spiritual enterprise, one has to uproot tendencies of multiplicity. One who can do this, who can destroy the darkness of multiplicity from the heart of a disciple, not just by words or advice, but by action, truly acts as a *guru*. Truly such a person is an unconditional ocean of grace. Remember, as long as your sense of divisiveness is not removed, you cannot escape from the hands of death. The *śrutis* say that those that view variety, that is multiplicity in this world, go from death to death. As long as one views multiplicity, the pressure of innumerable births and deaths and terrible lashes of joy and sorrow are not removed.

Let me mention something else here. Those who oppose the idea of forms, try to blow them away as imaginary. Let them remember that 'supreme energy' that is expressed in the form of a woman, whose hands and feet are described here, is not a regular form, but has the characteristics of form. It has the properties of a face without a face, or of a hand without one. In other words, 'with the properties of all the senses, without any of the senses'[15]. Or, as has been said, 'moves and holds with no hands or feet, sees without eyes and hears without ears.' To explain this mystery, this form and its parts are being described. The expression of great energy or supreme principle is without senses, yet has the properties of all the senses. This is the purpose of describing the hands, feet and other organs.

Leaving behind the body, senses and mind, a modern *Vedāntist*, who is a seeker on the path of negation, can rise to intellect and view the great energy, seeing it as without any senses, yet with the properties of all senses. They will then realize the worth of these words of the *Caṇḍī*, 'united into the form of a woman' (*ekasthaṁ tadvunnārī*). Arriving here, devotion appears spontaneously. This is not just the devotion of shedding a few tears. It is true devotion. However, one may declare negation, observing the vastness of the intellectual sheath, the greatness, the spread and the properties of divinity, one cannot but declare it to be one's sole refuge. When this sense of refuge and refugee arises, the percept of true devotion is born. From this sense of refuge, the true character of intellect emerges.

Those who are on the path of *Sānkhya* or Yoga, when they meet this principle with form and flavor, and arrive at supreme principle, if they do not see it only as a principle, but as God, they will realize the mystery of this woman with form. Even though *Sānkhya* does not acknowledge God (*Īśvara*), the one who meets supreme principle is called '*janya īśvara*.' So, when one arrives at supreme principle, what is the objection to calling it God? All properties of Godhood are properly expressed here. Worship can

---

15 *sarvvendriya guṇāvāsāṁ*

only be done to God. There can be no worship of *paramātmā* or *puruṣa*. Once we arrive at Godhood, residing in *paramātmā* or *puruṣa*, that presence without characteristics (*nirguṇa*) becomes easily attainable. It is a self-attained state. It cannot be achieved by some method or technique. As long as you progress by some method or technique, so long you are a worshipper or a spiritual seeker. Worship or spiritual enterprise takes place within this great energy. This energy 'united into the form of a woman.'

In *Caṇḍī*, the episodes that the great sage Medhasa recited to Suratha and Samādhi, are spiritual mysteries confirmed by schools of philosophy. All this had to be said to explain it. Remember that the worldly person with the help of *samādhi* is experiencing the principles of *Caṇḍī* sitting near an intellectual formed *guru*. It has been said in Volume One that the *Caṇḍī* is the spiritual quest for the intellectual sheath (*vijñānamaya koṣa*). Whatever methods spiritual seekers advance through, they have to travel by the paths of *Sānkhya*, Yoga or *Vedānta*. The study of nondual *Brahmaṇ* of *Vedānta*, the analytical principles of *Sānkhya* and the eightfold limbs of Yoga are all paths pointed out by the sages. One cannot advance even a step by leaving these paths. We advance through them knowingly or unknowingly. This is expressed in the various episodes of the ancient texts (*purāṇa*).

Verse 14.

saumyena stanayoryugmaṁ madhyacaindreṇa cābhavat|
vāruṇena ca jaṅghorū nitambastejasā bhuvaḥ||

Translation:

The energy of the Moon formed her breasts, the energy of *Indra* her middle part, that of *Varuṇa* the flare of her hips and thighs, that of earth her buttocks.

Explanation:

The Moon is the presiding deity of the mind. The nature of the Moon is to pour nectar. So, the prominent breasts of Mother appeared from the energy of the Moon. The forms and flavors of the world that we live with, or the feelings of joy, sorrow, laughter and tears that we have, are nothing but mind. In common view, it appears that it is the mind that binds us. Even the texts say that 'it is mind that is the cause of bondage and liberation of humans.' But listen to what *Devī Māhātmya* has to say. 'The breasts of Mother are the mind.' It is something to think about. Generally, what is ignorant, sinful, narrow and divided is termed the mind. Yet this mind is the breast of Mother. What is the matter here? If the created, infant consciousness is not given the shelter of something relatively mobile and attractive, it is unable to have self-awareness. As long as this infant consciousness does not get a rousing vibration, it does not feel its existence. Look, when the mind of general people is stilled a little bit, they fall asleep. They cannot even keep awake the feeling 'I am.' The mind is like a supporting staff for the consciousness of worldly persons. As long as beings do not leave this imaginary infant state, that is, do not know themselves, then what is the greatest well-wisher of beings to do? They will be directed so that they do not lose themselves and that they grow and recognize their true selves. This is the action of a friend and well wisher.

Mother has not let loose the devil of mind to torment or give pain to a spiritual seeker. The loving Mother gives the nectar of her breasts every day, to keep you alive, to nourish you. For once, look at your mind. Mind where there is lust, anger, greed, delusion, hatred, jealousy, envy and malice, is the breast of Mother. Day and night, what are you doing with wanton behavior? You are suckling at the breast of Mother. At every moment, the mind takes on the form and flavor of material things. Yes, these are the breasts of Mother. This disturbance, this drive of lust and other tendencies, these nourish you daily. They are nectar from Mother. You enjoy the perceptions of the mind as material things, as a result, you suffer the pain of the venom of material things. Enjoy them as the breasts of Mother, the result will be divine nectar. This is not just poetic enthusiasm, it is a mystery of spiritual enterprise.

Look at it from another aspect. Another name for the Moon

is the ruler of medicine. Plants are nourished by the rays of the Moon, the result of which are crops or food. It is by food that the material body is protected and nourished. So, food like maternal breasts that sustain us, arise from the rays of the Moon. In this manner, whether in the physical sheath (*annamaya koṣa*) or the mental or intellectual sheath, we are suckling at the breast of Mother. If you can only keep this in mind, your life is honored. The need for spiritual enterprise is satisfied. 'What is our mind, is really the love of Mother.'

Seen from another side, the love of Mother condenses to appear as a pair of breasts on her. If one can comprehend this, the directive of the senses is diminished. Instead of seeing signs of desire in the breasts of women, practice seeing them as signs of condensed affection. Maternal love is so strong in the heart of a woman, it condenses and is expressed outside as her breasts. Because the affection of a man is not so strong, the breasts of a man are not so prominent.

This may be seen from a view of forms. It can be seen from a spiritual viewpoint that the flow of energy is not just inert light. The love of Mother is present in it. To express this, it is being said that 'her breasts were formed from the energy of the Moon.' We have to understand the same about the other parts of the body. Repeating this point is not necessary.

The midsection of the body of the goddess was formed from the energy of *Indra*. The word '*Indra*' is formed from the root '*ind*' signifying wealth. *Indra* is the king of the gods, the one who has all riches. Wealth is expressed in the midsection of the body. The earth and the other five worlds are expressed in the middle part of the body. From the *Mulādhāra* and other spinal centers, various riches, that is, special powers are expressed. So, the energy of *Indra* is described as the midsection of the body of Mother. (The mystery of special powers will be discussed later.)

The energy of *Varuṇa* formed the flare of her waist and her thighs and that of the earth formed her buttocks. Generally, awareness is especially expressed above the throat. The midsection is more inert. Even then, with special effort, awareness can be observed in the throat, heart, umbilicus, root of the genitals and *Mulādhāra*. But the lower parts of the body, the thighs and buttocks are more inert-natured. There is no special expression of awareness in them. So, the final result of nature, the energy of *Varuṇa* and *Vasundharā*, rulers of very inert natured water and earth, formed her thighs and buttocks. The senses do not flow very much in them. The action organs of the feet flow through the thighs, which were formed from the energy of the ruler of the oceans, *Varuṇa*. The buttocks were formed by the very inert-natured ruler of earth.

We have to especially remember here, that there is no expression of inert characteristics in these divine forms. They are all formed of awareness or expressive properties. There is no inertness anywhere in these bodies. That is why the whole form has been said to be created from the energy or special awareness of the gods. But when anything is divided, at first sight, it may appear to be inert. That is why the buttocks etc. are mentioned to have inertness. In reality, they are not inert. The Goddess was formed from the awareness that is perceived as inert material. The difference between our bodies and these divine bodies is one of inertness and awareness. The bodies of worldly persons are made of inert materials. Divine bodies are made of the awareness that resides in them.

This is true about special forms. Within the spiritual mystery, it can be seen that spiritual seekers can perceive the properties of body parts in the expression of Self as supreme principle because all properties of Self are expressed by them. Because the properties of all the parts exist on the subtle level, they are also expressed on the physical level. What is not in the causal, cannot be present in action. The properties of the causal are the beginning of all properties. That is why in the primal creative principle all properties exist. Persons with the vision of Yoga can perceive this.

How is it possible to have no organs, yet have the properties of all organs? This question may arise in the minds of many. Although it may be impossible to explain this by language, I will say this. Think that you have arrived in front of a spirit of awareness. Here there are no eyes and other sense organs, yet the matter of vision and other senses exists. You feel as if it sees, hears and speaks. Do not think that this is imaginary because we use the word 'if', because the properties expressed here are way beyond the reign of imagination. It is in the arena of definitive tendency or intellect. Imaginary things of the mind, often do not result in action and are not expressed in the physical world. But in the intellectual plane, the 'if' is strong, stable, and definite. Another point is that mental imaginations are forgotten after some time. What is perceived here, is remembered for a very long time.

Verse 15.

brahmaṇastejasā pādau tadaṅgulyoharkatejasā|
vasūnāñca karāṅgulyaḥ kauberena ca nāsikā||

Translation:

Her feet were formed from the energy of *Brahmā*, her toes from the energy of *Sūrya* (the Sun), her fingers from the energy of the *Vāsus*, and her nose from the energy of *Kuvera.*

Explanation:

The rosy feet of Mother were formed from the red-hued energy of *Brahmā.* Although removed from this topic, I am here compelled to mention a well-known song by a spiritual seeker. Although only a portion of the song has a resemblance to this mantra, it is so beautiful and with such high feelings that any good-hearted person will be attracted by it. The authors working life also has a connection with this song. It is an advent song (*āgamanī*[16]). The goddess *Umā* is returning to the home of her father after a long time. Her mother *Menakā*, begins to lament, seeing her unadorned self. Then, *Umā* explains to her mother:

16 songs on arrival of the goddess for an annual celebration

Mother, do not even say that I have no adornments.
I am the only one in this world, who can boast of ornaments.
This universe is truly my tray of decorations, that Time puts on me morning, noon and evening; changing them again at night, so you may see both light and darkness;
Tell me, who else has such jewels? -1

Who says mother that your *Umā* has no jewels?
I wear flowers of stars strung on stilled lightning.
I wear a necklace made of a rainbow; Will I put on just an ordinary garland? -2

All know, that the lives of humans are my nose ring, like drops of water on a lotus leaf, they move all the time.
The ocean of knowledge, the *Upaniṣads* are my earrings.
My crown is supreme bliss[17], who removes the darkness of the world. –3

Everyone knows that a sign of courage is my bracelet, pearls of freedom form my bangles.
I cover myself with the cloth of *māyā*, always hidden.
I wear a chain of the seven oceans around my waist. -4

I put on ankle bells of the eight powers, that I love.
The holy-natured *Śrī* is my body scent.
Brahmā is the rosy color of my feet, *Keśava* the kohl for my eyes.
I chew on the betel-leaf of time forever. –5

All this *Govinda* has seen and will tell if asked.
I put on a mixture of choice dark clouds in my hair.
When the night is gone, I wear the young Sun on my forehead, I adorn myself with the rays of the Moon. –6

If one sees the view of Mother that is revealed to the spiritual seeker in this song, one will see that 'the energy of *Brahmā* formed her feet' and '*Brahmā* is the rosy color for my feet' are similar. A spiritual seeker who has seen Mother in this form can easily grasp the mysteries of *Caṇḍī*.

17 *Sadānanda- Śiva*

Whatever it is, *Brahmā* is the power of creation. This power of creation is the feet of Mother, that is, it is like her feet. To appear as creation, my immobile Mother has become mobile, one with movement. To go from a formless state to one with perceptions, and back to a formless state, is the cycle of creation for Mother, her divine play in this universe. So, to speak about her feet, her movements mean this principle of creation or *Brahmā*. The word '*jagat*' (universe) is derived from the root '*gam*' (movement). The meaning of the word '*pād*' (foot) is movement. I have been saying from the beginning that my Mother, although without organic senses, has all the properties of the senses. So even if she does not have material feet, she has the power of movement. My Mother is the nature of movement.

The mantra uses the dual number '*pādou*' to refer to her feet. The movement of Mother is two-fold. One is towards this universe, the other to Self. One is attractive, the other repulsive. This two-fold movement is called creation. It is by having this two-fold movement, that my Mother accomplishes the divine play of this universe. In this place, the word '*Brahmā*' means *Hiraṇyagarbha*, where creation, maintenance and dissolution occur.

Her toes were formed from the energy of the Sun. The Sun is a great physical expression of the principle of energy. The sensory organ of the principle of energy are the eyes or sight, and the action organs are the feet or movement. The power of movement finds its greatest effect in the toes. So, the energy of the Sun formed the toes of Mother.

'*vasūnāñca karāṅgulyaḥ*'- the power of the divine *Vāsus* formed her fingers. The word '*vasu*' means wealth. From materials of form and flavor to godhood, everything is wealth or *vasu*. It is the function of the hands or the organs of receiving. In one word they may be said to be called receivers. The hand organs are created to receive things. One has to understand this about all the organs. The *śrutis* say materials are superior to the senses (*indriyevyaḥ parahyarthāḥ*). The senses are needed for material things. First a form, then the eyes to appreciate form. First sound, then the ears. In the same way, first wealth then hands to accept it. The fingers are the greatest expression of receiving force, the final result of the receiving organ. It accepts all kinds of wealth. So, the energy of the *Vāsus* formed the fingers of Mother.

The energy of *Kuvera* formed her nose. The nose is the organ for smell. It is expressed from the right (*sāttvika*) part of the earth principle. The earth is one of the special members of *Kuvera Lokapālas*. Again, *Kuvera* is the ruler of wealth. The five-fold principles of materials are wealth. The earth principle holds all five-fold wealth. Because *Kuvera* is their ruler, his energy formed her nose. On the other hand, according to the *Cāndyogya Upaniṣad*, we see that *prāṇa* (life force) is the ruler of wealth. This life force coming into the physical world, appears as air, flowing as breath through the nose. This way, we can also say that the nose was formed from the energy of the ruler of wealth.

Verse 16.

tasyāstu dantāḥ sambhūtāḥ prājāpatyena tejasā|
nayanatritayaṁ jajñe tathā pāvakatejasā||

Translation:

Her teeth were formed from the energy of *Prajāpati* and that of fire formed her three eyes.

Explanation:

The expression of a blissful smile of the bliss-formed Mother is from her teeth. The one from whom the subjects of the world arise is *Prajāpati*. The six-fold changes that worldly persons undergo, of birth, etc. are Mother's smile. So, the teeth of Mother were formed from the energy of *Prajāpati*. On the other hand, the teeth do the work of chewing. The world annihilating game of the world destructive Mother is expressed by her teeth. That is why, when *Arjuna* was viewing the universal form[18], he was alarmed when he saw the world-devouring face with fearsome

18 *Bhāgavat Gitā*, Ch 11

teeth. It has been said in Volume One that we are nourishment for Mother. The *Vedānta sutras* say, 'the one that devours all that moves and does not move, is *Brahmaṇ*' (*attā caracara-grahanāt*). Because it removes, that is, destroys all the world, *ātmā*, Mother is '*attā*.' One who eats everything is called '*attā*.' *Prajāpati* is the helper of Mother in this act of dissolution. *Prajāpati* creates this food of the world of subjects with great joy and hands them over to the maintainer of this universe *Viṣṇu*, who prepares them accordingly and turns them over to the god of destruction, the intellectual formed *Śiva*. In turn, *Maheśvara* (*Śiva*), who is the single-minded possessor of the feet of Mother, takes this well-cooked fare and offers it to the mouth with terrifying teeth of '*attā*.' When you look at the sacrificial ceremony of this universe, your narrow mindedness, your weakness will be removed. See, that this universe is for the enjoyment of Mother. On seeing this, the sorrows of worldly persons will end.

Her three eyes are the Moon, the Sun and fire. These are the three eyes of the three-eyed Mother that view time. The sage does not mention the Sun and Moon here, but just the principle of energy in them. The eyes are the organs of expression. There are three; 1-the physical eye, by which the form of the material world is expressed, 2- the mental eye, by which part of the connected material and subtle matter is expressed and 3- the eye of knowledge by which physical and subtle, past and future, that is, the nature all known things is expressed. The central expression of the eyes of Mother is the significant nature by which the Sun and Moon are expressed. Only knowledge is its nature. That is why the mantra mentions that the eyes are formed from the energy of *Agṇi* (fire). The *śrutis* also say, 'all luminous things, in harmony with it, find their existence; all rest on the existence of it'[19] .

Look, Mother with her three eyes of the Moon, Sun and fire is always gazing at you with affection. The Sun is not just the Sun, it is the eye of Mother. The Moon is not the Moon; it is the eye of Mother. Fire is not fire; it is the eye of Mother. Just learning about

19 *tameva bhāntam anubhāti sarvaṁ, tasya bhāsā sarvamidaṁ vibhati, Kaṭha Upaniṣad*, 2.2.15

this produces no results. One has to truly try to understand them as the eyes of Mother. Fix your gaze on the eyes of Mother and call on her. Your life will be honored

---

Verse 17.

bhruvau ca sandhyayostejaḥ śravaṇāvanilasya ca|
anyeṣāṁ caiva devānāṁ sambhavastejasāṁ śivā||

Translation:

The eyebrows of Mother were formed from the energy of dusk and dawn, the ears from the energy of wind and her other parts from the energies of the other divinities. In this manner, there appeared, this blessed special figure of Mother.

Explanation:

The beauty of dawn and dusk are the eyebrows of Mother. That my Mother is always expressed as the beautiful natural world can be realized by looking at dawn and dusk. Although this greatness and beauty exists even in the smallest speck of sand, very few have the eyes to observe it. But, daybreak and end, take on such great beauty and express a small bit of the splendor of Mother, that it can be felt by all. The reason for speaking about beauty in mentioning the eyebrows is that they have a special place in the expression of the beauty of the body. If the eyebrows are shaved or colored, even though no other changes are made to the face, the appearance is greatly changed. The eyebrows are closely connected to bodily beauty. That is why the sage says, the eyebrows of Mother were formed from the energy of that deity, the consciousness that appears as the beauty of dawn and dusk.

Spiritually, we can see that the junction of beings and God (*Īśvara*) is one intersection of day and night, and the junction of *Īśvara* with *paramātmā* is another. The first is dawn, the end of the darkness of ignorance as a general worldly person, and the appearance of the beneficial spirit of knowledge. The other is dusk, the end of all specific knowledge and the entry into the unified spirit beyond perception. The children of Mother, see nothing else but beauty in her eyebrows, so, spiritual seekers are engrossed by the love of Mother in the meeting of worldly persons and God at dawn and that of God with *paramātmā* at dusk.

The ears of Mother were formed from the energy of the wind. Although sound appears from space (*ākāś*), it is conducted by air. Without air, one cannot perceive sound. So, the energy from the god of the winds formed her ears. In this manner, from the energies of the other gods, the other parts of Mother were formed. In this fashion, the blessed Mother appeared for the destruction of demons.

It has been mentioned previously, how special forms appear by the nature of expression. When the spirit of intelligence is expressed, that is, when the active and dark attributes (*rājasa* and *tāmasa*) are extinguished, and pure right spirit (*sattva*) is expressed, when a spiritual seeker gains the ability to reside in this expressive condition, then a form appears according to specific tendencies (*saṁskāra*) and bless seekers and gives them encouragement and honor. It is then that a spiritual seeker progresses rapidly towards liberation. I have said before that just by viewing the forms of gods and goddesses, one does not reach the end of the spiritual quest or the outcome of life. One does not obtain God or find liberation by just viewing divine forms. They are just the grace of the *guru* on the path of finding God or liberation. One has to know the nature of what appears as a divine form. Although this 'knowing or understanding' takes place because of grace, on finding God, some of his characteristics are bound to be expressed in the heart of a spiritual seeker.

When great longings for viewing any special form disappears from a spiritual seeker, then this mass of energy derived from all the gods transforms into the universal great form. A seeker realizes that this universe is the material form of God. The great devotee *Arjuna*, seeing this universal form, was moved beyond all doubt. Whether you call it a space of awareness (*cidākāś*) beyond *māyā*, or *Hiraṇyagarbha*, or supreme spirit, makes no difference.

As long as this true nature with characteristics of all senses does not appear, doubt is not removed. To explain this well, the *Caṇḍī* goes into detail about the formation of the body of Mother.

The wooden figure of *Jagannāth* that is installed in Puruṣottama[20] is a physical image of this characteristic of a form devoid of all senses but with the nature of all senses. To show this difficult concept that there are no sense organs, yet there are the characteristics of all organs, cannot be expressed in anything other than this figure of *Jagannāth*, with no hands or feet. How beautiful are these wooden forms of existence, awareness and bliss of *Jagannāth*, *Subhadrā* and *Balarām*? There are suggestions of hands, feet, eyes and ears, without any definitive parts. Honored is the one who established this. At the edge of the ocean of delusion, a great entity exists, 'takes and moves without hands or feet, sees without eyes, hears without ears.' The characteristics of color and position do not exist. Everything is equal, with the same flavor. In its nearness to equality, all differences of color and caste end. There is no ceremony, no worship, only the view and only enjoyment. Nowhere but in India, are seen so many methods of bringing extra-perceptual things within the arena of the senses. Some proof of how the sages of this land, the spiritual seekers, loved this entity beyond speech and mind, how they were bound by deep love to that Supreme being, is evident in the various pilgrimages, the many forms of gods and goddesses in this land and the household deities. We cannot imagine what happens when this extra-sensory love becomes dense. How enchanting it appears in the physical world. As long as we have physical bodies, we are not attracted much to things beyond the material. It does not have to be mentioned, how fond we are of the material world. Our bodies are the best example of how fond we are of this physical world. So, it is natural that we will bring our beloved into this physical world and show it affection and service and enjoy it. This is so beautiful that even thinking of it, we are overcome by wonder and joy.

---

20 Puri, in state of Oḍissa

Those who think that pilgrimages and deities are fantasies of the ignorant and trickery by selfish *Brāhmins* for earning money, and blow these things away, should calmly think about these ideas. I cannot say that there is no ignorance, error or deceit in this at all. But, there is no way to ignore the fact that a sense of great truth and dense love is ingrained in the people of this land. The pilgrimages and forms of deities are the brightest proofs. Although many people harbor wrong ideas about God by worshipping physical forms of deities, seeing divine characters in plays and theaters and listening to the tales of traveling bards, yet, from these ideas, they can move toward the right concepts. It is because of a lack of proper learning that these errors happen. So, I say, do not try to destroy. Arouse that which exists, enliven it. You do not have to learn anew or discover anything. Try to understand what exists. Understand it yourself and then explain it to others. Then ignorance in this land will go away. The great sages did not leave much to be said or expressed that we still have to discover with our brains. We would be honored by following their advice and practicing their rules and injunctions.

Verse 18.

tatah samastadevānāṁ tejoraśisamudbhavām|
tāṁ vilokya mudaṁ prāpuramarā mahiṣārdditāḥ||

Translation:

After this, the gods who were tormented by the attacks of *Mahiṣāsura*, seeing the Goddess formed from the mass of their energies, were very pleased.

Explanation:

The gods were tormented by the attacks of *Mahiṣāsura*. Special awareness established in the senses was perturbed by the attacks of the tendencies of stored actions (*saṁskāra*). This is why Mother appeared. Without being oppressed by *Mahiṣa*, the one who is derived from the energies does not appear. All beings have to experience this oppression or attack. 'I am being tortured by these senses that have turned towards worldly things.' As soon as this percept forms properly in the heart, Mother appears in her terrible form. If the child is under attack, is Mother not angered? This is not an fictitious Mother, but a real one. As long as you see that you are calling Mother in distress, but Mother does not appear, understand that you are not sufficiently distressed, just acting like one. This is not to be criticized. One day, acting this way, true distress may appear.

Mother repeatedly torments us with *Mahiṣa*. As long as this torment does not reach our perception, as long as we do not see worldly things as transient and ailing, so long, she appears as torment. Then, when this worldly life, holding up this body, this movement among body, senses, mind and intelligence, all appear to be a great torment, then one says with tearful eyes, 'Mother! We cannot tolerate this anymore. We are your oppressed children. Mother, appear here at once. Our life is so painful, that we cannot bear it anymore. This is torment, but we have no way to save ourselves from it.' When these feelings appear in the heart, then Mother appears in her form as savior. By just repeating 'You are the savior of all. We seek your refuge and are weak and distressed'[21] does not produce any results. One has to truly seek refuge, be deprived and distressed. When these three signs appear in you, Mother will appear in her form as savior. The form of Mother will appear from the spirits of the host of gods established in your senses. The gods will be happy. You will discover great joy.

Verse 19.

śūlaṁ śūlādviniṣkṛṣya dadou tasai pinākdhṛk|
cakrañca dattavān kṛṣṇaḥ samutpādya svacakrataḥ||

Translation:

The trident bearing *Śiva* attracting another trident from his own, offered it to the Goddess. In the same manner, *Kṛṣṇa* produced a discus (*cakra*) from his own and gave it to her.

21 *śaraṇāgata dīnārtta paritrāṇā parāyaṇā*, *Devī Māhātmya*, Chapter 11

Explanation:

In eleven mantras beginning with this one, the offering of weapons by the gods is described. Each god has a specific weapon. Each weapon is the power of a specific divinity. Remember that a specific perceptual awareness is a divinity. Although this has been mentioned before, if this core principle is forgotten, the main issue will be difficult to understand. That is why it is being repeated on occasion. Just as awareness is named a divinity when it is expressed as a specific percept (*bhāv*), in the same manner, the power of expressing that percept, that is, the power due to which awareness is divided and expressed in a specific manner is the weapon of that divinity. One has to understand the offering of the weapons as the offering of individual powers. The emergence of energy of the gods that have been described before was the expression of each god. This offering of weapons is that of providing the power of each. Understanding this will make one realize the mystery of offering weapons. This will be clarified later.

What is this offering of power? Understanding the divided power of each one as undivided supreme energy is the offering of power. When we realize that only the all-powerful energy of Mother is expressed through each of us, power is offered. The small portion of the ocean of power that we have demarcated, in other words, what we call human prowess (*puruṣkār*), is nothing but the power of Mother. Realizing that *puruṣkār* is accomplished by one who is the only person (*puruṣa*), is the offering of power. It is not enough to say 'O Lord! seated in my heart, I act as directed by you.'[22] One has to realize this. One has to truly see the ruler of the senses in one's heart. Before one envisions *Hṛṣikeśa* as Lord, just saying it would be untruthful. This vision of the Lord and offering of power are the same. Power is offered if we understand that the undivided consciousness that is Mother, is expressed as our senses, as mind, intelligence and ego, as five breaths, as earth, water and the five elements.

---

22 *tvyā Hṛṣikeśa hṛdisthitena, yathā niyuktahhasmi tathā karomi* (*Pāṇḍava Gitā*)

This does not take place in one day. In the beginning, one has to act as if these powers are our own, and one by one, offer them at the feet of Mother. It is begun with leaves, flowers, fruits or other ceremonial offerings. Then religious services, fasts and such austerities and paths of Yoga like *yama* and *niyama* follow. Finally, one arrives at self-study (*svādhyāya*) or a ceremony of knowledge. Then a spiritual seeker studies Self, that is, finds undivided knowledge or *paramātmā.* This is the final offering. Self cannot be found without self-surrender. It does not happen. As long as you do not realize 'Self in all beings and all beings in Self'[23], you have to understand that self-surrender has not occurred. To offer 'I' at the feet of Mother, one has to see the rule of Mother in every action. One has to say 'I offer myself to the will of God' always and offer one's self. Acting in this manner, one attains the ability to discover Self. The offering of powers is an intermediate condition. We see that this power of sight is that of Mother. Mother! You reside in me as the inner viewer and are expressed as the power of sight. These sounds that we hear, that power of hearing is Mother. In this manner, the power of smell, touch, taste and reception, movement, speech, generation and elimination, the powers of the action organs are all that of Mother. Again, the inner forces of memory, imagination, ego and conscience are all Mother. In this way, when all special powers are understood to be that of Mother, then all powers are truly offered to Mother. After this one can offer oneself. The sense of worldly person vanishes after self-surrender and a sense of supreme bliss emerges.

Mother! We have not learned to give anything. We only say that 'this is not ours, this is yours.' In practice, we hold on to everything tightly. We keep on holding on to this small 'I', which is repeatedly crushed by birth and death, anguished by the heat of worldly life. So, we cannot give you anything, do not wish to, cannot. To offer our mind, intelligence and ego at your feet are subtle things, very far away. We cannot freely offer at your feet even what is inconsequential, very physical, mere wealth, clothing

23 *Bhāgavat Gitā,* 6:29

and ornaments. We are narrow, living within small boundaries. Alas! Thinking about this, rents the heart apart. You deliver beneficence, night and day, you wish for us our best, saying 'fix your mind on me, let your thoughts dwell on me'[24]. But we do not pay attention to your blessings. If we listened, then would we be so hesitant to offer you material things, as the first steps of the ceremony of offering mind and intelligence? We think that if we give you anything, if we offer something to you, it will be a waste. We are stingy even in offering you material things that are distantly related to us, we who have to offer our 'I'-ness. O Mother, remove our narrow-mindedness. Make us worthy of ceremonial offerings. Then will we slowly through the offering of power, acquire the rights to surrender ourselves, we will be honored to be the children of Mother. Whatever is given to you, is returned to us a thousand-fold. Having proof of this hundreds of times, we cannot hold this firmly in our hearts. You are *ātmā*. When will we understand that giving to you is the same as giving to ourselves? Because we do not understand this, you appear in the form of torment by *Mahiṣa* and hit us in our core a hundred times to awaken us. Favorable times have come for the gods, so they can offer their weapons of power to you and be relieved.

When individual powers are drapped in pride, that is, they appear as 'my power', so long they rise and fall. So long, they appear as beginning and end. But the day that worldly persons understand that the centers of energy are all drops in the ocean of supreme energy, can they any longer hold them to be 'my energy'? Then they naturally have a desire to offer their energy. Or, by then, there is no offering, only vision. You are everything. Everything of me is you, everything of mine is yours. I did not see this for so long. My knowledge, wealth, children, senses, fame, I was engrossed by all these, so I have been repeatedly wounded by demons. For so long, I have been so distressed by my 'I'-ness, by the pride of my being, by applying my forces against demons. Mother, I cannot carry on anymore. Now is the time to accept your powers and save ourselves from thsee attacks by demons.

24 *Bhāgavat Gitā,* 12:8

There is a beautiful story in the *Kena Upaniṣad.* Once, the gods became very proud after defeating some demons. At that time, Mother appeared as *Haimavatī* and asked *Agṇi*, the god of fire, 'what strengths do you have?' He replied that he could burn down the whole world. Mother said 'Good, burn this spray of grass.' Applying all his power, *Agṇi* failed to do so. In the same manner, the gods of wind and water all failed to move the spray of grass with their powers. In the end, they understood that they had no strength of their own, they were empowered by the power of *Haimavatī.*

Spiritual seekers have to decide whether the narrative of the appearance of the Goddess from the energies of the gods and the offering of the weapons to her are according to the revealed texts (*śrutis*). Whatever it is, we will try to understand the meaning of this mantra.

Lord *Śiva*, extracted a lance from his own and offered it to the Goddess. *Śiva* is the *guru* of intellectual form, a figure of pure knowledge. The trident is his weapon. The force of knowledge is triadic. Knowledge is expressed as the triad, knower, what is known and knowing. 'I see a tree.' Here I am the knower, the tree is the known and the sense about trees is knowledge. Generally, knowledge is expressed in this triadic manner. Where there is knowledge, there is this triad. So, there is a trident in the hand of *Śiva*. (Although there is knowledge without the triad, that is a different matter.) This triadic percept of knowledge is a special expression of supreme energy. Realizing it is the offering of the trident. Even realizing that the force due to which knowledge becomes triadic is that of *Mahāmāyā*, does not completely banish the triad. That is why it is said that a lance was extracted from another. The trident of *Śiva* remains with him, only the affection and ownership of it are removed. The offering of the discus (*cakra*) by *Viṣṇu* in the next part should be understood similarly.

A spiritual seeker should also see that one's undivided knowledge is always reflected as the form and flavor of material things. It is divided into a triad of knower, known and knowledge.

The one who appears in this triadic form is Mother. Do not be proud of 'my knowledge.' Try to understand that the knowledge formed Mother is appearing in this fashion through you. This is the mystery of the offering of the trident by *Śiva*.

Viṣṇu produced a discus from his own and offered it to the Goddess. *Viṣṇu* is the universal life force. The meaning of '*cakra*' has been expounded in Volume One. This worldly life is the *cakra* of *Viṣṇu*. Until now, one was proud of the ownership of a stable, worldly life in the form of the *Sudarśana*[25] *cakra*, so one had to suffer the attacks of the *asura Mahiṣa*. Now, understanding it to be the energy of Mother, *Viṣṇu* offers it to her and is reassured. You should also see that this small worldly life, this family, wife and children, that you take care of and are proud of, is ignorance. The force that is expressed through you as your care and attention is Mother. Cherish her, offer her what is hers. When you properly understand that Mother resides inside you as energy, then the offerings are carried out correctly. When you succeed in these offerings, you will see that worries of the world are unburdened from your shoulders.

Verse 20.

śaṅkhañca varuṇaḥ śaktiṁ dadou tasyai hutāśanaḥ|
māruto dattavāṁścāpaṁ baṇapūrṇe tatheṣudhī||

Translation:

Varuṇa gave the Goddess a conch shell, *Agṇi* gave her power and *Vāyu* (air) gave a bow and two quivers of arrows.

Explanation:

After the chief of the gods, *Śiva* and *Viṣṇu* were honored by offering their powers at the feet of Mother, other gods followed. *Varuṇa* is the lord of the waters. The percept that resides in the combined waters, that is the consciousness established in water, is the god *Varuṇa*. He offered a conch shell. There is controversy

25 good looking; name of the *cakra* held by *Viṣṇu*

about the word '*śaṅkha.*' Some say that the conch shell is a weapon of *Viṣṇu*. The previous mantra speaks about *Viṣṇu* offering a discus. Then the first word in this mantra is '*śaṅkha*,' so one has to understand it to be a weapon of *Viṣṇu*. According to this view, one has to take the meaning that both *Varuṇa* and *Agṇi* offered their powers. It will be said later that the ruler of the waters, *Varuṇa* offered a snare. This is a well-known weapon of *Varuṇa*. (Its meaning will be expounded later.) Others say that because the word '*cakrañca*' ends with the suffix '*ca*', it signifies 'and' meaning both the discus and mace of *Viṣṇu*. In solving this controversy, some have enumerated the eighteen weapons in the hands of the eighteen-armed form of *Mahālakṣmi* described in *Vaikṛtik Rahasya*. Even that does not clarify the problem. Whatever it is, we will take the conch shell to represent the power of primal sound (*nāda*). Then, whether it is offered by *Viṣṇu* or whether it is offered by *Varuṇa*, does not matter. But, the offering by *Viṣṇu* seems to be more appropriate. The conch shell represents the nonmanifest power of primal sound, from which manifest sound in this universe is expressed. To realize that the power is that of Mother is the offering of the conch to her. The mystery of primal sound (*nāda*) will be explained later.

The power of water is to moisten or wet and that of fire is to burn. Understanding that both these powers are those of Mother, one can fathom the mystery of the offering of weapons by *Agṇi* and *Varuṇa*. Until now, consciousness established in water and the principle of energy was confined to the pride of wetting and burning. Now that is removed. In the same manner, the god of the winds *Māruta* gave a bow and two quivers of arrows. Bow and arrows are the indicators of energy flow. The quiver is a container for arrows. The flow of energy manifests in two directions, internal and external. So, the mantra mentions two quivers. The consciousness in which the sphere of air in which the earth is situated, is the god of air. His power is to flow. So long, the power was seen to be 'mine.' Now by offering it at the feet of Mother, he discovers true energy.

As a spiritual seeker, you will also see that the forces of water, fire and air in your physical body are the varied manifestations of unique, supreme energy. Offer the forces to the one whose energy is expressed through you. You will see that you are not just a worldly person afflicted by life. You are much more than that. How will you offer all this? First, let us take water. Perceive the portion of you that is water. (Those used to the establishment of truth will find this easy.) Say 'Water is truth' and hold this feeling in your heart. (It is easier to do this by concentrating on the seed mantra of *Varuṇa* in the *Svādhisthāna* spinal center.[26]) When this sense of water becomes strong, cherish it as Mother, as *ātmā*. Then envision it outside, that is, worship it as *Brahmaṇ*. Look, this spirit of water is inside the earth as underground streams, on the surface as rivers and seas, in the trees as sap, on mountains as waterfalls and in the sky as clouds. See that from your body to everything inside the earth, to the skies, there is the spirit of water. Look and say, 'This water resides as nectar in all beings, all beings reside in water as divine nectar.'[27] Look and see water inside and outside, above below, nothing but water. Then say, 'I am this, I am Self, all this is *Brahmaṇ*, all this is *amṛtam* (divine nectar), this is All.'

In this way, feel the principle of fire. Begin from the heat of the body and the fire in the stomach. (It is easier to do this by concentrating on the seed mantra of *Agṇi* in the *Maṇipura* spinal center.[28]) Say 'fire is truth' and extend the feeling of fire as heat inside the earth, in all things on earth, as submarine eruptions, in forest fires, in the light of the Sun, Moon and stars, everywhere. From your body to as far as the eye of knowledge can extend, see that there is nothing but *Agṇi*. Feeling this spirit of fire in all the world, say with devotion, 'This fire resides as nectar in all beings, all beings reside in fire as divine nectar.' Slowly your feelings will become imbued with fire. Then say 'I am this, I am Self, all this is *Brahmaṇ*, all this is *amṛtam*, this is All.'

In the same manner, for the principle of air, say 'air is truth.'

---

26 second spinal center, seed mantra *vaṁ*

27 *ayam atma sarveśam bhutanam madhu, Brihadāraṇyaka Upaniśad* 2.5.14

28 third spinal center, seed mantra *raṁ*

Then see that from your breath to the flow of air all over your body, to all over land, sea and sky, all of it is air. (It is easier to do this by concentrating on the seed mantra of air in the *Anāhata* center.[29]) Feeling that there is nothing but air inside and outside you, say with the sages of the *Upaniṣads*, 'This air resides as the nectar in all beings, all beings reside in air as divine nectar.' Look and see that Mother who you want, who you have searched for lifetimes, that Mother is present before you in the form of universal air. Offer yourself to her, cherish it as *ātmā*. Say 'I am this, I am Self, all this is *Brahmaṇ*, all this is *amṛtam* (divine nectar), this is All.'

When you get used to this, you will understand the mystery of the offering of the weapons by the gods. Revealing these secrets of spiritual effort in a book, in this manner, has the risk of disrespect to the words of teachers of *Vedānta,* by falling into the hands of those without rights to them. Considering the present time, place and people, one cannot refrain from doing this. If among a thousand persons, even one advances on this path, or begins to see these principles as true and cherishes them, then even in the regret for my action against tradition, there will be a chance for joy.

Verse 21.

vajramindraḥ samutpādya kuliśādamarādhipaḥ
dadou tasyai sahasrākṣo ghaṇṭāmairāvatādgajāt

Translation:

The king of the gods, the thousand-eyed *Indra*, produced thunder from his thunder and brought a gong from the elephant *Airāvata*, offering them to the Goddess.

Explanation:

Indra is the king of the gods. Thunder or lightning is his weapon or power. Modern scientists now agree that our home, this earth has electrical properties. Although it appears to be insentient

29 Fourth spinal center, at the level of the heart, seed mantra *yaṁ*

in their eyes, we understand it as a material expression of the power of awareness. The spirit of consciousness that is materially expressed as electric energy, the consciousness established in the energy of electricity is named the god *Indra*. Previously, in the fifth mantra, the gods had been explained as being established in the senses. Here they are described as energies. A thoughtful reader will see no conflict in this. The god *Indra* has to be understood from the direction of the senses, as the organ of movement and from the direction of energy, as that of the power of electricity. In reality, movement and electricity are linked. The god *Indra* understood the worldwide electric energy or that of thunder as his own, so he had to suffer banishment from heaven by *Mahiṣa*. Now, *Indra* has offered it at the feet of Mother and is beginning the destruction of *Mahiṣāsura*. The complete realization that control over the power of thunder by *Indra* is not his own is the offering of thunder. The weapon remains that of *Indra*, only the idea of his ownership is removed. One has to understand in the same manner the offering of the other weapons. This has been mentioned previously.

A spiritual seeker should notice that from the electricity in one's body, to the worldwide field of electricity in water, earth and sky, all is the sentient Mother. With simplicity and truth, call it Mother. See that this electricity resides as nectar in all beings. All beings reside in it as divine ambrosia. The world is divine nectar. Only pure bliss of self-sacrifice. Each the dearest of the other, nectar, *ātmā*, all very dear. Look how Mother loves us and how we love Mother. See, Mother in our hearts and we in the heart of Mother. We are the nectar of Mother and Mother is our nectar. Do you feel like weeping? Weep and say, O Mother, you are our life force. Look at the exchange of *prāṇa*. I am your life force and you are mine. Will you understand this principle? Tell this inert electric force, 'I am that, I am that Self, all this is *Brahmaṇ*, all this is divine nectar, all this is truth.' You will see how easy it is to destroy the *asura Mahiṣa*. But that is another topic.

Indra gave a gong from the elephant *Airāvata*. The root '*ir*' means speed or pace. The word '*irāvan*' means 'with speed.' A child of '*irāvan*' or relation to it is called *Airāvata*. The mount of *Indra* is *Airāvata*. Another name for *Indra* is a rider of the clouds (*meghabāhan*). Clouds and *Airāvata* are not different. Then why is *Airāvata* called an elephant? We have said that *Indra* is the god of thunder, that is electric power. The director of this electric force is *Airāvata*. The physical material that is used to conduct the electric force is called the elephant *Airāvata*. Although many things in the world conduct this energy, it is chiefly carried or conducted by clouds. Clouds often look like elephants in color and shape. Even now, when waterspouts are formed during tornadoes, people say it is the descent of *Airāvata* from heaven. The dark, black clouds bend as if by the weight of water, and due to the strong current of air, a pillar of water rises like the trunk of an elephant and touches the cloud. From a distance, this looks as if *Airāvata* has descended from heaven and is drinking. Whatever it is, that which conducts electricity also conducts sound, because sound comes from movement or vibration, so *Airāvata* has a gong. The god *Indra* offered the sound of thunder together with lightning. That is, he realized that the sound of thunder is also the power of Mother. This is the mystery of offering the gong.

To remove any doubts the reader may have, I have to repeat that by seeing these explanations of *Indra* and *Airāvata*, let no one doubt the existence of *Indra* on an elephant, holding lightning. Although the author of *Purvvamīmāṁsā* philosophy, the sage *Jaimini*, disregarded divine forms and only accepted gods in the form of mantra, we cannot deny special forms. Because then we have to acknowledge the absence of an all-powerful Mother. Also, these special forms can be envisioned. (We have discussed previously how such forms appear.) The mantra-natured forms of the gods mentioned by *Jaimini* are also not illogical, as divine forms are perceptual. The special percepts of a spiritual seeker, (such percepts are nothing but awareness), condense to be expressed as special forms. The mantras are expressions of these special perceptions. When we say perception, we have to consider a sound (*śabda* or word) based on it. There cannot be perceptions without *śabda*. Only the nature beyond perception can be said to be beyond sound. Sounds are mantras. The sound that arouses the perception of a particular divinity is the mantra of that divinity. So, it is not wrong to call the mantra a form of the divinity. Some say that if gods have forms, there are two problems. First, a god cannot accept worship at the same time in different places, and second, if the thunder-holding god *Indra*, seated on an elephant were to appear in the place of worship, the clay images or containers would be destroyed. (Such arguments are present in *Mīmāṁsā* philosophy.) We have to reply that such objections are inconsequential because the deities appear in the hearts of each spiritual seeker in subtle form. Therefore, there is no objection to their accepting worship in many places together. Then, the body of the gods is not physical like ours, that their appearance would shatter material containers. The forms of the deities are sentient, that is, they are built of awareness. By the chill of devotion of spiritual seekers, by strong prayers, the divine perceptions in their hearts condense and appear outside. Some may argue that if the gods exist in a subtle form in each being, then they are dividedly many. Just one god such as *Indra* becomes innumerable. The scriptural texts do not say this. It is true. However, just as consciousness is one, yet is expressed in different ways in each being, this is similar. We have previously discussed these principles of the gods.

The reason for saying so much about the forms of gods is because there are a group of people who only accept spiritual principles. There is another group that discards divine forms and such things as allegories. Then there is another group, who do not try to understand the proper mysteries of ancient tales and think that gods are like us, have homes and weddings and are formed of the five elements. All of this is only a lesser degree of knowledge. So, we have to repeatedly discuss these principles. This controversy can be avoided by remembering one thing before one enters into the mysteries of scriptural texts. The physical, subtle and causal[30] are all true. The compatibility of all three

30 *sthul, sūkṣma, kāraṇ*

together brings one to the proper conclusions. Of these three, one has to pay special attention to the causal. The physical and subtle have to be directed towards the causal. Drawing any conclusions from the physical or subtle without attention to the causal will be erroneous. The physical should be directed to the subtle, and the subtle directed to the causal. In this manner, the meaning of scriptural texts will not be erroneous. For the perception of the reader, I will say what these three, physical, subtle and causal are. The causal is *paramātmā*, pure consciousness, the subtle is energy (*śakti*), *māyā* or nature and the physical is action, that is, this phenomenal world of beings.

Let us now return to our topic. The divine world is subtle. Although divine forms may be perceived physically, they are part of the subtle world. Electricity is physical. The consciousness that is expressed as electricity is the power of *Indra*. If one meditates on this special consciousness and wishes to see the form of *Indra*, then one can view this meditative form. It does not happen in any other manner, never has.

Verse 22.

kāladaṇḍād yamo daṇḍaṁ pāśañcāmbupatirdadou|
prajāpatiścākṣamālāṁ dadou brahmā kamaṇḍalum||

Translation:

Yama gave a staff, from his (own) staff of Time. (In the same manner) *Varuṇa* gave a rope snare, *Prajāpati* a rosary and *Brahmaṇ* gave a watering pot (*kamaṇḍalu*).

Explanation:

Yama is the lord of death. Consciousness that is expressed as death is *Yama*. This lord of death is the controller of all worldly persons, so he is called *Yama* (control). His weapon is a staff or club of Time. With his staff of Time, he controls beings, in whatever unruly manner they keep traveling. So, this is the weapon of *Yama*.

The lord of the waters is *Varuṇa*. The offering of his energy, of a conch shell, has been mentioned before. Now it speaks about the offering of his main weapon, a rope snare (*pāśa*). This is a rope that binds. Affection or infatuation binds worldly persons, so it is a snare. Affection is born from the fluid principle, so, the special weapon of *Varuṇa* is a snare. One can argue that beings are not only bound by affection, that hate can bind too. This is true, but hate is but a transformation of affection. Where affection is impeded, it is expressed as hate.

Prajāpati gave a rosary. The garland of fifty primary alphabets is a rosary. This universe is made of sound. Those who perform the maternal gesture ritual (*mātrikā nyāsa*) will understand that the body is built from the fifty letters of the alphabet. I have said before that the condensation of perception is form (*murtti*), perceptions are clusters of sound and sounds are groups of letters. In this way, the world of beings, and their subjects are created from the letters of the alphabet. So, the energy of *Prajāpati* is a rosary.

Brahmā gave a watering pot (*kamaṇḍalu*). The container where the nonmanifest seeds of creation reside is a watering pot. The reason that we go through repeated births and deaths, or constantly suffer disturbances of perception is the expressions of these nonmanifest seeds. This container where the nonmanifest seeds of creation are stored is the watering pot of *Brahmā*.

In this manner, *Yama*, *Varuṇa*, *Prajāpati* and *Brahmā* offered a staff of time, a snare, a rosary of letters and a watering pot. They understood that their forces were that of Mother. The spiritual seeker has to also offer fear of death, affection, the physical and subtle power of creation of the body and the unexpressed tendencies (*saṁskāra*) at the feet of Mother, to be freed from entanglement and ego, and to go forward on the path of liberation. It has been mentioned before, the way to offer these things. Showing each individually would increase the size of this book. A lack of patience is also not impossible.

Verse 23.

samastaromakūpeṣu nijaraśmīn divākaraḥ|
kālaśca dattavān khaḍgaṁ tasyāścarmma ca nirmmalam||

Translation:

The Sun gave his rays of light to each pore of the Goddess. Time (*Kāla*) gave a scimitar and a pure covering pelt.

Explanation:

The expressive power of the Sun illuminated each pore of Mother, all over her body. The Sun god understood that the energy of expression by which he expressed the world was that of Mother and nothing else. He had no power of his own. This is the meaning of the offering of the rays of the Sun to the body of Mother. The *Upaniṣad* says, 'there, the Sun does not shine' and 'your light illuminates everything'[31].

Time (*Kāla*) gave her a scimitar and a pelt. *Kāla* is the consciousness of Time in which this universe exists. Time is the container for this universe; there is no container for time. Before, this the lord of death (*Yama*) gave the staff of time to the Goddess. That was the nature of the power of destruction. Here one is to understand time to be of the nature as the container of this universe, the great Time (*Mahākāla*). It will not be beside the point here, to discuss a little about time. Time is expressed to us as the trinity of past, present and future. In reality, time is one, and undivided, eternally as the present. 'The universe is'; in this case, the 'is' is an indicator of time, that is, it signifies the existence of this universe in the container of present time. In the same way, in 'this universe was' or the 'universe will be', time is perceived to be the container. It is the same everywhere else. Although we sometimes apply meaning to 'time is' and give it some vague sense, it is an empty alternate knowledge. When we say 'time is', it means a containership (*adhikaraṇ*) for time. But there is no container for time. Time is the eternal container. There can be no past and future in this container. What we call to be past

31 *Muṇḍaka Upaniṣad*, 2.2.11

and future is also understood by the present tense 'is.' Then the question will be, why can we not perceive the past and the future as present? The main reasons are memory and hope. Our memory, imagination and hope are the three physical expressions of time. If we can wipe out these three from inside, then there would be no perception of time. In dreamless sleep, none of these three remain, so we do not have the perception of time. The conviction of the past grows from memory and of the future from hope. Those who are visionaries of three times (*trikāladarśi*), remove these from their hearts. That is why they know the past and future. None of our imaginations are pure. They are mixed with memories of the past and hopes for the future. They narrow our power of knowledge and so keep the past and future unperceived.

Whatever it is, the container of this universe, Time, offered a dividing scimitar and covering pelt. These are the two powers of Time. One is separation from pure consciousness, and the other its non-expression. In the beginning, direction and time are envisioned in *paramātmā*. When *paramātmā* expresses itself as Time, it feels itself to be separated from pure consciousness. This is a scimitar. With this separation, pure consciousness is covered. This is a pelt. Seen from another angle, it is Time that separates everything and hides its self-nature. These may be called a scimitar and a pelt. For so long, Time was attached to these two by affection. Today he is honored to offer them at the feet of Mother.

You should also offer your sense of time at the feet of Mother. Try to understand your memories, imagination and hope as Mother. When memories of the past or the enticing hopes of the future come to pain you or encourage you, then weep and say 'O Mother, why are you, who is always the present, arising in my heart as memory or hope? Why are you tearing my heart apart? O, Mother! Stand in your nature beyond time. Wipe out the pictures of past and future forever. Give me peace.' If you weep in this manner, you will discover nature beyond Time and find peace.

Verse 24.

kṣirodaścāmalaṁ hāramajare ca tathāmbare|
cūḍāmaṇiṁ tathā divyaṁ kuṇḍale kaṭakāni ca||

Verse 25.

arddhacandraṁ tathā śubhraṁ keyūrān sarvvabāhuṣu|
nūpurau vimalau tadvad graiveyakamanuttamam|
añgulīyakaratnāni samastāsvaṅgulīṣu ca||

Translation:

The milk ocean gave her a beautiful neckband, ever-new pair of clothes, a crown for her head, divine earrings, bangles, a half-moon, armlets, ankle bells, a wonderful jeweled necklace and rings of precious stones for her fingers.

Explanation:

The milk ocean is pure right attribute (*sattva guṇa*). It is the expression of pure attribute of knowledge unaffected by active and static attributes (*rājasa* and *tāmasa*). It is said that seven oceans exist in the human body. Here we will briefly look at these seven oceans. (1) Pure right attribute - the cream or milk ocean, (2) the right attribute slightly tinged by the active one - the butter ocean, (3) the right attribute slightly tinged by the static one - the yogurt ocean, (4) the active attribute – the wine ocean, (5) the active attribute tinged by the right one - syrup ocean, (6) the active covered by the static one – the salt ocean, (7) the static attribute – the water ocean. These attributes (*guṇas*) are eternal and infinite, so they are described as oceans (*samudra*). Besides this, from the origin of the word '*samudra'*, this comparison is valid. The root '*und*' is used with the meaning of wetting. Because it wets, it is called *samudra*. The three attributes (*guṇas*) are like the oceans as they completely wet the pure consciousness with a fluid of divine play. With the differences in their connections, they are divided into seven. These are the seven seas[32] described in the ancient texts (*Purāṇa*).

---

32 *lavaṇekṣusurāsarpirdahidugdhajalāntakāḥ*

It is incorrect to view the absence of the seven seas in this universe because we envision them in the human body. It has been said before that divine creation is so beautiful that everything present in this universe is present in the body of each being. It is as if each of our bodies is like a tiny universe. If we analyze this well, we can learn about the mysteries of this universe. The *śrutis* also say that 'knowing Self, one knows everything.'

Whatever it is, the ocean of milk is mentioned here and is most important. It is a store of infinite riches. The gods churned this ocean and were honored to find various jewels and divine nectar (*amṛta*). On the other hand, when the spirit of intelligence is purified, it gives rise to various yogic powers. Besides this, a special discovery is divine nectar. Consuming this nectar, beings become immortal. Only *paramātmā* is *amṛta*. When intelligence (*buddhi*) is purified, intellect about *paramātmā* arises. The tendencies (*saṁskāra*) of birth and death are removed and beings become immortal. Generally, disturbances due to the active attribute and the covering due to the static attribute, narrow the expression of the spirit of intelligence. By intense focus on God, by the grace of Mother, when these are subdued, various yogic powers appear. One who is engrossed with greed for such riches is barred from finding divine nectar. Instead, poison is created. Then, the intellectual formed *Maheśvara*, the *guru* appears and imbibing that poison, pours divine nectar for the disciples, making them immortal. That is why do not enter into the spiritual battle in the hope of finding yogic powers. Only self-sacrifice and self-offering will end this battle. Sacrifice yourself at the feet of Mother, you will find Mother. Yogic powers, grime from the road, will come by themselves. Ignore them and run crying 'Mother.' Offer yourself at the feet of Mother. You will discover *Brāhmaṇ*, you will find eternal peace. But that is something else.

Let us discuss the ornaments that the ocean of milk gave.

(1) a beautiful neckband, (2) ever-new pair of clothing, (3) a crown for her head, (4) divine earrings, (5) bangles, (6) an auspicious half-moon, (7) armlets, (8) ankle bells, (9) a wonderful

jeweled necklace and (10) rings of precious stones for her fingers. The ocean of milk, an infinite store of invaluable jewels, was honored to offer these ornaments for Mother. Many have riches, but if they do not adorn Mother, if they are not offered for the ceremonial worship of Mother, if they are held by ego as 'my wealth', then one has to suffer the trouble of acquiring, saving and needlessly losing that wealth. The demons steal that wealth by guile or by strength. If anyone can take it as the wealth of Mother and surrender one's ego, then one can see that pure peace due to the proper use of wealth, slowly advances one on the path to immortality. That is why, today, the ocean of milk tries to adorn the body of Mother with all its wealth.

(1) The beautiful neckband is the power of pure expression. When the spirit of intelligence is clarified, then the power of expression is intact. All material expressions end in intelligence. There is no material expression beyond intelligence. Because of a disturbance of the active principle (*rājasa*), the power of expression of beings is very weak. Only a small part of whatever is brought in front of them is revealed. Say you look at a tree. Your intelligence or power of expression tells you 'this is a tree.' But you only view a small facet of the tree. You do not learn its past and future condition, its internal flow of sap. This is due to murkiness in the spirit of knowledge. It does not happen when right attribute (*sattva guṇa*) is pure. All parts of things then appear together. This power is the beautiful neckband. Realizing that this is but a power of Mother, that we have no pride in its ownership, is offering it to Mother. This is the secret of the ocean of milk offering a beautiful neckband to Mother. One has to understand similarly about the other ornaments. We will not repeatedly speak about the mystery of offering, but just mention the spiritual principle of these adornments.

(2) The pair of eternal apparel: *māyā* and subsidiary knowledge (*avidyā*) are coverings of the beautiful form of Mother. It was mentioned before that Mother said,

'I cover myself with the cloth of *māyā*, hiding always.' The power of *māyā* arises where Mother is imbued with the sense of Godhood. Where she is imbued by a sense of worldly persons, she is covered by lesser knowledge (*avidyā*). Both these are eternal, that is why the mantra uses the adjective '*ajara*' (without destruction). When pure right attribute is expressed, then the nature of *māyā* and *avidyā* and how they are coverings of Mother may be understood.

(3) A divine crown: This is the divine power of knowledge by which, all principles of this universe can be understood without restriction. We normally move within confined knowledge. It is mixed knowledge. When we have knowledge of a tree, we have a mixed collection of knowledge about its trunk, branches, leaves, flowers, bark, color, etc. We do not have complete knowledge of its tree-ness. In this manner, the true nature of things is not known by worldly persons. When divine power of knowledge is found, this confinement does not remain. Then, the nature of each thing is completely revealed. This is a definite sign of pureness of the spirit of knowledge.

(4) Earrings: The ability to hear sounds from far away and the unvoiced sound inside (*anāhata*) is the divine power of hearing. This is the proper adornment for the ears.

(5) Bangles: These are indicative of the divine power of receiving. The power to receive things from a distant place while residing in another has been named bangles (*kataka*).

(6) An auspicious half-moon: an ornament for the forehead, a divine light. The special light of intellect arises from the spinal center at the level of the eyebrows (*Ajñā cakra*). By its effect, remote and subtle things can be easily observed. It is called divine sight or the power of remote viewing. In the Yoga literature, it has been called *praprṭtyāloka*.

(7) Armlets (*keyura*): arm adornments, the power to hold. This is the divine power to hold. It is by this power that *Śrī Kṛṣṇa* held up mount Govardhana.

(8) Ankle bells (*nupura*): ornaments for the feet, the power of divine movement. With this power, one can travel to inaccessible lands, enter into the earth or rocks or easily escape from confinement. There are stories that when the saint Trailañga Swami was placed in a prison cell, he came out of it easily. This is the power of divine movement.

(9) A necklace: This is divine voice. One whose intelligence is pure has a pleasing voice. Their words appear sweet to all people. People are not annoyed even when they are cursing. This is called the gift of voice.

(10) Rings of precious stones: the divine power of touch. By this power, remote and subtle objects can be felt and their hardness or softness etc. determined.

When the principle of intelligence is purified, true knowledge (*prātiva*) appears. The Yoga Sutras say 'this true knowledge is everything.' When this knowledge appears, all kinds of yogic powers are acquired. I have said before that pure right attribute is the ocean of milk. Consider all the jewels or supernatural powers in it as powers of Mother or her ornaments. Offering them to her frees a spiritual seeker of ego. Those who are truly seeking liberation, those who are engrossed in the love of Mother, may also because of past tendencies achieve such yogic powers. Without a sense of ownership in them, they do not interfere in supernatural acts. These seekers have the nature of supplicants, they offer their selves at the feet of Mother and remain serene. They carry out the actions in the world like machine-driven manikins. Despite that, occasionally their divine powers become evident. This is not due to ego, but because of encouragement by Mother. Those who are truly engrossed by love of Mother, do not have a drop of desire to express special powers to become famous in this world. The accolades of this world do not reach them. Having surrendered their selves to supreme power, they rise high above praise and criticism of this world. But that again is something else.

Verse 26.

viśvakarmā dadau tasyai paraśuñcātinirmalam|
astrāṇyanekarūpāṇi tathābhedyaṁ ca daṁśanam||

Translation:

Viśvakarmā gave her a pristine axe, many other weapons and an impenetrable armor.

Explanation:

Viśvakarmā is a divine builder or carpenter. The *śrutis* say that '*tvastā* gives form' (*tvastā rūpaṇi piṁsatu*[33]). It is *Viśvakarmā* who creates form and name in this world. The one who defines undistorted root nature by name and form is *Viśvakarmā*. Just as a sculptor hews a piece of stone into different shapes or things, *Viśvakarmā* expresses nonmanifest nature into various names and forms. Realizing that this power of organizing the world is that of Mother, is the offering of the axe and other weapons by *Viśvakarmā*. There is a special significance in the offering of an impenetrable armor. Even though *Viśvakarmā* creates this variety in the world and enters it, he remains undistorted. He is like a warrior in a suit of armor, who is not hurt, even though he injures innumerable enemies. Although *Viśvakarmā* transforms into many names and forms, he remains undistorted in his eternal, pure, free nature. This is due to an impenetrable armor. Seeing this as the power of Mother is offering her this armor.

Verse 27.

amlānapaṅkajāṁ mālāṁ śirasyurasi cāparām|
adadajjaladhistasyai paṅkajañcātiśobhanam||

33 *Ṛk Veda*, 10.184.01

Translation:

The ocean gave her fresh lotus garlands to wear on her head and around her neck. Other than this it gave another beautiful lotus (to hold in her hand).

Explanation:

Jaladhi- the ocean of water. It was mentioned before, in connection with the seven oceans, that the static attribute (*tāmasa*) was the ocean of water. The lotus garland is the host of tendencies (*saṁskāra*). The root '*paṅka*' means both boggy soil and sins. So, one born of sins can be called *paṅkaja* (lotus). What is soil or sins? The sense of 'I' is sinful. The sense of 'I'-ness in the body and such is the root sin. So, it has been said 'my sinfulness' (*pāpoahaṁ*). The sense of 'I'-ness or Self in what is not Self is the root of all sins. All sins in this world are based on this sense of 'I.' Not only sins but what is called piety in general, is also based on this 'self-sin.' In this light, piety is included in sin. Just as, worldly happiness, in the view of conscience, is nothing but sorrow, because it has the fault of resultant change. In the eyes of Self-knowledge, a sense of non-Self is nothing but sinful. The philosophical term for this sin and piety is *saṁskāra*. They arise from '*pāpoahaṁ*', so they can be called lotuses (*paṅkaja*). Because tendencies are innumerable, the word garland has been used in the mantra. This *saṁskāra*, in the language of *Vedānta*, is *māyā*, in the language of *Sānkhya* it is *prakṛti* (nature), in *Mīmāṁsā* it is *apūrvva*, by *Naiāiks* it is *adṛṣta* (fate). *Saṁskāras* are eternal, so the mantra uses the adjective fresh (*amlāna*). For the liberated person, *māyā* or *prakṛti* just moves aside. But they are not destroyed or wasted, they flow eternally, so they are fresh. Ācārya Śankara has said in the commentary to the *Upaniṣads*, 'the results of actions are eternal' (*amṛtaṁ karmmaphalam*).

Whatever it is, these lotus garlands or queues of tendencies are held by inert principle. Expression or exposure is the property of right tendency (*sattva*), inspiration or movement is the property of active tendency (*rājasa*), and immobility or stasis is the property of the static tendency (*tāmasa*). The tendencies inherent or in the form of seeds in *tāmasa* are activated by *rājasa*. As a result of that, the property of expression of Self by right attribute is aroused. So, static tendency or the ocean of water is able to adorn Mother with a fresh lotus garland. Remember that if you can truly surrender at the feet of Mother, then the tendencies by which you are always troubled, that appear as eternal bonds, will turn into adornments for Mother.

There are other mysteries in this mantra. There is mention of offering two lotus garlands and another lotus. They signify the threefold states of *saṁskāra*s. These tendencies are divided into three kinds, future, stored and prior (*āgāmī, sañcita, prāravdha*). This has been mentioned before. When one finds Mother, or meets Self, future and stored tendencies are respectively, removed and destroyed. Only the prior (*prāravdha*) remains. This is destroyed by endurance. Future tendencies are displayed as an adornment for the head of Mother. Stored tendencies adorn her chest. Only prior tendencies are left. Although they are a bunch of tendencies, they are eroded in one lifetime. That is why the prior tendencies have not been called a garland but as one lotus. It is displayed in her hand, as a lotus of divine play. In reality, every event in the life of a viewer of Self is divine play (*lilā*), because they do not carry out actions from love or hatred like people in general. They carry out worldly actions by offering them at the feet of Mother, like machines operated by her hands. So, this lotus is said to be in her hand. There is a statement that says, 'The life of those who have seen Self is but divine play.'

Verse 28.

himavān vāhanaṁ siṁhaṁ ratnāni vividhāni ca|
dadāvaśūnyaṁ surayā pānapātraṁ dhanādhipaḥ||

Translation:

Himavān gave the Goddess a lion to ride and many gems. The wealthy *Kuvera* gave a chalice full of wine.

Explanation:

A condensed sense of the physical body is *Himavān*. The Himālayā mountains are the greatest emblem of physicality or inertness. The human body is the greatest mark of physicality or body sense. Beings are so bound up by thinking that 'I' am this body, that they cannot but be said to be unconscious as a great mountain.

The lion is the mount for the Goddess. This has been discussed in detail in Volume One. When humans begin to have enmity towards their sense of body, then they may be said to have the characteristics of a lion. This enmity towards the state as a general being and the attempt to arouse the perception of the supreme state (*Brahmaṇ*) is only possible with a human body. That is why humans are the greatest among beings. The lion is the greatest of animals. When humans can begin to understand this state of being as a mount for Mother, that is, as an instrument under the direction of the power of Mother, then this offering of a lion is accomplished. As long as the principle of nonduality is not realized, as long as it is not perceived that 'I am Mother', so long, there is enmity towards the state as a worldly person. After finding Mother, this does not remain. It is transformed into a mount for Mother.

The many gems signify the variety of results of action. The human body is the proper field of action or Kurukṣetra[34]. Actions are carried out with this body. That is, all applicable actions are completed as ceremonies for the worship of Mother. Other bodies, like those of gods or animals, are only for experiencing results (*bhoga*), they cannot fulfill actions. When a spiritual seeker is accomplished in the mantra 'from morning to evening, from evening to morning, all that I do, O Mother of this universe, are all in your worship.' When all actions are for the worship of Mother and the results of all acts are for the satisfaction of Mother, then it is the offering of many. This invaluable advice for offering the results of actions has been given by the Lord to *Arjuna* in the *Gitā*. Weak beings like us, find success in the offering by *Himavān*

34 battlefield in *Mahābhārata*

of many gems at the feet of Mother in *Devī Māhātmya*. That is why we have said, *Gitā* is spiritual effort, *Caṇḍī* is the outcome. Whatever it is, just as humans greedy for gems dive into deep oceans disregarding their lives, they dive into the difficult ocean of action eager for results. So, the fruits of action are gems. Offer these gems at the feet of Mother and find freedom from the binds of the results of action.

Something of note here is that, without the offering of the lion, gems cannot be offered. First, the state of worldly person has to be realized as a mount for Mother. Then it is seen that the results of action are offered by themselves. No separate effort has to be made for them. Take your ego as controller of being and bow at the feet of Mother, you will see that despite not attending to the results of actions, you are instrumental in carrying out varied acts.

The king of wealth is the power of life. Life is the king of all wealth. He is always engrossed in drinking the wine of joy of material things. He has not understood for so long where this wine comes from. Who is this satisfaction of enjoyment of desire and wealth? They have been driven out of heaven because they do not know this. Because of the torment during all this time, he now understands that the chalice, full of the wine of material things, is nothing else but Mother. Knowing that the joy of material things is nothing but the bliss of *Brahmaṇ*, the lord of wealth is honored to offer the chalice, filled with the joy of material things, in a ceremony of *Brahmaṇ*, to *Brahmaṇ* formed Mother.

Verse 29.

śeṣaśca sarvanāgeśo mahāmaṇivibhūṣitam|
nāgahāraṁ dadau tasyai dhatte yaḥ pṛthivīmimām||

Translation:

The one who supports this earth, the ruler of all serpents, *Śeṣa nāga* (*Ananta*), offered the Goddess a serpent necklace adorned with invaluable gems.

Explanation:

The remaining nectar of the seeds of tendencies is *Śeṣa*. In the language of Yoga, it is called a store of actions (*karmmāśaya*). This store determines the race, life span and fate of worldly persons. This is possible in an earthly body because this store of actions always holds on to the sense of earthly perceptions. That is why the mantra says 'the one who supports the earth' (*dhatte yaḥ pṛthivīmimām*). All actions that we carry out, consciously or unconsciously, germinate from this subtle container of seeds of action. During each lifetime, new stores of seeds of action are built up. So, in each lifetime new actions are conducted. Because this is the last stage of action, these seeds of tendencies are called '*śeṣa'* (final).

Why is it called a serpent and the king of serpents? Action means the breakout of some form of energy. All actions like seeing and hearing are expressions of some form of energy. When these energies are nonmanifest or in the form of seeds, their nature is not perceived. The spirit of energy is felt when they are expressed as actions. When energy is expressed, that is, when it appears as a flow of action, its movement is like a serpent. The meaning of the root '*sṛp*' is convoluted movement. The word *sarpa* (snake) is also applied to creatures with convoluted movements. The flow of energy does not travel in a straight line. This has also been proved by modern science of inert substances. (To us, energy is not inert. We understand energy to be awareness or the nature of consciousness.) Whatever that be, we have many divine forms that have serpent ornaments or are seated on them.

The secret is that energy is condensed and expressed in material form (*murtti*). This flow of energy is indicated by the ornamental serpent. Comprehending this truth, the energy of worldly persons is called *Kulakuṇḍalinī*. When spiritual seekers carry out special actions, they can directly perceive that a flow of energy ascends upwards like a serpent, or travels downwards.

Whatever it is from the store of actions all energies large and small are expressed. That is why *Śeṣa* has been called the king of all serpents. He gave Mother a serpent necklace adorned with valuable gems. *Kulakuṇḍalinī* adorned with the fruits of liberation is the serpent necklace adorned with great gems. Although there is nothing that is either bondage or liberation, because, supreme Self (*paramātmā*) is the nature of eternal freedom. In a state of worldly person, there is bondage and freedom. It is in the truth defined *Brahmaṇ* that the state of worldly person is conceived.

The *Mulādhāra* (lowest spinal center) is the store of actions. The state as a worldly person resides in it. The perception of worldly person is *Kulakuṇḍalinī*. Do not imagine it to be a snake and be led astray. It is a worldly person that is liberated, so the head of *Kulakuṇḍalin* is adorned with the great gem of liberation. The energy of beings goes towards *Brahmaṇ* with a serpentine movement, so it is called a serpent. Realizing that this energy of worldly persons is only Mother, is the offering of a serpent necklace. Tell the serpent-formed Mother sleeping in the *Mulādhāra*, "Mother! When will you arise? When will these worldly bonds fall away? Mother! Those who are yogis, those who have the spiritual powers of restraint and so on, attempt to arouse you by different means. We have no power, we have no spiritual effort. Does that mean that you will sleep forever? Awaken and stand in your supreme form and affectionately pick up this child." Pray in this simple fashion. You will see *Kulakuṇḍalinī* awaken and your state of being adorn Mother as a necklace with a gem of freedom. You are merged with Mother.

Verse 30.

anyairapi surairdevī bhūṣaṇairāyudhaistathā|
sammānitā nanādoccaiḥ sāṭṭahāsaṁ muhurmuhuḥ||

Translation:

Honored in this manner by various adornments and weapons from the gods, the Goddess repeatedly laughed loudly and made powerful calls.

Explanation:

After speaking of the offering of energies by the principal gods, the sage ends by mentioning the offering of adornments and weapons by the other gods. This is what happens. When worldly persons desire Mother, their mind, intelligence, senses and limbs, all atoms of their physical bodies vibrate with the name of Mother. One becomes so used to the name of Mother, *Praṇava* and other mantras one unconsciously repeats holy names (*japa*). *Japa* is carried out without effort, just like breathing. One should not understand *japa* to be done only with a rosary or with the fingers. The reminiscence of Mother or her greatness is true *japa*. A special sign of *japa* is yogic union. This condition slowly becomes dense. Individual powers become united and are expressed as the desired deity of one's tendencies (*saṁskāra*). Or a universal conscious entity is perceived. At this time, a spiritual aspirant realizes that this is the only ruler and enjoyer, the supreme Lord. Even though it is One, it enshrines all perceptions and is followed by all perceptions. What I prided myself on for all this time, my body, my mind, my intelligence, this ego by which I was firmly bound, were all ignorance. Now, by the grace of Mother, I can say that there is nothing but Mother. Mother of all nature, Mother of all gods, and Mother of all powers, my Mother exists as worldly person, God and *Brahmaṇ* eternally.

When one is established in the great truth that 'there is nothing but Mother', the bonds of ego fall away. Then, whatever spiritual aspirants have, clothing, adornments, or weapons, they offer at the feet of Mother. All the things that one had been proud of before, that one cherished, are with open heart, all offered to honor Mother. Does Mother have dishonor that the gods have to honor her with adornments and weapons? No, that is not so. My Mother is above honor and dishonor. But the gods, by worshipping her are honored. Although the root '*mān*' means to worship, here, the word 'honored' is used in the sense of worship[35]. Even then, here we will take the meaning of the word 'honor' to mean what is

35 actions carried out for the pleasure of an honored person (*pujā*)

generally known as 'agreement' or 'acceptance.' When Mother is completely accepted, she is honored.

O, Mother! Let your dear children understand that just by acknowledging your existence, they obey you and you are honored. If beings traveling on the path of life just remember that 'you are', then their lives are worthy. We say that 'God is', but act just the opposite. In how many of the actions that we carry out from sunrise to sunset, do we keep in mind that we are in the presence of God? One does not have to ask a Hindu woman if she has a husband, because her looks and ways reveal the presence of her husband. In the same manner, all acts and demeanors of those who have accepted the existence of the husband of this universe, reveal the presence of the divine spirit. Mother! We do not even accept your spirit of existence; how can we say 'reveal yourself to us'? How can those who do not even believe in your existence desire your view? Maybe we weep to say 'Mother, show yourself!' We shed tears and appear as devotees in the eyes of others. Maybe we loudly shout your praises and think ourselves to be worthy. But the great truth is this, we have not truly accepted your nature. So, I say, Mother! I do not want to understand your nature. I do not want to be honored by seeing your unimaginably, beautiful form. Only, let me accept you, that you are mine. If I know nothing else about you, give me faith in the existence that 'you are.' Let me accept your spirit. Let my mind, intelligence and senses say together, 'Mother is true.' Strong truths arise in the heart, that my wife is, my children are, life is, my body is. But really, if we say no to these existences, it will not matter, as they are ignorance. But that which truly 'is', whose spirit is so dense that if once we turn towards it, the spirit of this universe, these small set of 'is' completely vanishes. Yet we have not been able to believe in that existence. What could be a sorrier state than that?

O, Mother! For much time, many lifetimes, we have been suffering insufferable pressure just for this one thing. Just because we do not accept you, we have birth and death, sorrow and suffering. This torture by *Mahiṣāsura*, this torment by tiny desires is there for many, many days. We are afflicted by them. We cannot bear it anymore. Because you hide your nature, we cannot accept you. We suffer from the pain of these three worlds. But, no more. Reveal yourself and see how much your dear children are tormented by the woes of life.

Look! The moment that you accept the nature of Mother, the moment that you understand that you have a Mother who removes your sorrow, the moment you realize it, consider yourself to be tormented by demons, and lay your deluded vision on an unknowable spirit and say 'Come, Mother, I am tormented', Mother appears immediately. That is why the mantra says, 'laughed loudly and made powerful calls.' Mother roared, and filled the horizons with her loud laughter. Mother appeared in her terrible form. "Who is it that attacks my children? Fear not. I am your Mother, I have appeared. You will not be tormented any more. You no longer have to be trodden by non-self or inertness. I will destroy all perception of inertness, all demons. They cannot save themselves."

Hear these words of Mother, her loud voice and laughter and your life will be honored. Do not think that these are a play of words or an overflow of emotions. The day you truly understand yourself to be struck by the torment of demons, you will believe in the existence of Mother. You will truly seek refuge and wait for the appearance of Mother. You will then understand how true is her appearance as a savior. But that is something else.

When divided consciousness that is perceived because of its connection to objects becomes united and is perceived as undivided consciousness, a spiritual seeker sees that there is no expression of any special *dharma* in it. Yet, it is illuminated by an inexpressible blissful spirit. Until this time, like a blind person, one had to use the stick of material things to arouse Self. This is no longer necessary. A spiritual seeker can be immersed in existential consciousness, or an ocean of awareness, discard all narrowness and be encouraged by the complete, dense spirit of Self. Oh! How beautiful and desirable is such a condition. Although one cannot remain in this place for very long, even then, the memory of the little time that can be spent here, can keep a seeker in bliss. Seeing a desired divinity in that undivided spirit also makes it worthwhile for a seeker.

The special form that appears here from the combined energy of the host of gods is said in the *Vaikṛtik Rahasya* to be the figure of *Mahālakṣmī*. This appearance is with all riches and power, a complete figure of enjoyment, *bhogamurtti*. So, she is called *Bhogamāyā*. The dark form that appeared for the destruction of *Madhu* and *Kaiṭabha*, in Chapter One, was *Mahākālī* or *Yogamāyā*. She appeared in that form to remove the sleep of Yoga of *Viṣṇu*. In this chapter, we see the appearance of a gloriously enjoyable form of Mother. By appearing in this form of *Mahālakṣmī* from the combined energy of all the gods, on one hand, she increases the joy of the gods. On the other hand, by destroying demons, she removes obstacles from the path of liberation for worldly persons. Much more of these mysteries will be revealed.

Verse 31.

tasyā nādena ghoreṇa kṛtsnamāpūritaṁ nabhaḥ|
amāyatātimahatā pratiśabdo mahānabhūt||

Verse 32.

cukṣubhuḥ sakalā lokāḥ samudrāśca cakampire|
cacāla vasudhā celuḥ sakalāśca mahīdharāḥ||

Translation:

Space was filled with deafening sounds made by her (the Goddess). Great echoes appeared of that immeasurable, immense sound. All the worlds were in turmoil, the oceans vibrated, the earth moved and the mountains shifted.

Explanation:

When individual energies come together, individual sounds (*nāda*) also combine. Just as the great energy of creation-maintenance- dissolution residing in each worldly person and appearing as various senses and perceptions seems divided, one supreme sound in expressing different perceptions appears as different sounds, molded by the throat, palate, tongue, teeth and lips. Just as energy is one and undivided, so is primal sound (*nāda*). As long as this undivided energy or *nāda* is not discovered, it is expressed as various feelings and sounds. Energy (*śakti*) is imperceptible, its first expression is *nāda*. Both *nāda* and *śakti* are of the same nature. Wherever energy is expressed there is *nāda*. Spiritual seekers, by the grace of Mother, discover this supreme sound whenever they discover energy. All things found in this world, or all percepts that appear inside, are all sound. There are no materials or percepts without sound. So long, worldly persons were addicted to individual special sounds, so there was the torment of multiplicity, of *Mahiṣāsura*. But today, because of special acts, one has discovered undivided sound. It is that of Mother. Nonmanifest Mother has appeared in the form of sound. At first, it appears as a universal note (*anāhata nāda*), it fills all space. Later it echoes in each molecule of the body and the body appears to be filled by it. In this condition, the entire world appears to be one undivided note. The bliss that a spiritual seeker enjoys by uniting with this undivided note cannot be described. It is the great sound of Mother. By it, all worlds are in turmoil, the oceans vibrate, the earth moves and mountains shift.

The word '*loka*' is derived from the root '*luk*' meaning 'to see.' What can be seen or known is *loka*. That is, what is expressed by a special name and form is *loka*. In other words, all that can be received or taken is *loka*. The oceans, by a mixture of different attributes, are seven-fold. This has been mentioned before. The earth (*vasudhā*) is the earthly body. Because it holds *vasu*, that is infinite gems of knowledge, it is called *vasudhā*. The mountains (*mahidhara*) are condensed inertness. The final result of inertness is '*mahi*', the one who bears it. The consciousness that expresses it is *mahidhara*. All these are in turmoil, are moved. It is as if this magic imagined by *māyā* is not to persist. The terrible note from *sadcidānanda* has arisen. This sound may trample all divisiveness and the variety of perceptions and merge them into one kingdom of consciousness. It seems as if the rule of inertness is to end. So, they are moved and they vibrate. Such is the wonderful effect of the sound that comes from the voice of Mother and pierces the seven worlds.

Have you ever heard this call from Mother, this great attractive voice? Until you have complete faith in the existence of Mother until you offer yourself at the feet of Mother, will you be able to hear that call? Even if you do, will you be able to feel its greatness? This incredible call in the field of blissful awareness, this unique note, although terrifying, although great and immeasurable, is sweet. It is a note that arouses the heart. It is the assurance of the terrible voice of *Caṇḍī*. It is truly without comparison. Mother! You are calling night and day with an unvoiced *anāhata* note from inside our hearts. We do not hear your call. In the midst of the noise from this world, the disturbances of senses searching for material things, this call does not reach our ears. That is why Mother, we children, do not come back home. Although there is severe heat outside, we burn in fires of sorrow, yet we are engrossed in play with toys of delusion. With reddened eyes and pretending to be angry, you are calling us, but our deluded play does not end.

Why do we not hear your call? Why do you not call so we may hear? Call so that even our deaf may hear. We have heard that those that hear your call travel on shoreless oceans. Let us hear that call, Mother. The note that made the *gopis* of Vṛndāvana run without fear and shame, the note that made the birds and animals anxious, that made the river *Yamunā* rush, let us hear that sound. Let us hear the sound of that enchanting flute just once. We will leave these shores of material things and go afloat on the ocean of scandal of *Śyam*. Crying 'Mother', we will run like calves who are lost.

There are differences between that sound and this sound by Mother. Those were attractive notes of a flute. This is a terrible noise to protect tormented children from the fear of demons. The primal sound (*nāda*) is the same, but it is expressed differently in different places, times and persons. What appears to children as an enchanting call of attraction, can be expressed as a mantra for the destruction of terrible enemies. Mother has appeared in her terrible form. To destroy demons, Mother is adorned by great wealth of the energies of this world. Although in the eyes of the children, this is a figure of assurance and joy, in the eyes of the enemies it is terrible and provokes fear. In this case, the roar of Mother is terrible. This will be explained later.

When a spiritual seeker lets out a roar like a lion to call Mother, when one is initiated in the mantra of truth and aroused by truth, when one makes the sound of truth to be rescued from all weaknesses, then that sound makes all space vibrate. An inert body is given life, each molecule is empowered by a feeling of truth. Standing at the center of truth, say loudly, 'Hail to truth, hail to Mother', so that the whole world, inert and living vibrates with that call. Let the world get rid of inertness and take on life. Call Mother so that the tendencies of senses are frightened. Like brave children, to bring fear into the hearts of the demons, call Mother. One day, the whole world will call Mother and that dense sound will unite heaven and earth. I will stand afar and viewing that scene be overwhelmed with joy. That day will surely come.

Whatever that be, we need to discuss here a bit about the principles of primal sound (*nāda*). This *nāda* is *Brahmaṇ*. Immersed in the principle of this sound, one can envision Supreme being (*Brahmaṇ*) or climb onto the lap of Mother. How is this possible? First, remember that this universe is the imagination of *Brahmaṇ*. The *śrutis* also say 'just as imagined before' (*yathā pūrvvamkalpayat*). Imagination is a characteristic of the mind. Resolve and imagination are actions of the mind. What is imagined in the mind is a collection of words (sounds). There is little imagination without words. If there were no words, there would be little imagination. Imagination is a following of words in the mind. Saying that '*Brahmaṇ* imagined' is to say that *Brahmaṇ* made some sound, such as Sun, Moon, tree, plant, men, animals, world and so on. These mental imaginations are the visible world. So, this world is of the nature of sound.

From different aspect, it can be seen that things of the world are called materials (*padārtha*). In grammar, words are called '*pada*.' The meaning (*artha*) of *pada* is *padārtha*. A *pada* is a collection of alphabetic letters. They are also sound. Each *pada* or word has meaning. That meaning is a divine sign. It is an external sign of this sound defining a meaning. '*Vṛkṣa*' (tree) is a word. It is a collection of letters. It appears in the mind or voice as sound (*śavda*). According to grammar, what is *śavda* is not only a collection of letters but also of the nature of sound. The word '*vṛkṣa*' has a meaning and is an external sign of an object with branches and leaves. Pronouncing the word '*vṛkṣa*' brings cognizance of such an object. If we observe our mental activity in relation to any such thing, we will see that they are perceptions of the nature of sound. The *śrutis* also say that what is perceived as material is formed by words or sound (*bācāramvanaṁ nāmadheyaṁ vikāraḥ*). So, there is no doubt that this world is a collection of sounds. According to *Vedānta*, this universe is only a form of names. Names (*nām*) are sound or *nāda*.

This sound (*nāda*) is twofold. It has the nature of a note and of a word. *Nāda* from instruments like a conch or a drum is of the nature of a musical tone. Even with this, beings are aroused by joy, sorrow or anger. This can be seen regularly. In the battle of Kurukṣetra, the sounds from the conch shells of the *Pāndavas* struck fear in the hearts of their opponents. When sounds from inert instruments have such abilities, why is it surprising that the sounds out of sentient machines, that is, living beings are able to create and maintain this world? King Duryodhana said 'I will not give away a part of my kingdom, even the size of the tip of a needle.' With these words, the entire host of kings in *Bhārata* willingly, like a swarm of insects, gave themselves up in self-sacrifice in the fires of battle. There are many other examples in this world. On the other hand, the same word, by a difference in pronunciation or by a change in tone may arouse different feelings in an audience. If the brother of the wife is called '*śyālā*[36]' in a

36 brother-in-law in Bengali, also used as a swear word

humorous tone, it elicits a smile. The same word said to him in a rough voice, will make him return much, to the speaker with added interest. This is a rule in this world. The world is built of sound, is conducted by sound, and is destroyed by sound. This world is but sound.

Each molecule has a natural tone. It is from this natural tone that atomic vibrations are conducted. This natural sound is like the first letter of the alphabet '*a*.' The root or natural primal sound (*nāda*) of this universe is like a string of '*a*' sounds pronounced together in the same note and pitch. This is the primitive note. The Lord has also said, among the letters I am '*a*'[37]. When *Brahmaṇ* imagines the creation of this universe, then this '*a*' specially vibrates or moves. Then it sounds like a prolonged letter '*u*.' When the imagination of creation ceases, then the movement or vibration is silenced and the sound changes to a '*m m m*.' This '*Aum*' or *Oṁ* is the primal note of creation. Spiritual seekers, closing their sense of outward hearing, or by other acts, hear this primal note from the *Anāhata* center. This primal note has universal appeal. This heart-rousing '*Oṁ*' sound seems like Mother calling us to come to Her. It is so beautiful, it cannot be described. One has to say that 'it goes through the ears to the heart and makes one anxious.' Whatever that be, just as a musical instrument has basic notes that are expressed as different melodies by the fingers of the musician, this primal note appears as the variety of this universe, by interactions with the three attributes (*guṇas*).

It was mentioned in Volume One that this universe is vibrations of energy. The various vibrations of the supreme energy that resides in the heart of knowledge appear as the form and flavor of things. Vibrations are based on sound. That is, vibrations appear from primal sound. One can test this. The vibration of contraction and relaxation of the muscles of our limbs is based on sound. By the rousing of anger or desire, the muscles of the different parts, appear to vibrate unnaturally. The cause of such vibrations is the sound or note of those tendencies. When the sounds of desire

37 *Bhāgabata Gitā,* 10:39

or anger appear in the mind or the voice, then these external vibrations appear in the different parts of the body. In the same manner, divine feelings can often cause movements of the body parts of the spiritual seeker. This will be discussed later. That our flow of thoughts and perceptions is in the form of primal sound and that it appears as different vibrations of the supreme energy cannot be doubted.

The knowledgeable sages of the past were so practiced in primal sound and the principles of vibrations, that they could merely by applying sounds make different forces appear and fulfill their goals. *Vedic* and later *Tāntrika* mantras, are incredible discoveries of the knowledge of these principles of primal sound and vibrations. With the help of these mantras, even in this age of disbelief and lack of knowledge of this truth, many incredible, direct results can be achieved. Even now, many illiterate healers in this land can heal some diseases by reciting mantras and carrying out various improbable events that astound people.

A short time ago, a servant from the western part of the land, seemed to have died of a snake bite in our area. At least, the doctors examined his body and declared him to be dead. Thereafter, his relatives were taking him to the cremation ground in the evening. On the way, they met a friend of the deceased. The friend learning of his death by snake bite asked them not to cremate him. He then appeared at the cremation ground and tied a rope around the toe of the deceased, kept pulling on it and recited some mantras, occasionally tapping the head of the deceased. After three hours of carrying this out, the body began to show signs of life. After trying all night in this manner with the recital of mantras, the man recovered and returned home. When he recounted this story to me, the wound on his toe had not healed.

The author has also without applying any yogic powers, just by the effect of mantras healed many patients from dog bites. Some other diseases can also be healed by the effect of the power of mantras. Whatever it is, a mantra is primal sound. We have to honor the knowledge of those who discovered the close association of the healing powers with these sounds. Great was their compassion. Some special acts and the view of cherished forms can be carried out by the application of the power of mantras. Many now agree that primal sound has such powers. But finding someone who has properly entered the principles of this primal sound and has mastered them is rare.

Just as the material world is expressed from nonmanifest nature, material or expressed sound appears from nonmanifest primal sound. The balance of the three attributes (*guṇas*) is nature (*prakṛti*). Even in that condition, one has to acknowledge the existence of primal sound. Otherwise, vibrations between the *guṇas* cannot take place. I have said before that wherever there is vibration or energy, there is the spirit of primal sound. But this primal sound is beyond perception, so the scriptural authors call it '*parā*.' Just as *prakṛti* has a name '*parā*', just as *Brahmaṇ* is called '*parā*', so is the nonmanifest primal sound called '*parā vāk*.' The first result or vibration of *prakṛti* is the supreme principle (*mahat tattva*). It is the arena of expression of all worldly materials. The primal sound here is called *paśyantī*. Only yogis, that is, those who can take their sense of Self into this supreme principle can perceive the nature of this sound. Because it is not perceived by the sense of hearing, it is called *paśyantī*. After this *madhyamā*. This can be perceived in the intellectual (*manomaya*) plane. With some degree of stillness, by attention to one's perception of resolution and alternation, one can perceive this sound. It is noiseless, yet a sound. After this, when the perceptions are more condensed, a vibration appears in the throat, palate and lips. As a result of this, manifest or material sound is expressed. The scriptural authors call it *vaikharī*. This is common to all animals and is perceived by the sense of hearing. The ancient sages, instead of using the word '*nāda*', have applied the word '*vāk*,' '*nāda*' and '*vāk*' are the same. In this case, the word '*vāk*' is not used in the sense of the organ of speech. The word '*vāk*' is in the feminine gender, so all four words, *parā*, *paśyantī*, *madhymā* and *vaikharī* are feminine. *Vaikharī vāk* is divided into three kinds as *udātta, anudātta* and *svarit*. It is not necessary to discuss all of this here.

Another specialty of Aryan scriptural texts is that the alphabet expressing *nāda* or *vāk* is called *akṣara*. *Gitā* says that *akṣara* is Supreme being[38]. The same word '*akṣara*' that denotes Supreme being, is in this land, the word for alphabet. No better knowledge about the principle of *nāda* has been discovered anywhere else. There is something else to know. The fifty letters of the vowels and consonants of the alphabet are called *mātṛkā*. My *Mahāmāyā* Mother, who is the form of creation-maintenance-dissolution, is eternally expressed as alphabetic sound. In the meditation hymn of Mother, it says, 'the face, limbs and body of Mother are formed by the letters of the alphabet.' Where do you go searching for Mother? Look! Every sound coming out of your voice is Mother. All the various sounds you hear in this world are Mother. The mantra of a cherished deity you perform on the rosary, this mantra is Mother. The unexpressed words in your mind, your thoughts, are Mother. You call Mother, that word is Mother. There is no difference between a name and what is named. You do not see Mother because you do not want to. My Mother is visible everywhere as sound. You do not see because of the lack of desire. But that is another matter.

The body of each being and all materials are created from the fifty letters that form Mother. *Tāntrika* gestures (*nyāsa*) are based on this fact. Many recite the mantra '*aṁ namoh* to the forehead' etc. and touch their fingers to that location to complete the *nyāsa*. But this does not bring the full results of *nyāsa*. Because of a lack of attention to the purpose of the injunctions, these body movements are turned into mere contortions. I will give some hints here. Even if just one person advances with them, it will be worth it. Perceptual energy has to be taken to the forehead and other body parts. Until a vibration is perceived, the mantra should be slowly recited (without raising the voice). Mental recitation is the best. In the beginning, this practice may be difficult and a little painful. After a few days, the difficulty is gone and perception can be conducted by will. At the same time, pronounce these seed mantras so that they appear to become one with perception of the

---

38 *akṣaraṁ param brahma, Bhāgavat Gitā,* 8.3

vibrations. In this manner, when all three, mantra, vibration and gesture ring with the same tune, you will know that the *nyāsa* has been accomplished. During the conduction of this conscious *nyāsa*, there is an incredible feeling of happiness. There are other results. The feeling that one is just a physical body is removed. The body sense completely relaxes. It is also a way to remove illnesses. Besides this, a spiritual seeker accomplished in *nyāsa* can receive some other special powers.

Verse 33.

jayeti devāśca mudā tāmūcuḥ siṁhavāhinīm|
tuṣṭuvurmunayaścaināṁ bhaktinamrātmamūrtayaḥ||

Translation:

The host of gods, in great joy, loudly praised the rider of the lion. Sages sang hymns with devoted hearts and respectful postures.

Explanation:

After a long time, the gods are ready to have their desires fulfilled. Before this, their individual forces felt separated from supreme energy. Although they tried to prevent attacks by the demons, they failed. Now that feeling has been removed. Divided energies have surrendered to supreme force. The gods are joyous, there are sounds of victory. Let me explain. When the sense of Self is gathered into supreme principle or the intellectual sheath, one discovers one's personality or ego (*asmitā*). In this condition, the expression of the different senses or various worldly matters do not seem to be separate entities. They all appear to be special layers of personality. The separate awareness of the senses of the gods does not appear to have independent control. Everything is under one supreme control. The supreme power of Mother appears as a figure riding a lion. A spiritual seeker who wants to end worldly life is a lion. The seeker then truly harbors violence towards the state as a worldly person. Common people accept him as the greatest of men. His body is turned into an instrument or carrier for the power of Mother. What wonderful influences. In this condition, on one hand, the terrible sounds of Mother, her words of assurance, bring terror to the demons. On the other hand, they bring unending joy in the hearts of the gods. So, the mantra says that the joyful shouts of the gods crying 'victory to Mother', rang to the horizons. The sages who had been silent for so long, to expressions of the right attribute, ended their silence and sang praises to Mother. Respectfully reciting hymns of praise, they bowed their body and mind at the feet of Mother.

When you too in your heart perceive the presence of Mother, then with full belief, raise sounds of victory to Mother. The moment that you see that you have a glimpse of truth, a drop of the grace of Mother, at that moment, to remove doubts, disbelief and weaknesses in your heart, raise sounds of victory in joy and with devotion, recite hymns of praise. When you do this for some days, you will see that your heart becomes pure. It turns into a throne for Mother. No other easier way has been found to purify the heart. The sages of the days of the *Upaniṣad* advised us to purify the heart in this manner.

Verse 34.

dṛṣṭvā samastaṁ saṅkṣubdhaṁ trailokyamamarārayaḥ|
sannaddhākhilasainyāste samuttasthurudāyudhāḥ||

Translation:

Seeing all the three worlds perturbed, the enemies of the gods gathered with innumerable well-armed militia, prepared for battle.

Explanation:

After describing to king Suratha how the gods were arrayed, sage Medhasa drew the attention of the king to the demons. Look, the terrible sound from Mother, the sounds of victory from the gods and the sounds of hymns by the sages, came together and shook all three worlds. The three worlds, earth, middle and upper[39], the three lower spinal centers, were perturbed by this

39 *bhu, bhubaḥ, svaḥ*: earth, astral world and heaven

sound. These three lower centers are centers of expression for demons. The enemies of the gods, the *asuras*, who are the cause of repeated birth and death, readied themselves to oppose this effort by arming themselves with their weapons. Before this, the demons had repeatedly defeated the gods. So, this time, with their past tendencies, they rise with hopes of success. Alas! The demons do not know that this time it is not the gods, but Mother who appears on the battlefield.

Verse 35.

āḥ kimetaditi krodhādābhāṣya mahiṣāsuraḥ|
abhyadhāvata taṁ śabdamaśeṣairasurairvṛtaḥ||

Translation:

"Ah! What is this?" Uttering these words angrily, *Mahiṣāsura*, surrounded by uncountable demons, moved towards the source of the noise.

Explanation:

After all this time, the roar from Mother, mingled with the shouts of joy of the gods has brought fear and concern to the heart of *Mahiṣāsura*. The word '*āḥ*' is used to show a feeling of anger and pain. The sound from Mother has risen to bring pain in the heart of the collection of past tendencies (*saṁskāra*) of active attribute (*rājasa*). It has been mentioned before, that the three attributes (*guṇas*) have a guardian-guarded characteristic within themselves. When right attribute (*sattva*) is expressed, others are guarded. When other attributes are guarded they are also disturbed. This is what is described here. Noticing the appearance of *sattva*, *rājasa* arises to oppose it. Hearing the sounds of victory that perturb the three worlds, saying 'Where is this sound coming from?', *Mahiṣāsura*, with his helpers, rapidly went to look for it. Later, we will see the names of the other demons. You too will see that when you perform repetition of mantras, chant hymns or otherwise sing praises of Mother, the stored tendencies of the material world, unnoticed, oppose your spiritual enterprise.

Verse 36.

sa dadarśa tato devīṁ vyāptalokatrayāṁ tviṣā|
pādākrāntyā natabhuvaṁ kirīṭollikhitāmbarām||

Verse 37.

kṣobhitāśeṣapātālāṁ dhanurjyāniḥsvanena tām|
diśo bhujasahasreṇa samantādvyāpya saṁsthitām||

Translation:

After this, *Mahiṣāsura* saw the figure of the goddess. Her beauty flooded the three worlds. Her footsteps compressed the earth. Her crown touched the skies. The sounds from her bowstring perturbed the lower worlds. Her thousand hands filled all directions of space.

Explanation:

Before this, whenever *Mahiṣāsura* fought with the gods, he would see individual forces stand and battle with him. Each time, they had been defeated. But what does he see now? He sees the figure of a goddess. The Goddess, illuminated, self-expressed, the supreme power of awareness. Casting his look at her, he understood that by her presence, she expressed all three worlds. *Mahiṣāsura* is also an expression of her appearance, such was her beauty, such was her power of expression. 'When it shines, everything shines by it, all things shine in its light'[40]. Not only does her beauty illuminate all the worlds, the earth is compressed by her footsteps. Earth is inert. By the footsteps of the eternal one, by the influence of her power of movement, by her incredible energy, the principle of earth or inertness is downed, is made inexpressible. By the expression of awareness of the power of Mother, nothing appears to be inert. This is why Mother compresses the earth with her footsteps (*pādākrāntyā natabhuvaṁ*). Because expression is characterized by movement, the movement word '*pāda*' is applied. The word can also mean 'rays.' By the rise of the all-

40 *tameva bhāntam anubhāti sarvaṃ, tasya bhāsā sarvamidaṃ vibhāti*; *Kaṭhā Upaniṣad*, 2.2.15

pervading power of expression of Mother, the nature of earth (*bhu*), its principle or nature of inertness nearly disappears. The word '*natabhubaṁ*' is used to point to this sense of disappearance. The crown adorning her head is the percept of purity. It touches the skies. The nature of perception is like the sky, detached and all-encompassing. But the sky is inert, perception is of the nature of awareness. This is why the scriptures say, 'awareness piercing the sky of *Brahmaṇ* is greater than *Brahmaṇ*.'

The twang of the bowstrings of Mother perturbed all the lower worlds. This sound of the bowstring is the sound of *Praṇava* (*Oṁ*). The *śrutis* say, '*Praṇava* is the bow, Self is the arrow, and *Brahmaṇ* is the target'[41]. By the sound of *Praṇava*, seven layers of ignorance are perturbed. There are seven lower levels (*pātāl*), so the mantra says 'without end.' The seven layers of ignorance, bound, more bound, most bound, ignorant, more ignorant, most ignorant and inert, are known respectively as *atal, vital, sutal, talātal, rasātal, pātāl* and *mahital*. By the appearance of Mother in the form of awareness, by the sound of *Praṇava* of consciousness, all worlds of ignorance, the land of the demons or serpent world are moved. Just as the seven layers of ignorance are called the seven underworlds, the seven layers of knowledge are called the seven upper worlds (heavens). Although off-topic, I mention here the seven heavens, desire of freedom, greater desire of freedom, greatest desire of freedom, knower of *Brahmaṇ*, great knower of *Brahmaṇ*, greater knower of *Brahmaṇ*, greatest knower of *Brahmaṇ*, these seven layers of knowledge are the seven upper worlds.

The thousands or innumerable arms of Mother fill all directions, to the horizons. Generally, the directions appear to be empty or space. But, with the appearance of Mother, there is no sense of direction. Everything is imbued by Mother. A dense nature of awareness is illuminated everywhere. There is nothing empty, everything appears to be full. All characteristics that appear with Mother are evident in this mantra. When spiritual

41 *Muṅḍaka Upaniṣad*, 2.2.4

seekers find Mother, that is, envision Mother, these characteristics appear in them. Their consciousness or 'I'-ness appears to fill the three worlds. Inertness disappears. An expansive sense like the sky covers everything. With the soundless *Praṇava*, all ignorance, doubt and inertness are removed. One realizes that only the nature of consciousness exists everywhere.

As long as Mother is not seen in this manner, a proper spiritual enterprise has not even begun. Standing at this place, one has to target the arrow of self towards *Brahmaṇ*. When my Mother revealed in this fashion, there is a means for the torment by demons to end.

Verse 38.

tataḥ pravavṛte yuddhaṁ tayā devyā suradviṣām|
śastrāstrairbahudhā muktairādīpitadigantaram||

Translation:

The demons began to fight. The energy from the many weapons lit up the horizons.

Explanation:

Now the battle against enemies of the gods begins with Mother. If you say, what is battle for Mother? The demons may be destroyed just by her wishes. Where is the need for battle? In answer to that, it has to be said that there is a need. This battle is a joyful game between mother and child. This battle of mother and child is wondrous and beautiful. The children want to be engrossed by material things. Mother wants to make them leave by force and picks them up onto her lap. The divine play that takes place at this time, appears outwardly as a battle. For the children who are spiritual seekers, nothing more has to be said explicitly.

We see in *Gitā*, that *Arjuna* says to the Lord, 'Tell me definitely, that by which I can reach for what is right.' Even in such a place, there was a feeling of 'I' reaching for what is right. So, Mother appeared as a charioteer, as a *guru*, and maintaining control by *Arjuna*, had *Viṣma*, *Droṇa* and others killed by him. But we see in *Caṇḍī*, that the children are like naked babes on the lap of Mother. All control has been offered at her feet. There is no separate 'I.' Even if there is, it is a toy for Mother. Here it is Mother in happiness and sorrow, in joy and sadness, desire and anger, compassion and forgiveness and in hatred and jealousy. Here the child does not want to live without its Mother. So, Mother has to appear on the field of battle. Mother has to arm herself with many weapons and take a stance for the good of her children. Although the demons may be destroyed merely by her wishes, even then, Mother dresses according to the *saṁskāra* of the children and carries out a battle.

Even the clan of demons are children of Mother. Our senses as worldly persons are properly demons. She has encouraged the torment of demons so that we will call for her. We have called for Mother. In sorrow, sadness, torment or happiness, in whatever fashion, we have called for Mother. Can she stay still any longer? She will come and pick us up. She will now destroy our past tendencies, the bands of *asuras*. Seeing this, we will joyfully raise cries of 'victory to Mother' ringing to the horizons. Come all you children of Mother, with a million voices truly call Mother.

O! With what words will I tell you how Mother goes into battle. Those who in the words of *Sānkhya* call this *prakṛti* (Nature), have to look and see. Until *prakṛti* turns towards salvation, there is no hope of liberty. When *prakṛti* moves towards *puruṣa,* then the elements (*bhutas*) and senses and other principles become weak and turn towards dissolution. In the language of the devotee, this is a war game between Mother and child. Those who seek to close the externally faced tendencies with the help of Yoga should also see how a great internal attractive force disempowers externally faced tendencies and brings them towards dissolution. In the words of the child, this is a game with Mother. Again, there is no harm by those who are *Vedāntists*, in calling this universe a mirage, imagined from ignorance. You will see that when this ignorance or *māyā* becomes immersed in bright knowledge of *Brahmaṇ*, then sky and other elements, eyes and other senses, *prāṇa* and other breaths, disappear into supreme intellect. You will then see that self-expression of intellect, slowly dims the expression of materials by *māyā*. This in the language of *Caṇḍī* is the battle by Mother. Here, we do not want to call *māyā* or *prakṛti* false or inert. *Māyā* is *Brahmaṇ*, *Brahmaṇ* is *māyā*. *Brahmaṇ* without *māyā* and *puruṣa* without *prakṛti* is beyond enterprise and perception. When the intellect of *Brahmaṇ* is discovered by forward intelligence, that is, by a spirit of pure intelligence, it is still bound to *māyā*. Reaching this point makes human life and effort worthwhile. After this, further nature, that is, *Brahmaṇ* without *māyā* or *puruṣa* without *prakṛti* unfolds by itself. This has been said many times before. Whatever it is, we know that Mother appears in battle. In Volume One, we explained the mantra 'You are the nature of all; the balanced, the active and the dark attributes (*guṇas*) characterize your natural form'[42]. You have understood the nature of Self as Mother. You are used to cherishing the nature of Self, to show it devotion and worship. Does saying 'Mother', remind you of this? Then you will understand, will perceive that Mother is fighting. The mystery of the weapons will be explained later.

Verse 39.

mahiṣāsurasenānīścikṣurākhyo mahāsuraḥ|
yuyudhe cāmaraścānyaiścaturaṅgabalānvitaḥ||

Translation:

The leaders of the warriors of *Mahiṣāsura*, *Cikṣura* and *Cāmara*, together with other demons, began fighting with four armed divisions.

Explanation:

Cikṣura and *Cāmara* are two of the generals of *Mahiṣāsura*. Their battle is described in detail in the *Devī Bhāgavat Puraṇa*.

42 *prakṛtistañca sarvvasya guṇatrayabibhāvinī*, Chapter 1, Verse 57

Cikṣura is a force of distraction. The name is formed from the root '*cikṣ*' meaning distraction. *Cāmara* is a force of concealment. The name is formed from the root '*cam*' meaning to consume. On one hand, they move the children away from *Brahmamayi* Mother, on the other hand, they conceal her. Who cannot see Mother, Self, 'I'? Night and day, when awake or in any other state, who does one see? One always views Self, 'I', Mother. Even then, when looking, why do they not see. Why do they not understand? It is because of attacks by *Cikṣura* and *Cāmara*. On one hand, disturbance or a force of distraction does not let one see Mother, on the other, a force of concealment covers Mother. Let me explain this in more detail.

You see a tree. This is existence (*cit*) or *ātmā* in the form of a tree. But not observing Self, you only see the name and form of a tree. The one who distracts you from your true Self and attracts you to name and form is *Cikṣura*. The name and form or knowledge of materials that covers true existence or Self, and does not let you see, is called *Cāmara*. Or, say you see a piece of ice. Although you know it to be a condensed form of water, in your perception, it appears as a piece of white stone. Even though you want to focus on the molecules of water, the one who distracts your vision with a special form is the great *asura Cikṣura*. He is one of the generals of *Mahiṣāsura*. With him is the ruler of concealment, *Cāmara*. He enchants one with the beauty of name and form, cheating you of true nature. Look again. There are toys made of sugar, elephants and horses with so many names and forms. Although they are sugar, we do not comprehend. We are engrossed by name and form. We are cheated of the true nature of things. This is the attack by these demons.

Now try to understand the degree of this torment. You are Suratha. You have found the *guru*. By respectfully listening to and thinking of the words of Brahmarṣi Medhasa, you have understood that this universe is nothing but Mother or Self. Yet, after understanding this, hearing advice and thinking of this thousands of times, we experience it as only this universe. This is by whose attacks? This is from *Cikṣura* and *Cāmara*. Because the powers of distraction and concealment have not been removed from spirit, we are not able to take this universe as Self, as Mother. Only for the little time that you specially try and forcefully hold it as Mother, are they subdued. In the next moment they begin to act again. In this fashion, not for a day or two, but for a long time, this torment by the demons continues. So, it was said in the beginning that for a full hundred years, the battle raged between gods and demons. Yet, the demons were not destroyed. But, fear no more. Mother has appeared in battle. The one who had appeared as distraction and concealment has now come to end them too. So, why is there anxiety any more?

One day, in a delusion of joy you asked for this. Without blindfolds on your eyes and running about here and there, you would not find happiness. So, Mother, in her affection, covered your eyes with the power of concealment, and as the power of distraction satisfied all your needs. Having played this game for many lifetimes, now you say like a child, 'Mother I do not want multiplicity anymore, there is no joy in it.' So, by the grace of Mother, *Madhu* and *Kaiṭabha* have been destroyed. But, the multiplicity you had still desired, that which you have not yet enjoyed, you now pray that the distraction and concealment at the root of your stored tendencies also be removed. What you one day asked for from Mother, now you want her to remove. Do you mean this? You ask for it and then in the next moment want it removed. That is why Mother looks at you. Do you truly want that the powers of distraction and concealment be removed forever? Running here and there with blindfolded eyes stop forever? Is that what you truly want? No, that is false, that is not what you want. You want that both Mother and the world coexist. You want that 'I will enjoy the world with Mother.' That is why she does not appear in battle. But, when the child truly says 'Mother! I do not want this world anymore. I do not want things of form and flavor, body, sense, mind and intelligence. I want only you. I want my eternal, tranquil, formless Mother, only you', then Mother battles for the children who say this with a simplicity. For them, she destroys *Cikṣura* and *Cāmara*. You must say this too. You have become

Suratha. Samādhi is your companion. *Guru* Medhasa is helping you, he is your shelter. You too must say, 'truly I do not want this world.' You will see Mother battle for you.

Whatever it is, the mantra mentions four divisions of power of *Cikṣura* and *Cāmara*. We will now try to understand this. The four divisions are elephants, chariots, horsemen and foot soldiers., Pain, action, misfortune and fate of beings are stored by the powers of distraction and concealment. The elephant represents pain, the horses action, the footmen misfortune and the chariots fate. Accompanied by these four divisions, the generals of *Mahiṣāsura* appear on the battlefield. Worldly persons not only suffer from these two generals, distraction and concealment, but also feel torment by the four divisions of soldiers.

The first is pain. The tendencies of spirit are painful. What is known as happiness in this world, is in the eyes of those with conscience, sorrow or pain, because worldly happiness appears with a crown of pain. On one hand, it is temporary, on the other, having the possibility of ending in the future, the duration of enjoyment is also painful. The second is action. The root of pain is action. Pain appears from action. The tri-fold nature of action has been explained before. Third, misfortune, the word (*bipāka*) signifies termination. The flow of tendencies of spirit always terminates. The fourth is fate or hope. It is called the store of action. The fine resolutions of action are stored in it. It is conducted by the forces of distraction and concealment. This is the nature of beings. These four divisions conducted by distraction and concealment can be called worldly persons.

Let me be more explicit. Look at who you are. First, you have blindfolded your eyes. Who am I? Not knowing the answer, you have already accepted ignorance. This is the primary concealment. Residing in this concealment of ignorance, you are daily running after form and flavor. This is distraction. As a result of this, you suffer the pains of happiness and sorrow for many lifetimes. From this pain, action or repeated contact between materials and senses takes place. These actions terminate and produce seeds of pain.

These seeds then form the subtle store of actions. Think about this calmly. This is your state as a worldly person. If you can for once be freed from the hands of these four troopers, that is, discover Supreme being, become free of pain, action, misfortune and fate, then you will be free from the state as a worldly person. Supreme Mother, to free you from this bondage of being, is getting ready to destroy *Cikṣura* and *Cāmara* and their four divisions of soldiers.

Verse 40.

rathānāmayutaiḥ ṣaḍbhirudagrākhyo mahāsuraḥ|
ayudhyatāyutānāñca sahasreṇa mahāhanuḥ||

Translation:

The *asura* named *Udagra* came to battle with sixty thousand chariots and the *asura Mahāhanu* came to battle with ten million chariots.

Explanation:

The demon forces are being described. Other than *Cikṣura* and *Cāmara*, great demons like *Udagra* and *Mahāhanu* appeared on the battlefield. We will learn their names and strengths in time. The word '*ut*' means upward and '*agra*' means head. This is *Udagra.* The pride of ego is the demon *Udagra.* He does not want to lower his head. Knowing that there is, or can be, no controller other than Mother, even after a hundred thousand direct and indirect proofs, worldly persons do not lower their head of ego held high or do not want to. Understand this feeling to be the *asura Udagra.* One might be concerned that this has been said before. Only after beings have offered their control at the feet of Mother, does she appear in battle. Then from where does the *asura* of ego appear? In answer, I have said that movement of nature is twofold, attraction and repulsion. Because of the attractive force, despite the presence of pride in the state of being, inner feelings of surrender appear. If this surrender is complete then there is liberation. There are no more battles. As long as war rages, we have to understand that we have not surrendered completely, not found knowledge of

Self. When beings become aware of the control by Mother and get ready to surrender, but cannot because their ego hinders them, they weep and say to her 'I have not been able to surrender. O, Mother! Make me fit to surrender to you.' When this perception comes in the right manner, when there is no duplicity, when like a simple-hearted child one surrenders to Mother, then she arranges to destroy the *asura Udagra*.

Whatever it is, this *asura* is not without power. It comes to battle with sixty thousand chariots[43]. What are the sixty thousand chariots? The *śrutis* say that the body is the chariot. There are six body sheaths, physical, physiological, mental, intelligent, intellectual and blissful. *Paramātmā* is as if covered by these six layers. These six bodies are the chariots of the demon *Udagra*. Although *Vedānta* mentions five sheaths, by separating the intellectual sheath into intelligent and intellectual (*jñana* and *vijñana*), six body sheaths are also well known in the scriptural texts. The intelligent sheath can be called *buddhi* and the intellectual sheath great spirit (*mahadātmā*).

The sheath built or nourished from the transformation of food materials is called the physical or material sheath (*annamaya koṣa*). It is the first chariot of *Udagra*. Worldly persons initially think that this physical body is 'I.' It is the initial shelter of their ego. As long as the body remains, one has to understand that a portion of ego remains. The moment that all pride for the body disappears, the body falls. Whatever high state may be reached in *samādhi*, a small seed remains. So, one returns to the perception of the body. But it is needless to say that the body perception of a self-realized soul is very different from that of a common worldly person. A self-realized person is forever free from fear of death. By this one sign, it may be said that they do not have pride for their body. But worldly persons are afraid of death, so they hold on to pride for their bodies. One may say that self-realized beings retain a bit of pride for the body, for the erosion of stored actions, for the removal of darkness in this world, because of their compassion, or

43 six *ayuta* = sixty thousand

to bring freedom to a few favored companions. It does not matter, but that is something else.

Another chariot of *Udagra* is the physiological (*prāṇamaya*) sheath. This is the sheath by which the physical body retains the power of life. Commonly it is called *prāṇa* and the other five breaths. But basically, they are not just physical breaths. The force of life is the proper *prāṇamaya* layer. The sense of self of worldly persons is also confined here. Third, is the *manomaya* sheath, or the mind and the senses. In this layer, one feels oneself to be mind and senses. Fourth, is the sheath of intelligence or knowledge. This layer is the shelter for the expression of all material things. That I am with knowledge and that I know all material things, is a source of pride for this sheath. Then the intellectual (*vijñānamaya*) sheath. Here both physical and subtle matters are revealed. It is the fifth site for ego. Finally, the blissful sheath. This is the sixth place of pride of ego. These six special chariots, by innumerable names and forms, physical and subtle, are seen as innumerable kinds. That is why the mantra uses the word *ayuta* (ten thousand) to signify innumerable. Or, the word '*ayuta*' may mean 'not united', that is, different from Supreme being. Forgetting that only Mother is properly 'I', worldly persons forgetfully are bound by ego to a six-layered body. This is the spiritual mystery of the sixty thousand chariots of the demon *Udagra*.

The physical or mental power of beings is *Mahāhanu*. What is generally known as self-drive (*puruṣākār*) is called *Mahāhanu*. Until this self-drive of beings is not ended by repeated opposition by the divine, it is all-powerful. 'By hard work, I have achieved knowledge or acquired wealth, or I have found knowledge of Self by severe spiritual enterprise.' These perceptions are those of *Mahāhanu*. It has a million chariots (a thousand *ayutas*). In these places, the numbers stand for innumerable. The actions from connections of the senses to material things are innumerable. This is why the word 'thousands' is used here. The word '*ayuta*' means not united. This was said before. Not understanding that the one providing the 'drive' in self-drive is Mother, carrying out all the actions of senses, is the battle by *Mahāhanu* with a million chariots. This is the spiritual secret.

Verse 41.

pañcāśadbhiśca niyutairasilomā mahāsuraḥ|
ayutānāṁ śataiḥ ṣaḍbhirbāṣkalo yuyudhe raṇe||

Translation:

The great *asura Asilomā* and *Bāskala*, came to battle with respectively fifty million and sixty million chariots.

Explanation:

Asilomā means one who has hair like swords. The body can be injured when one comes close to him. By spiritual vision, it may be called malice. Malice is rightly *Asilomā*. Not only does it injure others, but like a wildfire, it destroys those that seek its shelter. Jealousy and envy are included in this. Intolerance of the good of others makes people narrow-minded and disturbed. Many great souls are sad at the sorrow of others and shed tears seeing those of others. But it is rare to find people who are genuinely happy at the happiness of others, who with a simplicity, smile when others smile. Why does this happen? Because of the attack by the demon *Asilomā*.

On the other hand, we have to understand that those who willfully practice malice towards material things, as a means of renunciation for seeking God, are also being tormented by this demon *Asilomā*. Because attraction and malice are both chains. Just as great attraction to material things is a hindrance to finding God, so is any great repulsion to them. One day, the end of attraction takes place in the divine. It is difficult for the repulsion of things to end in the divine. Yes, *Kaṁsa*, *Śiśupāl* and *Dantavakra* harbored true malice. Their malice being focused on God brought them liberation. But that is impossible for people in general because their spirits are very weak.

Whatever that is, the number of chariots of this *asura Asilomā* is fifty million (*niyuta*). The feeling of malice spreads based on form, flavor and the five characteristics. Pointing to their innumerable variations, large numbers are cited. Or, the word '*niyuta*' may mean 'not united.' Spiritually the words '*ayuta*' and '*niyuta*' mean a state of emptiness without union with *paramātmā.* At every moment, our eyes and five senses and our speech and five work organs, are united with five material characteristics. Among them, some are in our favor, others are against us. A change in spirit because of unfavorable contact is malice. It is expressed by both senses of knowledge and action. The ten senses and the five materials multiplied together, appear as fifty different kinds of malice. So, the mantra uses the word, fifty million. As long as one has a sense of non-Self, that is, one feels things to be different from Mother, this sense of malice is impossible to remove. The word '*bāskala*' means the desire to enjoy. The torment of this demon appears to us as repeated births and deaths. From eternal times we have become used to enjoying this world, for many lifetimes we are enjoying this same world, but this desire does not end, so strong and unbeatable is this *asura.* The number of his chariots is sixty million (six *niyutas*). This body which is for the enjoyment of desires is the location for the demon *Bāskala.* In it, the six transformations, birth, existence, growth, change, deterioration and termination take place. Based on this six-fold changing body, one has to travel through a million births, by the force of desire. We have explained the word '*niyuta*' before.

Verse 42.

gajavājisahasrau ghairanekaiḥ parivāritaḥ|
vṛto rathānāṁ koṭyā ca yuddhe tasminnayudhyata||

Translation:

The demon named *Parivārita* came to the battleground surrounded by many thousands of elephants and horses, together with ten million chariots.

Explanation:

Parivārita is the sense of duty of looking after worldly business or family. It is a special *asura*. [In the commentary of a text published from Bombay, a different *asura* with this name is mentioned. This is also mentioned by the famed commentator, Gopal Chakravarty in *Tattva Prakāśikā*.] In general, some may find this disagreeable. Because, those who follow the tenets of society and *dharma*, find it their duty to look after their dependents. It is against *dharma* to not do so. It disrupts the rule of society and one acquires sin. This has been repeatedly advised in *Maṇu Saṁhitā* and other scriptural texts that follow the *Vedas*. But those that have entered into the principles of *Caṇḍī*, in whose hearts secrets of *Gitā* have been lit, in other words, those who seek liberation, who are past *dharma* and *adharma*, do not have what is known as duty. As long as ego or a state of worldly person remains and one does not see the illumination of supreme spirit in this universe, so long things like *dharma* and discrimination and such items remain. Those who are serene after merging their sense of being into the Self of Mother, have nothing remaining that can be called duty. Their bodies become a center of emergence of the power of Mother. They carry out actions, but not by any influence of duty. Then, tuning their voices to the melody of *Gitā*, they can say 'O, *Pārtha*, I have no duties at all in all three worlds'[44].

As long as there is a great desire to be here, but one has not yet reached this point, sense of duty appears as torment by a demons. The heart of a spiritual seeker wants to merge into greater life, but the demons *Parivārita* stands as duty and hinders this great union. It has been said in Volume One that acts of *dharma* are also bondages. This sense of duty of looking after one's family is also bondage. The word duty has with it a sense of ownership. One has a sense of duty before one is established in the complete knowledge that there is no other controller but Mother, there cannot be. One may be anxious about whether those who have realized the universal rule of Mother do not act from a sense of

44 *Bhāgavat Gitā,* 3:22

duty. In answer, all scriptures and philosophies declare that they carry out prescribed actions, but without any sense of ownership. They act like mechanical toys. This is a result of finding Mother. The external sign of a vision of Self is the destruction of ignorance that 'I am the ruler.' Although after this, a little bit of the sense of being or ego remains, it is a fangless serpent that cannot deliver venom.

There is something here that needs special attention. If one is greedy to stay away from the heavy burden of looking after one's family and all the troubles arising from it, and so in the name of religion, dress in ochre clothes, it is a sign of a sinful soul. If one is truly desirous of liberation, love of Self overflows its banks. Then Mother saves one from the attacks by the demon *Parivārita*. Be careful. Let no one leave the *dharma* of family without a direct sign from Mother or orders from a right *guru* and drown in *adharma*. As long as there is an argument about *dharma* and *adharma* in the heart, forsaking one's family is forbidden. One can stay within the family and still be a renunciate. This is easy and natural. But, when you are engrossed by the affection of Mother, have complete faith in the existence of Mother and rely on control by Mother, then you will feel that the demon *Parivārita* is tormenting you. Then with a sad heart, let Mother know, 'O Mother, I cannot bear this anymore. I understand a thousand times that only you are the ruler. Even then, this sense of duty comes as an *asura* and bothers me. I have no other place to speak of my joy and sorrow. Turn me free from this sense of duty towards family. I am bound by a hundred thousand duties because of the demand of that one duty. You are Mother. You are the only source for my freedom. You are the house of enjoyment for my open heart. You are everything to me. You will end all my hesitation. Why will I be a slave to the world after I hold on to you? You are the queen of queens. Why should I, who am your child, go from door to door begging for a handful of food?'

In this fashion, with a simplicity, let Mother know. You will see that in unseen ways, Mother will save you from this demon. Until Mother herself does not begin to kill this *asura*, do not foolishly try to do it yourself. Remember that Mother does not keep unfulfilled any longings of her children. That is why I say that there is no fault in asking anything from Mother if you can do so as a child asks Mother. If you ask like a mendicant, you have doubts about the existence of Mother. You ask from her as from a stepmother, like a doubtful beggar. You are anxious in case she refuses you. So, your results are as such. If you ask, do so like her child, not like a beggar. But that is another matter.

Whatever it is, the number of chariots of this *asura* is ten million, with thousands of elephants. The word '*gaja*' signifies bondage and '*bāji*' means fast. With this one duty of looking after one's family, there come innumerable duties in front of us. This is what binds people and makes them rush about like horses. This has been discussed before.

Verse 43.

biḍālākṣyohayutānāñca pañcāśadbhirathāyutaiḥ|
yuyudhuḥ saṁyuge tatra rathānāṁ parivāritaḥ||

Translation:

After this, the *asura* named *Biḍālākṣa* surrounded by five hundred thousand chariots began to fight on the battlefield.

Explanation:

Biḍālākṣa means one who has eyes (*akṣa*) like a cat (*biḍāla*). Spiritually this is the tendency for finding fault. The specialty of a cat's eyes is that the eyes are yellow and it can see equally by night and by day. Just as one with jaundiced eyes sees all the world to be colored yellow, so do worldly persons see a unique *Brahmaṇ* as things existing in this universe, even after understanding and discussing it a thousand times. 'All you see is nothing but *Brahmaṇ*. All this is Self. All the world is *Viṣṇu*. I cover all this world.' We have heard all this so many times and been so advised, yet we do not take this universe as Self, as Mother. This is the torment by the *asura Biḍālākṣa*. What can we do Mother? It is not only today but for many lifetimes that we are being cheated in this manner. That this visible world is nothing but you, is not always evident. The torment of jaundiced eyes in seeing existence as non-Self never ends. Just as by day, because of the torment of the cat-eye, we see unique sentient spirit in the shape of inert material things, by night we are enchanted by dreams of these inert things. In this manner, night and day we are tormented by the attacks of *Biḍālākṣa*.

But, Mother, now we have hope in our hearts. Because we have understood that this view of the universe is an attack by a demon. That is why you have appeared to destroy these demons. What do we have to fear anymore? O, Mother! Appear in every heart and destroy the demon *Biḍālākṣa* of fault-finding, this viewing of material things. Let the *dharma* of truth be established again in this world.

Even with a materialistic view, we may see that this demon *Biḍālākṣa*, or this fault-finding vision, disturbs people and is a cause of sorrow. We use a thousand eyes to see the fault of others. Alas, we do not realize that when we look at the faults of others, it comes and stains our hearts. We cannot easily realize, how happy one can be if we shut our eyes to the faults of others. So, I pray to Mother, to save myself from the torment by the demon *Biḍālākṣa*. May I not even mistakenly view the faults of others. All persons have faults and merits. O, Mother! May my eyes only fall on the merits of others. May I not stain my heart by discussing the faults of others. Mother, give me that strength.

This *Biḍālākṣa* has fifty *ayuta* (five hundred thousand) chariots. We receive *paramātmā* as five elements with ten sense organs. So, its material characters take on fifty different forms. Here *ayuta* means innumerable or ununited. This has been mentioned before in other mantras.

Verse 44.

anye ca tatrāyutaśo rathanāgahayairvṛtāḥ|
yuyudhuḥ saṁyuge devyā saha tatra mahāsurāḥ||

Translation:

The other great demons, began to fight with the Goddess surrounded by tens of thousands of elephants, horses and chariots.

Explanation:

In the previous mantras, the names and strengths of the principal demons have been described. Now other demons are mentioned, *Uddhata*, *Durdhara*, *Durmmukha* and *Karāla*. The destruction of *Ugrasya* and *Ugravirya* will be described in the next chapter. These names are meaningful. Smart spiritual aspirants will be able to discover these demons within themselves. The Yoga literature mentions that those with a vision of Yoga can see within themselves, gods, demons and places of pilgrimage. Brahmarṣi Medhasa points out and shows king Suratha that demons like *Cikṣura* and *Cāmara* are on the battlefield with all their strength. When human beings understand their inner favored tendencies as these demons, (just repeating this will not matter, one has to feel this in one's heart), they see that the demons instead of fighting with them are fighting with Mother. So, the mantra says '*devyā saha yuyudhuḥ*.' As long as you see that you are fighting with these demons, you have to understand that you have not found the proper means to destroy them. You are a child of Mother. Be seated in her heart and watch how these demons show themselves and how Mother destroys them. But that is something else.

Verse 45.

koṭikoṭisahasraistu rathānāṁ dantināṁ tathā|
hayānāṁ ca vṛto yuddhe tatrābhūnmahiṣāsura||

Translation:

In this manner, *Mahiṣāsura* surrounded by millions of chariots, elephants and horses, began to fight in battle.

Explanation:

A spiritual seeker should now look at the forces of these demons. In the body and your heart, demons have gathered forces and are destroying you. With their power, they have removed you from the kingdom of Self. What you thought to be just perceptions in your heart, you now see to be demons. This is how it happens. In the beginning, spiritual seekers like king Suratha, think that family, wealth and property are the main obstacles to spiritual enterprise. Then, after advancing a little, they understand that what they thought to be external obstacles were not so. The principal obstacles are percepts in the mind. If these could be shut out, then Mother would be found. As they slowly advance, they understand this in their hearts. These percepts are not small, they are great demons. With millions of warriors, *Mahiṣāsura* is trying to enclose us forever in the prison of this world. But the seeker is without fear and has hope because one has surrendered at the feet of Mother and is eagerly waiting to see the destruction of these demons.

As long as you perform spiritual enterprise under your control, practice *yama* and *niyama* to try to destroy these demons, so long there is the fear that this enterprise may fail because you still hold control. But, when Mother appears as spiritual enterprise, then there is no fear of failure. That is why I say, whatever you do, keep complete faith in the control of Mother, learn to have complete faith in her. You will see that some unfathomable power will remove all your obstacles. Not only is the spiritual path of the seeker who has faith in Mother without obstacles, his daily life is also free of them.

Verse 46.

tomarairbhindipālaiśca śaktibhirmusalaistathā|
yuyudhuḥ saṁyuge devyā khaḍgaiḥ paraśupaṭṭiśaiḥ||

Translation:

The demons began to fight with the Goddess using many different weapons, *tomara, bhindipāla, śakti, musala, kaḍga, paraśu* and *paṭṭiśa.*

Explanation:

Just as we find the names of demons like *Cikṣura* and *Cāmara*, there is mention of seven different principal weapons. For those who do not agree with a demon named *Parivārita*, there are seven chief demons. Because we accepted *Parivārita*, according to us, there are eight chief demons. We will settle this matter later. Let us first understand the spiritual mystery of these weapons.

Tomara: That which confers composite or unified perception is called *tomara*. The function of the weapon *tomara* is to bring together masses of perceptions and make them seem like one. This is the weapon of the great *asura Cikṣura*. It is the nature of the power of distraction to turn a wide range of perceptions into a narrow band of knowledge. You see a tree and you think that you see an object called a tree. In fact, it is not one entity. It is a temporary collection of a multitude of knowledge. You see a river flow. The flow you see at first glance is not the one you see at a second one. That part has moved far away. In these same manner, with a third and fourth glance, you do not see the previous parts of the flow. At each moment, new views come into your vision. But, you think of them as the same flow of water. A fast-moving flame appears to you as a steady line. Truly it is not a line. The rapidly moving flame appears as a line. See how the *asura Cikṣura* with his *tomara* weapon makes your atomic-sized mind enjoy the variety of this world. You can now understand why you cannot hold on to a perception longer than a moment. At every instant, how many hundred thousand perceptions arise in the spirit. There is no way to look at them separately. Different perceptions gather together and appear as one single thing. This is the effect of the weapon *tomara* used by *Cikṣura*. If one enters the inner kingdom calmly, one can see the effect of this weapon. Subtle disturbances are more terrible, but they can only be seen through the eyes of Yoga. This *tomara* weapon is very dangerous. One cannot make out where and how it causes injury. Yet it rips one apart. You see the smiling face of your child, and you are so happy. It does not let you understand that this view is a collection of temporary perceptions. It appears you have seen the face of a child. This narrow, combined view of things is the weapon *tomara*.

The next one is called *bhindipāla* because it nurtures or promotes divisiveness. It is the weapon of the great *asura Cāmara*. It is the nature of the power of concealment, to make one perceive material things, that which is non-Self, as different from *paramātmā.* Let us say that because of faith in the *guru* and the words of *Vedānta*, by the establishment of truth, you understand this universe to be *Brahmaṇ*. In a moment, by throwing his *bhindipāla* weapon, the *asura Cāmara* gives it the shape of this world. You understand this universe to be completely separate from *Brahmaṇ*. This is the terrible effect of this weapon.

The weapon of the demon *Udagra* is *śakti*. The ego or the sense of control of beings always sees its power in all actions. When one is in danger when traveling in life, and all self-driven actions fail, one turns upwards to seek help from some unknown power. Yet when actions succeed, one thinks them to be because of one's power. This is a trick of this weapon. Power only resides in consciousness. There is no other power. There cannot be. Seeing power in inert materials is the effect of this *śakti* weapon of the demon *Udagra*.

Muṣala (mace) the root '*muṣa*' means 'to steal.' It is called *muṣala* because it confers a sense of theft or robbery. It is the weapon of the great *asura Mahāhanu*. Not understanding that strength or capability is only with God, that nurture is only *Mahāmāyā* Mother, makes one think that mental power is the only way to accomplish things. This is the effect of this weapon. Its action is to rob the influence of divinity and promote perceptions of the individual.

Khaḍga (sword or scimitar) is a weapon of hesitancy. It is the weapon of *Asilomā*. The weapon of *Asilomā* should be an *asi* (sword). Although you and I are one and same, it is by the attack by this weapon that I imagine you to be different.

Paraśu, the root '*śu*' means 'to go.' It is called *paraśu* because it gives the perception of other. It is the weapon of the *asura Bāskala*. Desires are fulfilled by materials that are non-self, different from Self. When everything becomes Self, there is no seeing or hearing, so there is no fulfillment of desires. An attack by this weapon of *Bāskala* creates fondness for things that are non-self.

A *paṭṭiśa* is the weapon of the *asura Biḍālākṣa. Paṭṭiśa* is a kind of magical weapon. By its application vision is distorted, one sees darkness. With its evil sight, the darkness of ignorance becomes dense.

Other than this, there is the *asura Parivārita.* There is no special weapon named for his use in this mantra. The next mantra mentions the throwing of a *pāśa* (net). This is the weapon of *Parivārita.* It is by this sense of duty to family that bondage (*pāśa*) becomes tighter.

In this mantra also, the sage says that the demons fought with the Goddess, not with me, with Mother. When spiritual seekers surrender at the feet of God and see themselves as children in the lap of Mother, they see that the demons are fighting with Mother. One is only a motive, residing as a witness.

Seeing the spiritual meanings of these famous weapons, on one hand, one should not be suspicious of the usual meanings, on the other hand, one should not think that these are far-fetched and meaningless. The scriptural words are aimed at Self, this is the conclusion of all philosophies and all great sages. Where meaning is directly aimed at the Self, there is no doubt or argument. Where one has to find a meaning aimed towards Self, there is no need to bring doubts and arguments to these but to have complete respect for them. Self or 'Mother' is the subject of all the scriptural texts. This universe is for knowing 'I.' This should be firmly established in the heart.

Verse 47.

kecicca cikṣipuḥ śaktiḥ kecit pāśāṁstathāpare|
devīṁ khaḍgaprahāraistu te tāṁ hantuṁ pracakramuḥ||

Translation:

Some demons with power weapons (*śakti*), some with snares (*pāśa*) and some with scimitars (*khaḍga*) tried to kill the Goddess.

Explanation:

The word '*pāśa*' is formed from the root '*paś*' meaning bondage. It is like a rope used to bind. It has been said before that this is the weapon of the *asura Parivārita*. A spiritual seeker sees that when the bondage of the sense of duty wraps around from all sides, it seems as if the power of Mother is going to be subdued. Not only the sense of duty, but with other weapons, these demons are prepared to kill Mother.

Do not think that just by seeking shelter at the feet of Mother all your demonic tendencies will be uprooted. What effort Mother needs to destroy these tribes of demons is only known by the one you call Mother.

Do not ask why one who is all-powerful, the supreme one has to apply effort to destroy demons? It could be fulfilled just by wishing it so. Oh! She has no wishes of her own. She has to appear wishful because of your wishes. She has to act through your tendencies (*saṁskāra*), inspired by your wishes. She is Mother. She is your nature. She is swept up by her love for you. That is why her supreme nature does not have the opportunity to arise. You have kept her a powerless Mother of her forever bleak children. That is why in this battle with demons she has to suffer such trouble. If you could truly believe her to be the supreme power, then just by her wish, the demons would become nonexistent. Whenever you look at Mother, look at your heart. You will see that you have waves of doubt. Because you have doubts like, 'will Mother save me from this danger', you do not get instant results. Alas! We the children of the queen of queens, cannot call for Mother with the force we should. Why? Because we do not desire to do so. That is why we do not have faith. We harbor doubts. Just as we gradually call on Mother, she shows herself gradually. It is because of our doubts that Mother does not reveal herself. That is why she has to take so much trouble in this battle with demons. That is why these demons can throw weapons at her and her limbs bleed and her sentient body becomes dim. Oh! We are such ungrateful children. O, Mother! We are even unfit to ask for your forgiveness.

Verse 48.

sāpi devī tatastāni śastrāṇyastrāṇi caṇḍikā|
līlayaiva praciccheda nijaśastrāstravarṣiṇī||

Translation:

Devī Caṇḍīkā then used her weapons and easily destroyed those thrown by the demons.

Explanation:

Mother also has the various weapons that the demons carry. The gods have worshipped her with their weapons. Mother has nothing of her own. She has given everything to her children. Not just everything, even herself. She is so engrossed with her children that she has kept nothing for herself. She has given away everything and is naked. Mother, whose form is emptiness, whose nature is completeness, whose expression is light, only for you and for no one else, resides as your nature and lets you enjoy the world. Then, as the spirit of the gods, she fights with the demons. What can be lost in looking at her once?

I have said before that nature has two results, one external or centrifugal and the other internal or centripetal. On one side the power of gods and on the other the power of demons. Therefore, the weapons on each side are equal. As long as that part of power, that is, the weaponry, is held with pride as 'mine', so long, the gods are defeated in battle. But now, they have offered all their power at the feet of Mother. So, even though Mother has nothing of her own, she has now appeared in her figure as a warrior, armed with all her weapons.

In this manner, according to tendencies (*saṁskāra*) of a spiritual seeker, the form of Mother takes shape. Mother has no special form. Whatever form the children put her in, whatever form they desire to see her in, the affectionate Mother appears in that form. This is said to be the 'imagination of *Brahmaṇ* for the good of the seeker'[45]. Remember, this is not the imagination of a seeker, but that of *Brahmaṇ*. Children, look and see that for you, Mother now bears arms, carries all these weapons. She appears in her form as the destroyer of *Mahiṣāsura*. If you are truly her child, then your heart will quaver, tears will spring from your eyes and you will wish to vanish into the earth because of your ingratitude. You will call on Mother and say, "Let me forever be attacked by demons, leave me forever in the depths of hell. It will be better than you, the exquisite and eternally peaceful Mother, appearing on this disturbing field of battle with these demons, just because of me. You are having to bear this minuteness, this divisiveness just because of me. You have no special form. You have no role as controller or enjoyer. You are pure, unmarked, without outcome. Despite that, just because of me, you have to appear in this perceptible form. O, Mother! You are so filled by love."

Verse 49.

> *anāyastānanā devī stūyamānā surarṣibhiḥ|*
> *mumocāsuradeheṣu śastrāṇyastrāṇi ceśvarī||*

Translation:

The serene-faced Goddess, being praised by the gods and sages, appeared as supreme Goddess, that is, in her magnificent form, and began to shower weapons on the demons.

Explanation:

My Mother is always serene-faced. Even being wounded by the sharp arrows of these demons and suffering in terrible battles, my Mother is serene-faced. There is no sign of trouble on her face., There is always a smile on her ruby lips. From the time a spiritual seeker calls and understands Self as Mother, that day, she

45 *sādhkānaṁ hitārthāya brahmaṇo rūpakalpanā*

appears as the great Goddess and prepares to battle against these great demons. (Here, recount the explanation of mantras referring to the great Goddess and great demons in Volume One.) After a long time, you have now recognized Mother. That is why she is always smiling, praised by gods and sages. The gods and sages are singing verses of praise to Mother, reciting stories of the greatness of the Goddess. That is why even with the turmoil of battle, my Mother is smiling. Can you not see? When terrible tendencies of demons rise inside you, divine nature is wounded. At that time, divinities residing in you, gods seated in your senses, begin to call loudly for Mother and sing praises to her. In this manner, in memory of the great Goddess, satisfaction appears in the figure of the Goddess attacked by great demons. Then, hopelessness and weariness disappear. The heart fills with hope. Attacks by demons diminish. Such events take place in the heart of spiritual seekers every day.

We have mentioned before the loud recitation of praises. Even though repetitious, something more has to be said. You will see in scriptural texts, in the *Veda*, *Upaniṣad*, *Tantra* and *Purāṇa*, that hymns and praises are described as a chief means of worship. The worship, fire and funeral ceremonies mentioned in scriptural texts are just variations of hymns and praises, combined with offerings of materials. What is this singing of praises (*stuti*)? Declaring the nature of divinity is singing their praises. It cannot be said enough, how quickly this form of worship produces its effects. By this means, a combined practice of knowledge, devotion and action can be carried out. The result of other practices takes time, but the results of this external practice take place while carrying it out. Lord Gourāṅga adapted the recitation of praises with the accompaniment of musical instruments like drums and cymbals and added rhythm and tune to make it easier for even uneducated, materially oriented persons to turn easily towards God. The great scriptural texts like the *Upaniṣads* accepted the recitation of praises as a most important means of spiritual enterprise. In the time of the *Āryans*, worship was carried out with mantras of *Ṛk* and *Yajur Veda* and songs of *Sāma Veda*. In *Bhāgavat Gitā*, *Arjuna* sang praises on seeing the universal form. The gods tormented by *Rāvaṇa*, *Kumbhakarṇa* and *Kaṁsa* sang praises to *Viṣṇu* on the edge of the milk ocean. In *Caṇḍī*, the gods, tormented by demons, sang praises to Mother, the sounds ringing to the horizons. There are few chapters in the *Śrimat Bhāgavat* that do not mention some praises. Looking at the path of spiritual enterprise, from the days of the sages to modern times, it appears that even though methods have changed a lot, recitation of praises remains the same.

There appear to be two kinds of recitation of praises (*stuti*). One by those who are under attack and the other for gratitude. One, when in danger, and the other when the goal is reached. Much of the scriptural texts are filled with these two kinds of praises. The power of recitation of praises may be understood by spiritual seekers who have acquired mantra consciousness. (Mantra consciousness has been discussed in Volume One.) As long as mantras are not united with consciousness and do not have feeling and flavor, the results of recitation of praises are not directly perceptible. For a seeker with disturbances in the spirit, it is better to recite praises than pretend to meditate. One does not have to perform meditation, because it happens by itself. One cannot meditate on imperceptible things. When Mother appears, when she is perceptible, then a seeker is overwhelmed and with engrossed eyes, becomes overcome by love. This is meditation. Some may think that recitation of praises is external worship, so they are to be discarded. Only those who are always in a meditative frame, whose spirits are one-pointed and withdrawn can say this to be true. In modern times, the great Ācārya Śankara and Lord Gourāñga, either willfully or for the benefit of others, followed this path for those with disturbed spirits. Otherwise, the creation of so many directive texts, the spread of religion or the construction of monasteries could not have been accomplished. Whatever that be, it has been tested and seen that the results of recitation of praises are superior to a pretense of meditation. The recitation of hymns and praises is included within what the *Vedānta* scriptures call rumination (*manana*) and the yogic literature calls focus (*dhāraṇā*). I would like to speak about mediation later.

There are different ways of reciting hymns and praises, alone or together with a group of like-minded people. Lord Gourāñga often practiced the second type. It is rare to find a seeker who can sit alone in a secret place and keep the spirit turned towards God for a very long time. Those who think that just by going to a hidden place their spiritual effort will be great can examine themselves. They will see that when they are hinding and try to turn their spirit towards God, external sounds appear in their hearts. Closing the door of the room does not close the door to the heart. All kinds of thoughts about material things appear and distort one's focus on God. A little attention will show that outer quietness has not kept one alone or brought inner silence. Instead of that, if a few similar-minded persons get together and recite verses of praise with mantra consciousness, they may get a taste of inner quietness. At least, for a short time, they can be free of useless thoughts. Much hindrance appears from spiritual effort with people in opposition. There is no doubt that a quiet place is preferable to that. But, in the beginning, when one is together with a few persons of similar minds, one can see more utility than a quiet place. For those who have attained mantra consciousness, faults and obstacles in group spiritual enterprise cannot do any harm. By such group enterprise, by the grace of *guru*, the spirit of knowledge soon becomes pure and one finds mindfulness. Then a spiritual seeker can discover the center of spiritual effort and carry out the quest alone. Or, spiritual effort becomes so easy and natural that activities of daily living become part of a spiritual quest. Then, being alone or with others is of no consequence.

Whatever it is, it is wrong to doubt or argue with what the gods, sages, great souls and teachers have been carrying out from the beginning of creation. Even when one sees that praises are being sung outside to the almighty, one with inner vision sees that inside. a spiritual seeker has turned divine. If you are saying, 'O kind one, O peaceful one, O blessed one', if you say this with proper meaning, feeling and truth, then at that time, you will be kind, blessed and peaceful. These divine feelings will arise in your heart.

Someone sees the waters of Gangā and says "Oh! What dirty, murky water! How can one bathe in this!" Someone else says "Ah! My all-loving, sin-removing, giver of well-being, my mother Gangā", and goes and bathes in it. Think and see, at that moment which one of these benefits? One says, "That man is very proud, thinks no end of himself." Another says, "Let that be, but he cares for others, helping people who are in trouble." Think about who of these two benefits more. I have said before that it is your mind that is shaped outside as this universe. As you think, so will you find results. There is a great saying. When you sing praises of the Supreme being, you fill yourself with supremacy. What can be of greater benefit to mankind?

There is another group of people who say that God is beyond words and thought. How can one sing his praises? As proof, they cite the statement saying, 'how can one praise that which cannot be defined?' This is true. But have you perceived this undefined thing? Even if you have, you cannot say it. When you emerge from the nature of an undefined being, you too define it verbally. And if you have not, it is by this verbalized nature that you can reach the non-verbalized state. So, in both cases, you have to agree to recite hymns of praises. The Lord has said that 'speaking about the divine they always find satisfaction and pleasure'[46]. Let this take place. First, find him with words and thought, then will you find him beyond words and thought. First, develop a taste for a divine name, then will you find pleasure in divine spirit. No. Does that ever occur? As long as one does not develop a taste for divine spirit, one cannot develop a taste for divine name. That is why it is said that the great Lord Gourāñga, blessed Rūpa Gosvāmi at his highest spiritual point by saying, 'may you have a taste for the divine name.' Chanting or reciting a divine name night and day is not the sign of a taste for it. It is just the result of practice. When one acquires a taste for a divine name, there appears distaste for material things. A day comes, when chanting the divine name, distaste for material things appears in the heart, not only in words.

---

46 *kathayantaś ca māṁ nityaṁ tuṣhyanti ca ramanti ca, Bhāgavat Gitā,* 10:9

One will understand then that one has acquired a taste for a divine name. Paramahaṁsa Ramakṛṣṇa used to say, 'when one sees divine illumination, one acquires a taste for divine words and a distaste for desire and wealth.' But that is something else.

Whatever it is, that my Mother is serene-faced, always pleased and always smiling, can be especially perceived through hymns and praises. So, the mantra says, 'praised by gods and sages.' In this manner, with a smiling face, my Mother began to throw weapons at the demons. My Mother appeared in her supreme form as Goddess and prepared to end the power of demons. When she is praised, her form residing in all perceptions appears. Let me say more clearly. Always brighten your self-nature, inner spirit of Mother as nature of Supreme being, with hymns and praises. Never keep it bleak and frail. If you wish to feel the effect of the great words of *Bhāgavat Gitā*, 'raised up by Self, not weakened by it'[47]. always see Mother in her form as supreme Goddess. It does not happen in a day. By repeatedly pronouncing words of the greatness of God, that is, by hymns of praises, does it become easy. The more you believe in Mother as Goddess, the more easily will the power of the demons be destroyed. With it, the poverty striking your wishes, your sense as a mere worldly person will be removed.

What is a state of Godhood? It is the absence of being stricken by desire. The complete fulfillment of all desire is a state of God. The incompleteness of desire is poverty or a state as a worldly person. One cannot get rid of such a state without a view of supreme form. That is why one needs to perceive the nature of Self as supreme form. Hymns and praises are an easy and definitive way of doing this. Thoughts like 'I will be good, will be happy, will remove bad tendencies, will not be attracted to worldly things, will have faith in God, will show devotion', arise in our minds all the time. Why are these wishes not fulfilled? Why are these struck down? We do not call on Mother as supreme

---

47 *uddhared ātmanātmānaṁ nātmānam avasādayet*, *ibid*, 6:5

Goddess, even if we do, we do not have faith that she is supreme Goddess. She is not stricken by desires. We cannot agree to this in our hearts. So, our poverty does not end.

Verse 50.

sohapi kruddho dhutaśaṭo devyā vāhanakeśarī|
cacārāsurasainyeṣu vaneṣviva hutāśanaḥ||

Translation:

The lion, the mount of the Goddess, also became angry and swirling his mane moved among the demon warriors like a fiery blaze surging through a forest.

Explanation:

Mother is ready for battle in her form as the great Goddess. Therefore, her mount is also ready. I have said, when worldly persons take on the nature of a lion, that is, bear hostility towards their worldly states, then Mother takes on the form of a destroyer of demons and is established in it. Or, when Mother appears in her form as a destroyer of demons, then worldly persons cannot but take on the nature of lions. Today, Mother is ready for battle. So, the children are lion-natured, ready to destroy demons.

When spiritual seekers see that someone is forcefully pulling them away from all their worldly acts and occasionally, by some unknowable force, engaging them in a spiritual effort, they begin to carry out actions towards spiritual progress. Then, one has to understand that Mother has appeared on the field of battle. At that time, you too should apply your effort and wish to remove your sense as a worldly person. Then your lion nature will appear. Mother will honor you by placing her feet on you.

Those who say 'When Mother appears, we will be of the nature of lions. When she makes us, we will apply spiritual effort', have to understand that they are not yet free from the hands of weakness. Such feelings are to be decried. When carrying out actions in the world, one says, 'I am the doer', 'my effort' but in the case of remembering Mother, one depends on her. This is self-deception. Only feeble-minded persons apply such words of consolation and flow along blindly in their usual channels. Remember it is not possible for the weak to find Self (*nāyamātmā valahīnena labhya*[48]). Before beginning worldly acts, one has to see the control of God. But, one has to also see the control of God after the end of spiritual effort. In all worldly acts, there could be some failure. But, in spiritual effort, even a deep sigh is successful. Even the desire 'I will carry out spiritual enterprise' is not without success. That is why I said, take on the nature of a lion, Mother will establish herself on you. You will move among the demons like a forest fire.

The simile in this mantra is very beautiful. Dry branches rub together and create a fire in the forest that will consume the whole of it. The forest consumes itself. You should show violence to yourself. Show violence to your sense as a worldly person, your sense as a demon. Show aggression towards this pride of body and mind. This is your action, a natural act. What has been called self-nature in *Gitā*, is in *Devī Māhātmya* a lion. It is very satisfying for a spiritual seeker.

Verse 51.

niḥśvāsān mumuce yāṁśca yudhyamānā raṇehambikā|
ta eva sadyaḥ sambhūtā gaṇāḥ śatasahasraśaḥ|

Translation:

The air that Goddess *Amvikā* breathed out while in battle, immediately turned into hundreds of thousands of warriors (named *Gaṇa*) who fought the demons.

Explanation:

Mother has appeared in battle. This is perceived by any spiritual seeker who has surrendered. This has been mentioned many times. The breath of Mother is a great sign of this self-surrender. When a spiritual seeker begins to see the inspiration

48 *Munḍaka Upaniṣad*, 3.2.4

of Mother in every action, then slowly the mystery of this breath of *Amvikā* can be understood. Even breath is not one's own, it is from Mother. Mother resides within me in the form of breathing. The external sign of this is in-breath and out-breath. That which we neglect as mere breath, air flow, is the breath of Mother. Where do you run to look for Mother? Look, the breath that is working through your nostrils is telling you of the spirit of Mother. This is Mother, hold her here. Watching this movement, call her *mā*, you will find Mother. She will appear. Without effort, the air will be stilled in *kumbhaka*. Disturbances of the spirit will disappear. Finding true stillness and bliss, life will be honored. But that is something else.

Generally, breathing shows signs of disturbances of spirit. By watching one's breath, one can make out that spirit is disturbed. That is why many yogis try to remove such disturbances by external breath control (*prāṇāyāma*). By practicing *pūraka*, *recaka* and *kumbhaka*[49] they try to control their breath. These are very basic methods for making the spirit still. These methods may be able to quieten the spirit, but one cannot discover Self by them. Practicing these for a very long time, they become the goal of a practitioner. Although a quiet spirit is a sign of discovering Self, remember that one cannot do so just by quieting the spirit. Only those who seek Self and welcome it, will land on it. That is why the *śrutis* say, 'only those who seek it will find'[50]. 'In whatever manner I am worshipped, I do the same'[51]. If you look to quieten the spirit, that is what you will have. My Mother fulfills all our wishes. Not understanding that by discovering Mother, the spirit naturally becomes quiet, if one tries procedures to stop the breath, ignorance is not removed. One does not discover divine nectar. On the other hand, it is seen in many cases that for those who are householders and are not used to asceticism from childhood, these methods may lead to incurable physical problems.

49 names for parts of breath control in *Haṭha* Yoga

50 *yamevaiṣa vṛṇute tenaiva labhyaḥ*, *Kaṭha Upaniṣad*, 1.2.23

51 *Bhāgabata Gitā*, 4:11

Whatever it is, if one understands breath to be that of *Amvikā*, of Mother, they appear as warriors to aid Mother in destroying demons. How does one know that these breaths are of Mother? There will be signs in the breaths. These signs are the names of Mother, *Praṇava* (*Oṁ*) and other mantras. Those who are used to chanting holy names with each in and out-breath have a great aid towards controlling demonic tendencies. When you see your breath appear with the name of Mother, you will understand how the breath of *Amvikā* become *Gaṇa* warriors and destroy demons. This is made clearer in the next mantra.

One more thing. Realizing breath as that of Mother is true surrender. That I have nothing, even my breath is yours Mother, even my 'I' is you, you always reside as me. Your breath flows in my nostrils as mine. Oh my 'I.' Oh my 'I.' What bliss, what truth, what divine nectar! O children born of divine nectar, realize this truth. This joyous, ambrosial touch will enliven you from your toenails to the tips of your hair. There is no place to store this bliss, it is so great, so dense, so deep. Look. Your own self is Mother; perceive that your breath is not yours but from her, inside you. You will see your 'I'-ness disappear. The effort of many lifetimes to dissipate 'I' is accomplished with ease. Do not let this deep mystery that Mother now holds in front of her dear children with tears in her eyes, be ignored and turned into mere words, to be sold in the market. See that no one brings pain to the heart of Mother.

Verse 52.

yuyudhuste paraśubhirbhindipālāsipaṭṭiśaiḥ|
nāśayantohsuragaṇān devīśaktyupabṛṁhitāḥ||

Translation:

These warriors (named *Gaṇa*), being empowered by energy from the Goddess, began to battle and destroy the demons with their weapons, *paraśu*, *bhindipāla*, sword and *paṭṭiśa*.

Explanation:

As long as we take pride that it is our breath, we remain without power. From one moment to another, they move us towards death. When they appear as the breath of Mother, they are empowered by her. With great valor, they destroy demonic warriors and move towards eternal life. This is not just a play of words. If one can truly take and understand breath to be that of Mother, demonic tendencies can be subdued and one overcomes any fear of death. This is a well-tested truth. Whatever it is, the way to understand that these breaths are those of Mother has been mentioned before. It is *japa* (repetition of a divine name). Not a lifeless repetition, but one with awareness, a recitation of a conscious mantra. One does not have to carry out this *japa*. It is spontaneous. Just as one does not have to breathe by effort, this too is carried out effortlessly. It may not happen in one day, but careful practice from the beginning will make *japa* natural. The fruitfulness of self-surrender and consciousness of mantra is first noticed by a perception of the breath of Mother. One must remember that this is the backbone of spiritual effort. If one appears with these assets, all spiritual effort quickly yields results.

Those practicing renunciation (*sannyās*) perform the offering of *ajapā* to succeed in self-surrender. In brief, in one day and night, we carry out twenty-one thousand, six hundred *ajapās*, that is the repetition of the mantra '*haṁsa*' as in and out-breath. This is our 'I'-ness. If we look closely, the 'I'-ness of worldly person can be seen as a collection of in and out-breaths. This collection has to be divided into parts and offered to *guru*, *Gaṇeśa*, *Śiva*, *Viṣṇu* and others. When all of this is offered and given, nothing remains. So, there is nothing that is 'I'. In the end, only nondual spirit of *Brahmaṇ* remains. In many instances, this process is turned into a recitation of mantras. I do not know how much time it takes until the sense of 'I' is obliterated just by the recital of mantras. But there is no doubt that 'I'-ness is removed by the realization of breath as that of Mother.

By the words 'obliteration of I', do not think that there will be no 'I'. Remember, in the first volume with the example of a lamp, it was said that there are no multiple 'I's. The one Self-expressed through mind, intelligence and senses appear as many. If one can dissolve this 'I' imagined by ignorance, the true nature of 'I' can be found. One realizes that what is true 'I', the only one, Self, my Mother, is expressed eternally.

The material ceremonies mentioned in *Bhāgavat Gitā* are a step in this surrender of self. From the time that one slowly begins to have a little faith in the nature of divinity, this ceremony of material things, that is, the offering of material things begins. This is an early sign of the offering of Self. After days of doing this, one is no longer satisfied by just offering material things. One begins spiritual effort (*sādhanā*). This is a worship ceremony. The goal is to clean up oneself. When one notices that the 'I' is too soiled, too attached to material things, one cannot offer this impure thing at the feet of supreme purity. Then, one begins to try to purify oneself by serious spiritual effort. When one is a little pure, one is entitled to the ceremony of Yoga. Then one is in union with God and carries out all worldly acts as ceremonial worship. Even in this condition, 'I' is separate. After some days of a meeting with divinity, affection, attraction or devotion appears. When this devotion deepens, it turns into love. Then the ceremony of self-study (*svādhyāya*) is performed. One realizes the nature of Self. In this manner, great knowledge of meeting Self is accomplished. Such sacrifice of Self is called the dissolution of 'I.' This is the ultimate goal of the mantra 'forsaking all religions, seek shelter only in me'[52].

Do not think that if you surrender in this manner once, the worldly 'I' will no longer arise. You will return to yourself. God will make you lose yourself, merge with you, and then return your Self to you. At that time, this 'I' is very beautiful, very pure. It has no vanity, no attachments. It is established on a firm foundation of truth. At this time, whether it carries out prescribed actions, or undertakes inaction, under all conditions, it is like a machine run by the divine. This is the final stage of self-surrender.

---

52 *Bhāgavat Gitā,* 18:66

Whatever it is, the *Gaṇa* warriors, empowered by the strength of Mother, using breath powered by *Praṇava* and other mantras, used their weapons to demolish the demons. The meaning of these weapons like *bhindipāla* has been explained before. Although such meaning is applicable to demons, such meanings have been given for Mother also. So. it is not necessary to repeat them. That normal breath is a sign of disturbance of the spirit, supporting the demons, has been mentioned in the previous mantra. But, when breath becomes imbued with the name of Mother, is imbued by a consciousness of mantra recital, is realized as breath of Mother, they are destructive to the spirit of the demons. This is the demolition of the demons by *Gaṇa* warriors.

You can examine this. When your spirit is disturbed by different worldly thoughts, when demonic feelings come and attack you one after another, keep your attention on your breath. Keep repeating the divine name from breath to breath (*japa*), and at the same time feel that it is the breath of Mother inside you that travels through your nostrils. You will see that soon demonic feelings will be calmed and your spirit will be quiet. You will understand the results of these actions.

Verse 53.

avādayanta paṭahān gaṇāḥ śaṅkhāṁstathāpare|
mṛdaṅgāṁśca tathaivānye tasmin yuddhamahotsave||

Translation:

In this great celebratory battle, some of the *Gaṇa* warriors sounded kettle drums, some conch shells and some hand drums.

Explanation:

In this mantra, there is advice about a particular type of spiritual enterprise. Following the flow of breath, shutting out the function of hearing, if one moves to the heart center (*Anāhata cakra*) and resides there for some time, one can hear the sounds of drums and conch shells. Other than this one may hear sounds like those of crickets, frogs, thunder and bells. In the mantra, drums and conch shells are mentioned as the main ones. The other sounds are included with them. Different spiritual seekers do not hear the same sounds. By their differences in nature, these sounds differ. But most spiritual seekers can hear the sounds that are mentioned.

In this manner, when a cherished mantra unites with a specific sound (*nāda*) in *Anāhata*, a spiritual seeker can be confident about his repetition of a divine name (*japa*). This is mantra consciousness mentioned in *Tantra*. In this condition, one does not have to apply effort to repeat the name. *Japa* occurs by natural energy. When this primal sound appears, it produces incredible joy. It moves the spiritual seeker greatly. There is nothing else anywhere but the continuous sounds of drum and flute. How attractive is this sound? It tugs at your heart. This is the sound of the flute of *Śrī Kṛṣṇa*. By its attraction, the *gopis* left their homes and floated onto unknown seas. Truly this sound destroys one's duties. It turns people insane. When any of these sounds of flute or drums become natural, a spiritual seeker enjoys immense joy. When one unites *Praṇava* or other mantras with this primal sound, the spirit becomes quiet. The torment by demons is removed.

But, let me say something here. Let no one apply effort to hear these sounds. That would be an obstacle to finding truth. One does not discover truth just by hearing primal sounds. Progressing on the path of truth, these things appear by themselves. If you pay attention to the heart center (*Anāhata*) and wait with an anxious heart to hear the call of Mother, you will see that the sweet, attractive call of Mother appears in your ear. You too will reply by saying 'yes, Mother.' Always remember, our goal is to find Mother. Many things will appear on the path and then disappear. See everything, hear everything, but do not be addicted to any of it. Not just mere sounds, do not be attracted to even yogic powers.

Whatever it is, in this mantra the battle has been called a great celebration. Truly, in a battle in which Mother has appeared, in which the drum-beat of the warriors emerging from her breath is sounding, cannot be but called a celebration. Appearing in such a battle, the golden flag on top of my temple of freedom can be seen. In such a battle the power of the demons is removed. How can such a battle not be a celebration? Where is the harm in joining such a battle?

Verse 54.

tato devī triśūlena gadayā śaktivṛṣṭibhiḥ|
khaḍgādibhiśca śataśo nijaghāna mahāsurān||

Translation:

After this, the Goddess began to kill thousands of demons with blows of her trident, mace, *śakti* and scimitar.

Explanation:

The manner of battle by the lion and *Gaṇa* warriors have been recounted. Now the battle by Mother is described. First, come blows from her trident. What is a trident? It is threefold knowledge. The knower, what is known and knowledge, can be called a trident. It is a weapon of intellectual formed *Maheśvara* (*Śiva*). Before this, *Maheśvara* extracted a lance from his own and offered it to the Goddess. How are demons destroyed by a trident? When things of form and flavor, or desire and other tendencies, disturb the spirit, then a trident is aimed at them. That these things and the tendencies are nothing but triads have to be repeatedly resolved with firmness.

Let me explain more clearly. Let us say that you are enchanted by a beautiful form. Look at this beauty with close attention. This beauty is a matter of knowledge, of what is known. Of 'I know', the part 'I' is the knower, and the part 'know' is knowledge. They are three waves on the ocean of knowledge. In Volume One, in the explanation of the verses like 'all animals have knowledge about sensed material things'[53] it was said that all beings are part of an ocean of knowledge. Get close to this, that is hold it in your intelligence. Three waves of an undivided ocean of knowledge

53 Volume One, Chapter One, Verse 32

appear to us as knower, known and knowledge. Whether they are matters of form and flavor or tendencies of lust and anger, they are nothing but this triad. Such repeated analysis is the blow of a trident, that is the application of a triad. The force by whose influence, this ocean of knowledge forms waves of knower, known and knowledge, that force is the Goddess, my Mother. Keep your sight focused on Mother. See that on one side, she appears as demons of material things, on the other, wielding a trident, that is, applying this analysis of a triad, she destroys them. Because you are applying this triadic analysis, do not think that you are in control. It is Mother who expresses herself through these analytics. If one understands this mystery of the trident, and practices it repeatedly with firm resolve, so that it becomes one's nature, victory is assured in the spiritual battle.

After the trident, comes a mace (*gadā*). The root '*gad*' means expressed word. Just as demons can be destroyed by throwing a trident, (by applying the triad), so can their power be diminished by applying speech, by loudly reciting hymns of praises. Besides this, the destruction of demons by showering them with *śakti* (power) and scimitar is mentioned. Repeatedly remembering that the nature of demons is also a special expression of supreme power is showering them with *śakti*. As long as only material things or tendencies are observed, they are all-powerful demons. When they are understood to be the powers of Mother, then the power of the demons is diminished by a shower of *śakti*. To always remember that material things are just forms of energy, is the showering of power (*śakti*). Finally, the scimitar (*khaḍga*) is a weapon that cuts into two. Knowledge is a scimitar in the hands of Mother. Only by establishing the knowledge that there is nothing but *ātmā*, Mother everywhere is all sense of non-Self destroyed. By blows of this intellectual scimitar, all material expression, the sense of demons, is removed. If you are established in truth, if the establishment of truth is your nature, then whenever you are confronted by material things, your knowledge accepts them as truth, as Mother. This is a blow with a scimitar on these demons. In this manner, hundreds of them are destroyed.

Verse 55.

pātayāmāsa caivānyān ghaṇṭāsvanavimohitān|
asurān bhuvi pāśena baddhvā cānyānakarṣayat|

Translation:

Mother bemused some demons with the sound of her bell and threw them on the ground. She entangled some with a snare and pulled them down.

Explanation:

The sound of the bell is unvoiced (*anāhata*) *nāda*. In the battle by the *Gaṇa* warriors, the meaning of the sound of drums has been explained. The sounds of a bell are special. *Indra*, king of the gods, had wrought a bell from that of *Airāvata* and offered it to the Goddess. The sound of a bell is an easy means for removing distractions and practicing attention. When a large bell is struck, a prolonged sound like '*taṁṁṁ*' can be heard from afar. A similar prolonged sound like the letter '*m*' arises from the heart center (*Anāhata*). It is so sweet and attractive that one's spirit does not want to be distracted by external things. When *Praṇava* and other mantras are added to this '*m*' sound, then *japa* (repetition) takes place automatically. Spirit is engrossed with this *japa*. Perceptive power of the demons cannot emerge.

Besides this, Mother used another weapon, which is a snare (*pāśa*). Mother bound some demons in a snare of affection and pulled them towards her. If all the demons are destroyed, then her divine play (*lilā*) cannot continue. So, that some of them would help in her *lilā*, she brings them to her side. Listen, if the action of the active principle (*rājasa*) is halted, then right principle (*sattva*) cannot be expressed. The power of active principle that is favorable for the expression of intellectual nature has to be prevented from demonic expression and inducted to the right side. Also, if all tendencies of the spirit are completely shut off, the actions of the world will end. So, instead of destroying all of them, some have to be brought under control. Generally, beings are driven by tendencies of their senses, this is the torment by demons. Conquering the senses is a proper victory over demons. This can be achieved in many fashions. It is not accomplished only by weapons or by control. Sometimes they have to be given the enjoyment of desires of the right tendencies and included as helpers in spiritual effort. This is the secret of the entanglement of demons with a snare.

There is another word in this mantra that should be attended to. That is the word '*bhubi.*' The center of '*bhu*' or earth principle is the *Mulādhāra cakra*. The part of *rājasa* power that arouses the right principle is at the *Mulādhāra*. When restraint is applied to this center, the subtle sense of action is perceived as the entanglement of demons by the snare of Mother.

Verse 56.

kecid dvidhākṛtāstīkṣṇaiḥ khaḍgapātaistathāpare|
vipothitā nipātena gadayā bhuvi śerate||

Translation:

Some of the demons were divided into two by blows of a sharp scimitar. Some were broken apart by being thrown down and some fell to the ground by blows from her mace.

Explanation:

Here the sad state of the demons is being described. Some of the demons were rendered into two halves by a scimitar of knowledge. Some of them were destroyed by being struck down to the earth. There remained no signs of them. They disappeared into the nonmanifest. Some were laid to the ground by blows of her mace, that is, by conscious repetition of mantras or loud recitation of hymns. They resided in the earth principle that is the *Mulādhāra cakra*, to help the arousal of right tendency (*sattva*).

Verse 57.

vemuśca kecid rudhiraṁ musalena bhṛśaṁ hatāḥ|
kecinnipatitā bhūmau bhinnāḥ śūlena vakṣasi||

Translation:

Some of the demons being hit by her club, began to throw up blood. Some were stricken in the chest with her lance and fell to the ground.

Explanation:

Throwing up blood means becoming powerless. The power by which, the disturbance of active tendency (*rājasa*) appears in spirit is called blood. The active tendency is red. The power of *rājasa* is blood. So, throwing up blood means a lack of power of *rājasa*. The meaning of the trident has been explained before this. The significance of being thrown to the ground is that demonic tendencies, by blows from the weapons of Mother, like burnt seeds, unable to germinate, reside in the *Mulādhāra cakra*. As long as the body remains, they are not obliterated. But even then, they can no longer disempower the children of Mother with sorrow or enchantment.

Verse 58.

nirantarāḥ śaraugheṇa kṛtāḥ kecidraṇājire|
śyenānukāriṇaḥ prāṇān mumucustridaśārdanāḥ||

Translation:

Some of the demons on the battlefield, were struck by so many arrows (shot by Mother), that there was no space left on their bodies. The tormenters of the gods, the generals of these demons began to die in this manner.

Explanation:

When the power of demons disturbs the peace of the spirit of a spiritual seeker, when their hearts turn into battlefields, then arrows have to be shot repeatedly towards demonic tendencies.

Praṇava and other mantras, that is, the call for Mother are arrows, as propounded in *Upaniṣads* and other texts. 'O, Mother, you are here. You have taken a minuscule form and stand in my heart. You are Mother. Why have you taken this form and so anguish me? O Mother, appear in your tranquil and peaceful form. O, Mother!' In this manner, one has to repeatedly fire arrows, so that not a portion of tendencies remain. So frequently have the mantras to be recited, so frequently have arrows to be shot at the target of *Brahman*, that no interval remains. This is the significance of the words '*nirantarāḥ śaraugheṇa*.' If one can carry this out, demonic forces that destroy divine feelings of a seeker are demolished. The spiritual seeker can test whether demons can be conquered in this fashion. One may fail repeatedly, but final victory is assured.

Verse 59.

keṣāñcid bāhavaśchinnāśchinnagrīvāstathāpare|
śirāṁsi peturanyeṣāmanye madhye vidāritāḥ||

Translation:

The arms of some of the demons, the necks of some and the heads of others were torn apart. The mid-sections of some were pierced.

Explanation:

The tearing of arms signifies the end of receiving power. The removal of longings to receive matters of form and flavor born of desire are the tearing of the arms of demons. Dividing the neck is the inability to make sounds. The tendencies are born from the ability to voice words. Without words, perceptions do not appear. These things have been discussed before in detail. The basic ingredients of perception or tendencies are words. The significance of cutting the neck is the end of creating words. The piercing of the middle section is the end of creative action. Here this has to be taken as demonic action. Actions have three states. The first creation, then stability and then dissolution. The piercing of the mid parts of the demons has to be understood as the destruction of the stability of actions. When stability is gone, the creation and dissolution of actions also end.

Verse 60.

vicchinnajaṅghāstvapare peturur vvyāṁ mahāsurāḥ|
ekabāhvakṣicaraṇāḥ keciddevyā dvidhā kṛtāḥ||

Translation:

The hips of some demons were separated and they fell to the ground. Some were divided in half from head to buttock. Each half had one eye, one arm and one leg.

Explanation:

Division of the hips signifies an inability to move. Constant mobility of the tendencies is the ability of movement. Tendencies (*saṁskāra*) have special forms. These forms are perceptual. Desire or receiving are its arms, expressions are eyes, and movements are its feet. By dividing them into two, the special form of the tendencies was destroyed. By doing this, their ability to produce special results was removed.

Just as positive and negative electricity come together to create electric work, just as the expression of paternal and maternal forces in the right and left halves of our bodies come together to create our body for fulfilling desire, so do the opposing forces of attraction and repulsion come together to create perceptions or tendencies. If these powers are divided into two in the manner that *Bhima* divided *Jarāsandha*[54] then they lose the ability to produce action. Mother appearing in this battle with demons, divided some of them into two halves, to end their ability to create action.

---

54 in *Mahābhārata*

Verse 61.

chinnehapi cānye śirasi patitāḥ punarutthitāḥ|
kabandhā yuyudhurdevyā gṛhītaparamāyudhāḥ||

Verse 62.

nanṛtuścāpare tatra yuddhe tūryalayāśritāḥ|
kabandhāśchinnaśirasaḥ khaḍgaśaktyṛṣṭipāṇayaḥ||

Verse 63.

tiṣṭha tiṣṭheti bhāṣanto devīmanye mahāsurāḥ||

Translation:

Some other demons with their heads cut off, fell to the ground and picking up excellent weapons, arose as headless bodies to fight with the Goddess. Some of these headless bodies danced on the battlefield to the tune of trumpets. Other great demons with scimitars and swords in their hands, shouting 'wait, wait', had their heads cut off.

Explanation:

Some of the demonic tendencies are so strong that even if their heads are cut off, they do not stop fighting. By the grace of Mother, those spiritual seekers, who have had their desires uprooted, who are firmly established in knowledge of 'not having anything in the world to receive or deny', even they may be tormented by such headless demons. The ancient tales we hear, of the fall of the great seeker *Viśāmitra*, of disturbances of the spirit of *Parāśara*, of desire for revenge by *Durvvāsa*, are attacks by these headless demons. Even the gentle *avatara* Buddha was attacked by *Mārā*. Such things take place due to stored practices. They are not a hindrance to discovering Mother. We hear true or false stories of the weaknesses of so many hundreds of great souls. These should not be reasons for surprise or disrespect. Because they are temporary attacks by headless demons. These are proof that understanding the divine play of Mother is beyond the intelligence of people. These temporary weaknesses do not harm those who are truly following good. The Lord himself has said, 'those who do good never come to harm'[55]. Therefore, no one should judge great souls from an ordinary viewpoint. What may appear to be a fault or weakness in common view, maybe a deep mystery in a great one. What game Mother plays and in what manner may not be easy to determine with the power of common spirit.

Some of the demons danced to the tune and rhythm of battle music. When the desire by a spiritual seeker, for receiving external things ends, tendencies of material matters arise in the heart. Although they cannot create action in the material world, (being without desire, they are headless), even then, these demonic feelings continue dancing. Spiritual seekers can perceive this at all times. What has been described in *Gitā* as 'being called deceptive behavior'[56], is the dance of headless torsos in *Devī Māhātmya*. In the beginning, all spiritual seekers have to control their work senses. When external work senses are stilled, one sees that internal senses are not yet under control. What one does not carry out in action, is easily thought of in the mind. This has been called 'deception.' Without this deception, one cannot reach truthful behavior. Those who are established in truthful behavior, have all come through such deception. This is the dance by the headless demons. Desire and performance are absent, yet demonic tendencies arise in the spirit. They dance in tune with trumpets. The recital of *Praṇava* and other mantras are the music of battle. You may be repeating your cherished divine name, but inside many useless material things arise. Your chanting continues, at the same time, the dance of the demons continues. Let no one lose hope in this state, do not stop your martial music. As much as they dance, remember, they are headless torsos. Their dance will soon cease. Keep your eyes on Mother. Do not discredit yourself as a liar. One has to alight on truth beyond these lies. These lies, this dance by headless demons, are all disguises of Mother, her divine play. So, seeing your weakness, do not let your spirit flag.

---

55 *Bhāgavat Gitā,* 6:40

56 *ibid,* 3:6

Some great demons, carrying scimitars and other weapons, while crying 'wait, wait' to the Goddess were beheaded by her. When being attacked by some powerful adversary, a weaker person trying to hide will tell their opponents, 'Let it be, we will see later.' The intention is that at this point I cannot harm you, but given the right time and place, in the future, I will emerge again. Truly, by inhibition of a sense of action, the flare of tendencies is only checked. Given the proper opportunity, they arise as action again. 'Objects fall away from abstinent persons.' [57] By controlling the senses, the receiving of things end, but the love of desire remains. Finding opportunity, that is, given any loosening of control, torment by these demons begins again. Pointing to this feeling, they are saying to the Goddess, 'wait, wait.' At this point, a spiritual seeker is not only applying self-control but having surrendered at the feet of Mother, is without worry. Here, Mother has severed heads. She has destroyed any ability to produce action. The Lord has also said, 'seeing great spirit, desire for material things end.'[58] Here one adores the feet of Mother, is established in *paramātmā.* There is no scope of affection for material things. The mantra says, while they said 'wait, wait', the Goddess severed the heads of these great demons.

Verse 64.

pātitai rathanāgāśvairasuraiśca vasundharā|
agamyā sābhavattatra yatrābhūt sa mahāraṇaḥ||

Translation:

The ground where this great battle took place, covered by with fallen chariots, elephants, horses and demons, became inaccessible.

Explanation:

Truly, the ground, the spirit of a spiritual seeker becomes inaccessible. Although the earth is a store of innumerable riches,

57 *Bhāgavat Gitā,* 2:59

58 *ibid*

although it supports achievement, power, peace and other *vāsus*, despite that, because of the corpses of demons, it was inaccessible. Until the bodies of the demonic tendencies are not obliterated, one cannot look for hidden treasures in the ground, the land of spirit. The material instruments of the body that help to arouse demonic tendencies and demolish right percepts are chariots, elephants and horses carrying demons. The power of demons is gone, but their material parts remain. So, the arena of spirit is not yet calm. A spiritual seeker cannot as yet dive deep into spirit to look for jewels of special powers. When an old wound heals the scar does not disappear immediately. Although by the grace of Mother, disturbances of active tendency (*rājasa*) are calmed, the tendencies like the corpses of demons do not disappear. Spiritual seekers can experience this themselves. Although external desires of the spirit are gone, because of habit, their natural feelings are not removed. So, one does not realize the true, calm nature of spirit. That is why the mantra says that the earth was inaccessible.

Verse 65.

śoṇitaughā mahānadyaḥ sadyastatra visusruvuḥ|
madhye cāsurasainyasya vāraṇāsuravājinām||

Translation:

Between *asura* warriors, blood from elephants, demons and horses flowed like great rivers.

Explanation:

A river of blood flowed among the demons. What is a river of blood? It is the flow of the power of pure active tendency (*rājasa*). The color red is the outer expression of *rājasa*. The demons were so moved by this battle, that nothing other than a deep red flow of energy could be perceived. At this time, a spiritual seeker sees that the white space of spirit (*cidākāś*), turns a deep red and swells like a great river of blood. Because of repeated blows of demonic tendencies, specific demons cannot be seen. Only a deep red flow like that of blood, as a swell of energy of active principle, may be perceived. *Mulādhāra* and lower centers are at this time perceived as illuminated by red light. This is the 'great river of blood.'

Verse 66.

kṣaṇena tanmahāsainyamasurāṇāṁ tathāmbikā|
ninye kṣayaṁ yathā vahnistṛṇadārumahācayam||

Translation:

Just as a fire quickly turns a pile of wood into ashes, Mother *Amvikā* rapidly destroyed the huge army of demons.

Explanation:

There is a verse of this nature in the *Bhāgavat Gitā*, 'just as a blazing fire turns wood into ashes, so *Arjuna* does a fire of knowledge reduce all action to ashes.'[59] Here too we see that Mother appears in the affectionate form of *Amvikā* and destroys all demonic tendencies. We cannot agree with those who do not realize the true meaning of the words 'the world is false', and discarding the part that is 'the world', try to reach this state by analyzing 'I am *Brahmaṇ*.' Although no one can disagree that knowledge of *Brahmaṇ* is a destroyer of all action, just by saying that the world is false using analysis and removing it from sight, one does not discover divine nectar. What is found by analysis is not knowledge, it is a hint of knowledge. Knowledge means to know, to perceive. Until some matter is known, until then, there is no knowledge of it. One cannot erode action by lecture or study. One has to realize knowledge. *Īṣā Upaniṣad* says true knowledge (*vidyā*) and lesser knowledge (*avidyā*) are both required for liberation. By *avidyā*, one crosses over death and by *vidyā*, discovers divine nectar[60]. Tendencies of actions are *avidyā*. But, calling it false and closing one's eyes to it does not remove the fear of death. As long as there is variety in knowledge, so long it will

---

59 *Bhāgavat Gitā,* 4:37

60 *Īṣā Upaniṣad*, 11

send beings from death to death. You see a flow of action and you perceive variety, but you are creating new tendencies by repeating that it is all false. This can never remove the fear of death. One has to imbue a flow of action with supreme spirit (*Brahmaṇ*). There is no separate action, it is all *Brahmaṇ*. This knowledge has to be firmly established. When actions become imbued with *Brahmaṇ*, then tendencies (*saṁskāra*) of actions are removed. This is the first step. This is the realization of *Brahmaṇ* with characteristics (*saguṇa*), or crossing over the fear of death by *avidyā*. When this is accomplished, one can realize *Brahmaṇ* without characteristics (*nirguṇa*), or find divine nectar by *vidyā*. In this manner, beings taking refuge in *vidyā* and *avidyā*, are saved from death and are able to enjoy divine nectar.

Look and see how within moments, Mother destroys innumerable demons. The innumerable tendencies of actions that arise in your spirit are demons. They have to be each held and turned into tendencies of Mother. They each have to be realized as Mother in disguise. In this manner, when the tendencies of Mother become dense and only have the shape of tendencies, are they all imbued by Mother. All their form is of Mother. Then one can understand that these demons have been overcome by Mother. This does not take place in a day. It has to be practiced respectfully for a long time. This is the teaching of Yoga. However, you are a child of Mother. You are calling her. To find her is your goal in life. When your intense desire rests eternally in the heart of the sentient one, then do not pay attention to demons fighting in your spirit. Keep your eyes constantly on Mother. Call her, thinking yourself to be a tormented child. Be engrossed by the greatness of Mother. You will see that within moments, she will destroy all your demonic tendencies.

Verse 67.

sa ca siṁho mahānādamutsṛjan dhutakesaraḥ|
śarīrebhyohamarārīṇāmasūniva vicinvati||

Translation:

With loud roars and shaking its mane, the lion too, began to gather lives from the bodies of demons.

Explanation:

In this mantra, the establishment of life force (*prāṇa pratiṣṭhā*) is described. It is this establishment of life force that is the spiritual effort of this middle character. This is specifically brought up here. When one is established in life, then the knot of *prāṇa*, of *Viṣṇu* can be penetrated. This mystery is accessible to humble and respectful seekers in the lineage of a *guru*. On the other hand, those who have no firm belief in the nature of divinity, who do not have firm respect in the words of a *guru* or scriptural texts and those who do not have the channel of *suṣumṇā* open, will not benefit from these discussions. However, let us proceed. Let us remember our only refuge is at the feet of divine Mother, and try to unveil the mystery of this mantra. Mother, may you appear as intellect, may you clarify our path in this spiritual quest. Let blind ignorance of worldly persons be illuminated by a bright light of knowledge and devotion.

The mantra says that the lion began to gather lives from the bodies of demons. The lion is a worldly person that is an instrument for the expression of the power of Mother. I have said before that when a spiritual seeker, becomes violent towards his state as a worldly person when one attempts to remove the sense of body, then one can be called a lion. Mother, by the touch of her feet, honors one's life. Worldly persons, begin to gather life from their bodies. This is spiritual effort, this is the establishment of *prāṇa*. As long as one is engrossed with just the body, one is a common being. When one gathers up life from the body, one becomes the foremost of beings, a lion. The body is inert and life is conscious. Search for consciousness in the inert. Understanding that all inert things are a playground of consciousness is the establishment of life force.

Your young child is playing happily and you watch with enchanted eyes. Think about this. What do you understand as your child? Who is enchanting you? Is it a body or a life? Not the body. If it was just a lump of flesh and blood that enchanted you, if that was a portion of yourself, then one would not send it to the cemetery if life left it. So, who is your child? It is life, *prāṇa*. It is that, for which one is a being (*prāṇi*). Without it, a body is just a corpse. But, worldly persons, disregard this night and day, they do not pay attention to it. They stay with what is inert and play with corpses. Those who abandon life, disregard *Śiva*, and stay with a corpse (*śava*), how can they find what is good. Those who live in cremation grounds, who love cremation grounds, yet pay no attention to the dark Mother *Śyāmā* who dwells on it, how can they be free from illness, sorrow, death, laments and tears? Oh! You will be engrossed by name and form, will live on a cremation ground and yet speak about divine nectar. Can you ever find that divine nectar? Look, each body is a cemetery. As long as you do not pay attention to the one that occupies the body[61], so long you live in a cemetery. However well your dwelling may be decorated with precious things, illuminated by garlands of lights, resound with the voices of children and workers, if the sentient, living ruler of the house, divine Mother is not established in it, then it is just a cremation ground. In whatever fashion your body may be decorated with costly apparel, however it may be illuminated by knowledge and learning, whatever high office you may hold, if one pays no attention to Mother, if one does not take the body as a temple for Mother, then it is just a cemetery or a corpse. The one that inside you says 'I, I', the one which when it leaves your heart, they take your body outside as inauspicious, look at that Mother that lives on that cremation ground. See her in each material thing, in each body. You will find eternal prosperity, there will be nothing inauspicious in this world.

Those of you who seek the one that lives on cremation grounds, who carry out severe Yoga, austerities and spiritual effort, look how she resides in your heart eternally. Do not disregard this as something known. Search for it with firm belief and respect. You will find the one that lives on cemeteries. You see nothing and

---

61 *deha*- the body, *dehi*- the occupier

understand nothing. Who will you seek refuge with? That feeling you have of life, that perception that is living, the one that swells in joy and contracts in sorrow, look at it. Let tendencies of spirit flow to it, weep for it as Mother. Offer all your desires to it, speak to it of all your joy and sorrow. You will find the one that dwells on cremation grounds. Your life will be honored by the affection of the dark one, Mother *Śyāmā*.

When you say 'life' (*prāṇa*), a nonmanifest but true feeling arises in your heart. Move that feeling into every material. Visualize life force in each form, flavor, sound, touch and scent. Gather life from body to body. This is the establishment of life force (*prāṇa pratiṣṭhā*). Even though in the beginning, as in the establishment of truth, it appears to be mimicry, do not stop. After imitating it for some time, you will realize its true sense. Those who are used to the establishment of truth, whose inner space is steady, will feel this. Say, you are looking at a tree. By the establishment of truth, you perceive it as truth, as Mother, life, *prāṇa*. This is the nature of that truth. There is no truth without consciousness, there cannot be. No one has to be told what perception of life is, the feeling of life. Every person has a vague feeling of one's life. Imagine that same life is being seen in front as a tree. A vibration of life should arise on seeing the tree. By doing this in each object, a universal perception of life will arise. O how desirable, how sweet that is. This world is perceived as a dense, true material. That separation of form and flavor for each object disappears. That the world appears just as an impenetrable truth in common view goes away when life force is established. Then, one cannot find a separate spirit of this world, only condensed consciousness. The term 'dense spirit' that you may hear, can be felt when you reach this point. Truly it is denser than stone. Only a spiritual seeker accomplished in this establishment of life is capable of carrying out external worship, that is ceremonial worship (*pujā*) of a *murtti*. When life is established in a material form, it truly transforms into a sentient one. Mother, beyond word and mind, overcome by love for her children, appears in solid, condensed form, and accepts worship to honor her children. This is perceived by spiritual seekers who have established life force. But that is something else.

Whatever it is, a spiritual seeker has to gather life from the body. By doing this, one finds great life and one realizes that it is life that is formed into insentient materials. Not knowing, that the tiny feeling of consciousness that you have in your heart, is creator, maintainer, destroyer, great life-formed Mother, you suffer torments of sorrow, pain and death. It is because you keep great Mother empress dressed in poverty in your own home, that your weakness, your poverty is not removed. To get rid of these, one has to establish life in each piece of matter. Remember one cannot find life without giving life. Understand the world to be Mother, offer your life at her feet. It is your life that takes the shape of this world.

My life-natured Mother, I know that giving you my life will end any state as a worldly person. I know that if we offer all life at your feet, the torment of these demons will end. But we do not offer life at your feet. We are orphaned, weak, troubled and ignorant children. By your compassion, you have to take our lives. We do not know how to offer our lives. Our lives are bemused by the gain and loss of worldly things. How will we give you that? You are *Kṛṣṇa*. Apply your great power of attraction and unite the drops of our lives into an ocean of great life. Let us be honored. Let your name as great savior be glorious. We hear that as *Kṛṣṇa* in Vṛndāvana, you went to the homes of cow-herds, stole their butter and stole the hearts of *gopis*. You have to rob our hearts in the same manner. We will not give you our lives willingly. If you let us know of your arrival, we will banish you. In case we lose our hearts on seeing your all-enchanting form, we close our doors and stay inside. So, I tell you, come as a thief and steal our lives. Please come and rob our lives. Then we may taste eternity and cool our disturbed spirits. As long as we are not able to offer our hearts, let us weep in this manner. Out of her kindness, no not kindness, her affection, Mother will come one day and satisfy our desires.

Whatever it is, when you are used to seeing Mother in all this world, understanding that she is life is the establishment of life. When the feelings of demons enter one by one and erode the shores of peace, one has to grab each of them and see them as life. That it is life that comes in all these forms has to be practiced repeatedly and felt in the heart. Remember the example of a piece of confection in Volume One. Whatever the outer shape may be, one has to hold on to the feeling that it is nothing but life. This is the gathering of life from the bodies of the demons. Practicing this for some days will untie the knot of life. The ignorance that life is a tiny thing in the heart will disappear. You will then see that this infinite, diverse world is nothing but *prāṇa*. You will be engrossed by the great expanse of a life of Self. You will understand yourself to be beyond birth and death, forever at peace. The blissful state of a spiritual seeker that appears cannot be described in words.

There are two adjectives describing the lion in this mantra, '*mahānādamutsṛjan*' and '*dhutakesaraḥ*.' When the lion was gathering life from the bodies of the demons, it roared and shook its mane. The first is a sign of excitement and the second one of anger. To destroy the tendencies of demons, excitement and anger are needed. One has to stand against demonic nature with enthusiasm. The lion, blessed by a touch of the feet of Mother, and filled with great enthusiasm, acts out the anger and excitement of Mother. This is not a cause of bondage. It is a means or external sign of liberation. The spiritual seeker also needs to go forward, loudly calling Mother. When you see both inside and outside, the great expansion of your life, you cannot remain silent. You cannot think of yourself to be a weak being. Seeing the excitement of great life, you too will make the horizons resound with your call for Mother. This call for Mother by you will purify the air. Those who hear this cry will also move towards Mother to sacrifice themselves like insects flying into a flame. Oh! Even thinking of this makes my heart dance in excitement.

Verse 68.

devyā gaṇaiśca taistatra kṛtaṁ yuddhaṁ tathāsuraiḥ|
yathaiṣāṁ tutuṣurdevāḥ puṣpavṛṣṭimuco divi||

*iti mārkeṇḍeyapurāṇe savarṇike manv*antare *devīmāhātmye mahiṣāsurasainyavadhḥ|*

Translation:

On that battlefield, the warriors of the Goddess fought the demons so well, that the gods in heaven (being content) showered them with flowers.

Here ends this description of the destruction of the warriors of *Mahiṣāsura*, in *Devī Māhātmya*, from the ancient *Mārkeṇḍeya Purāṇa*, in the era of *Sāvarṇi*.

Explanation:

The battle by *Gaṇa* warriors has been explained before. The significance of showering flowers by the gods is that of blessings and transmission of power. When beings surrender at the feet of Mother and are empowered by Mother, take the sturdy weapon of the establishment of life, confront demons and fight as best they can, then the gods encourage them with their blessings and energy. As long as beings nurture the power of demons, the gods remain powerless. But once they dare to stand up against these demons, then the gods are encouraged and pleased. The *Gitā* says this too. Worldly persons nurture the energy of gods. The gods too look after the welfare of beings. They support each other.[62] As long as beings do not take this to heart, they cannot find blessings and power from the gods and improve. Today, by the blessing of Mother, even the breath of beings stands up against these demons. They are prepared to destroy the power of these demons. The gods bless them and give them power.

As you too travel in a spiritual quest, you will see that the gods give you the necessary power to move forward rapidly. As long as you stay away from a spiritual quest, thinking that you are

62 *Bhāgavat Gitā*, 3.11

weak and powerless, the path will appear difficult and thorny. But, if you put one step forward, you will see that God comes three steps towards you. Do not be afraid to move forward, saying 'I am a worldly person, I am enamored by material things, I love wealth and desire, so it is impossible for me to go forward on a spiritual quest.' Whatever condition anyone is in, one can still find God. Nothing needs to be taken or discarded. Becoming excited at the thought of finding him is enough to find him. Then all the gods stand in your favor and give you their blessing and power.

Come, fearful children. Come all you who are burnt by the fires of three worlds. Let us all get together and call for Mother. The gods will shower us with flowers. We will be honored.

Chapter 3

Destruction of *Mahiṣāsura*

Verse 1.

ṛṣiruvāca|
nihanyamānaṁ tatsainyamavalokya mahāsura|
senānīścikṣuraḥ kopād yayau yoddhumathāmbikām||

Translation:

The sage (*ṛṣi*) said, after this, seeing the demon warriors slain, their chief general, the great *asura Cikṣura*, angrily went forward to fight *Amvikā*.

Explanation:

Up to this point, the destruction of demonic warriors has been described. Now battles with demon generals and their deaths will be narrated. By the grace of Mother, by the influence of attractive force towards nature of Self, demonic tendencies have been disempowered. But, without the disappearance of the chief action forces of active tendency (*rājasa*), apprehension of torment by the tendencies of demons is not removed. They now come to the notice of spiritual aspirants. We have mentioned before that *Cikṣura* is the power of distraction. By the power of this influence, we do not see Mother. By this unconquered *asura Cikṣura*, before we can realize our true natures, we are expressed as matters of form and flavor. The trouble it takes to relieve oneself of this unconquered *asura* is probably more than that needed for anything else. To get rid of distraction, spiritual seekers carry out many kinds of yogic procedures, much severe austerity and practice. They think that if in some way this distraction of spirit can be removed, then the nature of *paramātmā* will be revealed. As an example, they mention the image of the Moon on water. Their conclusion is that when the waves on the water are stilled, a tranquil image of the Moon can be seen. No other effort is required. There is no doubt that their conclusion is based on truth. But, it is difficult to say if there are spiritual seekers who can completely rid themselves of the clutches of distraction. As long as we have a body we understand that we have distractions. The name of this distracted state is worldly existence. By serious control, austerity and prolonged practice, the degree of distraction may be lowered.

We have discovered directions for a different path that is well suited for the present time, place and those entitled. Mother has repeatedly signaled us to travel in this straight and simple direction. This is the Vedic path observed by the sages. We will not be bothered by distractions. We will surrender at the feet of Mother like simple-hearted children and reside with complete independence and full reliance. Whether it be a distraction or it is deceit or whatever torment, we will under all conditions keep faith on the feet of Mother and go forward. Mother will make arrangements that are needed for all of us. We are blissful, unclothed children on the lap of Mother. We do not need to analyze and consider all these various things. We neither have that right nor the ability. Come, let us call Mother and with complete faith leap into the affectionate heart of the great one. Mother will make us carry out all spiritual effort and enterprise. What is good or bad for us is understood much better by Mother than by us. Why should we spend night and day worrying about this? If there is a need for battle, Mother will fight. If distraction has to be removed, Mother will do so. We will be spectators. We will watch this divine play of Mother. In joy or sorrow, elation or grief, distraction or concentration, under all conditions, we are onlookers. We are joyous, naked children on the lap of Mother.

If we can understand well that the life in us is our Mother, that she is overcome by affection for her children, that she is always doing what is good for us, then what do we need to worry about? So, we see in this mantra, that the *asura* went to battle with *Amvikā* (*yayau yoddhumathāmbikām*). He did not come to fight with us. Whether it is distraction, or it is deception, arrogance, pride, conceit or delusion, why would it matter to me? There is no clash with me. I remain quiet and steady, a viewer of this divine game. The demons leave me alone and go to battle with *Amvikā*.

Look how easy it is for a yogi who has surrendered. The great *asura Cikṣura* goes to fight with Mother. The conditions of a self-surrendered yogi, accomplished in the pursuit of the mantra, 'take refuge only in me'[1], are described by this principle in *Caṇḍī*. This has been said repeatedly before and is being recounted here. Self-surrender is a spiritual effort. A spiritual seeker discovers this after traveling through many circumstances. When one is accomplished in this, body, mind and senses become instruments for Mother. In trying to show this, the sage of *Devī Māhātmya*, taking Suratha and Samādhi as examples, demonstrates this incredible mystery. Using the destruction of demons to express these spiritual principles, he tries to open the blind and ignorant eyes of this world.

In the previous verse, self-motivation (*puruṣkāra*) by the lion that has been described is not at odds with self-surrender or complete dependency. Because it is the power of Mother that appears through the body of worldly persons and appears as motivation. As long as beings do not taste surrender, they do not discover the true nature of self-effort. This *puruṣa* (male principle) of self-motivation is Mother. If you do not know this *puruṣa*, how can you see its achievement and action? Do not think even in your dreams that when one is dependent on Mother, one becomes inert. True activity appears in a self-surrendered yogi. That is why I say, practice self-surrender. Go forward with surrender. Remember, one cannot find Self without self-surrender. If you want to find great life, merge your little one into that of Mother. Forget your little 'I', hold with both hands 'I' that is Mother, *guru*. You will see how hundreds of demons are slain, how divine games are played out. But you will not be touched by ownership. You will have to do nothing. You will realize that you are but an observer, a witness. You will be freed from the imaginary puzzle of freedom from bondage.

---

1 *māmekaṁ śaraṇaṁ vraja, Bhāgavat Gitā,* 18:66

Verse 2.

sa devīṁ śaravarṣeṇa vavarṣa samarehasuraḥ|
yathā merugireḥ śṛñgaṁ toyavarṣeṇa toyadaḥ||

Translation:

Like clouds raining around the peaks of the high Sumeru mountain the demons showered arrows towards the Goddess on the battlefield.

Explanation:

The illustration used in this mantra is very beautiful. Clouds bring rain, but they cannot do so on the peaks of the Sumeru mountain because they are so high that clouds do not reach them. In the epic *Kumārsambhava*, poet Kālidasa says, 'the clouds are a skirt for the Himalayas', that is, they reach to the waist of the mountains and cannot go higher. The Sumeru peaks are so tall that the clouds cannot rain on the top of those peaks. In the same manner, innumerable arrows shot by the great *asura Cikṣura* could not reach the body of the Goddess.

The nature of my Mother is existence-awareness-bliss, beyond speech and thought, she is beyond the reach of mind, intelligence or senses. How can distractions of spirit touch her? So, the shower of arrows from *Cikṣura* did not touch her body. How can that which cannot be processed by the mind, whose nature and expression give nature and expression to the mind, be affected by mental disturbances? As long as one does not know the nature of Mother, so long is there fear of demons, so long is there arrangements and effort to prevent distraction. Mother is *ātmā*, eternally alone, eternally pure, eternally free. Just as distraction is a property of spirit, deterrence is also a property of spirit. Neither *samādhi* nor disturbance can rise above spirit. How can properties of spirit touch the body of the sentient one?

Verse 3.

tasya chitvā tato devī līlayaiva śarotkarān|
jaghāna turagān bāṇairyantārañcaiva vājinām||

Verse 4.

ciccheda ca dhanuḥ sadyo dhvajañcātisamucchṛtam|
vivyādha caiva gātreṣu chinnadhanvānamāśugaiḥ||

Translation:

The Goddess stopped the arrows (of *Cikṣura*) with ease and with her arrows destroyed his horses and charioteer. Then, with her arrows, she split his bow and tall pennant and struck the demon whose bow had been broken.

Explanation:

It was said in the previous mantra that the arrows of *Cikṣura* could not touch the body of Mother. Now the might of Mother is being described. Mother expressed the power of her Self by six actions: 1- stopping the arrows of *Cikṣura*, 2- destroying his horse, 3- killing his charioteer, 4- breaking his bow, 5- splitting his tall pennant, 6- hitting his body with arrows. Let us try to understand the secret of these six actions.

First, stopping the arrows of *Cikṣura*: The forces creating material disturbances in the spirit are the arrows of *Cikṣura*. The way to end them is to shoot arrows of establishment of life (*prāṇa pratiṣṭhā*). Whenever vibrations of materials appear in the spirit, understand them to be vibrations of the great spirit. My Mother living in me, as great existence expresses herself as material objects. Form and flavor, desire and wealth are my life, my Mother. Holding this percept for some time stops the vibrations of material things. This truth can be accomplished.

Second, the killing of the horses of *Cikṣura*: The word 'horses' represents the senses (*indriyas*). The *śrutis* say that the senses are like horses. Vibrations of material things in the field of spirit are brought by the horses of senses. The five sense objects are reached or enjoyed by these sense horses. By application of establishment of life force, material vibrations are seen as life and the forces of senses are enchanted by the spirit of life. This is the significance of killing the horses.

Third, killing the charioteer: Mind is the driver of the horses. When senses are perfused by life force, their driver, the mind is also imbued by life, because the things taken by the senses are brought to the mind. As long as eyes and other organs only carry form and flavor and present them to the mind, so long is it bemused by the divisiveness and inertness of material things. When the senses are imbued with life, they take life itself in the shape of form and flavor. So, all that is taken to the mind is of the nature of life. So, the perception of material things, of multiplicity and resolution-alternation ends. This is the mystery of the killing of the charioteer.

Fourth, the breaking of the bow: This is the end of the bow of action. With the establishment of life everywhere, seeing the expansion of great life inside and outside, the organs of actions are so engrossed that they stop acquiring material things. This is the breaking of the bow of *Cikṣura*.

Fifth, splitting the tall pennant: The sense of ego is a tall pennant. Seeing life force covering all this world, it is understood that all actions are carried out by it. 'I do not do anything, it is all carried out by my life-natured Mother.' Everything in the three worlds is under the control of life-natured Mother. When one is established in this knowledge, how can the pennant of ego still be standing?

Sixth, piercing the body of *Cikṣura* with arrows: When the great *asura Cikṣura* has his pennant broken and is without his charioteer, Mother finding the right opportunity, pierces his body with arrows. It has been said that the establishment of life force is the shooting of arrows by Mother. When the power of distraction becomes relatively weak, one has to practice this establishment of life force repeatedly. By this means, *Cikṣura*, the power of distraction, (becoming imbued with *prāṇa*), is forced to let go of any disturbances.

This is an incredible strategy of battle. Only spiritual seekers practiced in the art of establishment of life force can understand this secret. By day or night, if this battle is perceived even once, the spiritual path becomes easy. Before, when you are practicing the establishment of truth, speaking of Mother, you understood an entity with unknowable nature, you saw her to be far away. She was somewhere beyond this universe. You did not know her true nature. Now, by the grace of the *guru*, you know that the life force felt in your heart is Mother. It is so near, so dear, the one whose spirit gives you spirit, whose existence gives you existence, because of whom, your body, mind, senses, spouse, children, wealth and fame all exist, that life force is Mother. If at this moment she stood down from your heart, you would have nothing that is you. That life force is Mother. If you gather life in all materials, in all perceptions, you will understand that your tiny *prāṇa* is the life force of this universe. Again, noticing the distraction of spirit, if you practice the establishment of life force, you will understand that all this is spirit, all this distraction is all life force. There is nothing that is not a final resort of the life-natured Mother.

Verse 5.

sacchinnadhanvā viratho hatāśvo hatasārathiḥ|
abhyadhāvata tāṁ devīṁ khaḍgacarmadharohasuraḥ||

Translation:

When the bow of *Cikṣura* was snapped, his chariot broken and his horse and charioteer killed, the *asura* taking up a scimitar and shield ran towards Mother.

Explanation:

Understanding the significance of the scimitar (*khaḍga*) and shield (*carma*) the meaning of this mantra will become easy. The scimitar is a weapon to divide. Knowledge of divisiveness is a scimitar. The lack of realization that I and this universe have no separate spirit other than that of life force (*prāṇa*) or Mother, is the reason for the gathering of knowledge. It seems to appear that Mother is one and this existing world of beings is separate from her. Even after a thousand explanations, after a long study of scriptural texts, this sense of division is not removed from the heart. This is the weapon of distraction. This is the scimitar of *Cikşura*. It is the chief means of keeping one separated from Mother.

In general terms, a *carma*[2] is a shield. Murkiness that prevents union is like a shield. Just as divisiveness appears to keep beings separate from Self, dimness destroys any effort to remove divisiveness. When we leap forward, when we move in the hope of merging into the heart of Mother, then this dimness of being stands in front of us as a hindrance to union with Mother. Mother is eternal, pure, free *ātmā* and we are transient, impure, ignorant and non-self. So, we cannot unite with her. We cannot merge our burning heart with her all-loving one and become overcome by bliss. We sometimes say that there would be no need for liberation if we could stay enslaved and enjoy the love of Mother. Alas! It can never happen. To love Mother, to properly enjoy her affection, we have to be like her, eternal, pure and free. As long as even a trace of 'I' remains, we have to know that we have not understood that Mother is life force, we have not been able to merge our tiny life force into the great one of Mother. How can bound life force love free *ātmā*? This is why *Vaişṇava* philosophers say that 'beings can never become God. They will always remain beings. Even the thought of beings becoming God is sinful.' This is not without relevance. One cannot attain Godhood when even a drop of a state as a worldly person remains.

A state as a worldly person and the state of *Brahmaṇ* are as opposite as light and darkness. As long as a state of worldly person remains, one cannot achieve the state of *Brahmaṇ*. When one alights on *Brahmaṇ*, no trace of a worldly person remains. When beings alight on great, loving *paramātmā*, they are engrossed by love. In time this ripens and love becomes dense, overcoming

2 skin or leather

worldly persons so that they can find no other existence but that of *Brahmaṇ*. In this state, beings acquire feelings of *Brahmaṇ*. That is why in the Yoga of great knowledge, *Bhāgavat Gitā* says, 'those who worship me with devotion, reside in me, and I express myself especially in them'[3]. In this condition, there is only a thin line of difference between a worldly person and divinity. At each moment, undivided, nondual nature is revealed. This is a state of liberation as a worldly person. In a state without a body or *kaivalya*, even this line of division does not remain. There is complete love or supreme union.

Whatever it is, we have come a long way from our topic under discussion. The scimitar and shield of the great *asura Cikṣura*, that is, the knowledge of division and murkiness are great barriers to our arriving at a state of complete love. When you stand in front of Mother and say 'most loved of loved ones, my life force, *paramātmā*', and realize her to be your life force, *paramātmā,* who is it that separates you from the shelter of Mother? This is the demon carrying a scimitar and shield. Realize this torment in your heart.

Verse 6.

siṁhamāhatya khaḍgena tīkṣṇadhāreṇa mūrdhani|
ājaghāna bhuje savye devīmapyativegavān||

Translation:

The very agile, great *asura Cikṣura*, with his sharp scimitar, hit the lion on its head, and the left hand of the Goddess.

Explanation:

A scimitar is a sharp instrument. That Mother is one and I am another, is knowledge stored over many lifetimes. So, it is tough and sharp. What will happen by just saying 'I am *Brahmaṇ*, I am that'? One cannot find relief from strokes of this sharp sword. The first act of this divisive knowledge is to strike at the head

3 *Bhāgavat Gitā,* 9:29

of the lion, to divide the upper organ of the worldly person, the tendency for undivided knowledge. The first strike of *Cikṣura* is to the head of the lion. Worldly persons think that they are impure, they are tiny. How could they be *Brahmaṇ*? This is a great strategy of battle. If you review your own spiritual life, you will see how true is this strike by *Cikṣura* on the head of the lion. It is because of this that you reside so far away from Mother. Because of it, you suffer weights of many lives and deaths.

Then there is a blow to the left hand of Mother. My Mother suppresses enemies with her right hand and holds her children to her bosom with her left. She does not leave us for even a moment, so the demon hits her left hand to take us away from her. His goal is served if I can be moved from the heart of Mother. But we are not holding on to Mother. It is Mother who is holding us. So, the powerful demons fail.

From a spiritual viewpoint, it can be seen that there is an attractive force in the left hand of Mother. The movement of spirit towards Self is the attractive force of Mother. Because of an attractive force from *ātmā*, externally faced nature turns towards Self. This has been described as the *gopis* leaving their homes, attracted by music from the flute of *Śri Kṛṣṇa*, who is standing beneath the trees of Vṛndāvana. When this takes place on the inside, the external sign is called abstention or withdrawal. Then, attractions for material things slowly diminish. This withdrawal is the left hand of Mother. What on the inside is the attraction of Mother, is expressed outside as abstention. All religious scriptures speak of this renunciation. The right hand of Mother is action. There is no special need to speak of it here. If one understands the left hand then the right one is easily understood.

You can see if the *asura* can make the left hand of Mother weak and inactive, whether his goal is served or not. If he can remove me from the path of withdrawal, then I will be signing him a pledge of slavery. It is with this hope that *Cikṣura* strikes at the left hand of Mother. I have said that Mother holds us with her left hand. Now try to understand this too. It is by the path of abstention that a spiritual seeker progresses on a path of self-surrender. Offering all responsibility to Mother, one is without worry. What is the reason that you are not a bit concerned about the attack of this demon on your spirit, in the great battle that is waging? Mother holds you by the attraction of her left hand. You have surrendered and are in the bosom of Mother, so you are without worry and are confident. Even a hundred storms and troubles of this world cannot come and pain you because Mother holds you to her heart. It is to make you fall from there that *Cikṣura* strikes at her left hand.

Verse 7.

tasyāḥ khaḍgo bhujaṁ prāpya paphāla nṛpanandana|
tato jagrāha śūlaṁ sa kopādaruṇalocanaḥ||

Translation:

O king Suratha, the scimitar of the *asura* shattered when it touched the hand of Mother. Eyes red with anger, the demon picked up a lance.

Explanation:

The word '*paphāla*' is constructed from the root '*phal*' (breakage). The word means 'was broken.' Hoping to remove us from the hold of Mother, *Cikṣura* had tried to strike the left hand of Mother with his scimitar. He failed. He could not remove us from the attraction of Mother, or sway us from the path of withdrawal. Why? Because, it is not me that is holding on to Mother so that if I let go, the purpose of the *asura* is served. I have both hands raised, waving both hands of desire and withdrawal, shouting praises to Mother and dancing with joy. I have neither desire nor withdrawal. Seeing me with both hands raised, Mother holds me firmly. What do I have to fear? If the demon had struck my hand, I would have fallen. But this is the arm of Mother, so the scimitar shattered.

As long as you attempt to carry out a spiritual effort to find

Mother on your own, you will have to suffer blows from demons at every step. Do not think that a path of renunciation is the goal of life. On the other hand, do not become unruly under the influence of desire. Understand in your heart that you are in the folds of Mother. If withdrawal is needed, Mother will make it happen. If it is necessary to be protected from desire, Mother will take care of it. You only have to have a firm belief that 'I am sheltered, Mother is my refuge.'

Whatever it is, attempts by these demons have failed. Seeing that knowledge of divisiveness failed, the demon picked up a lance. What is this lance? It is the root of ignorance. 'I do not know myself'' is root ignorance. Innumerable lifetimes and deaths, innumerable worldly persons are based on this one ignorance. A lance (*śula*) is a sharp-pointed weapon of iron. This root ignorance is also very sharp, so it is difficult to understand its nature. All knowledge or ignorance of matter is seated at the sharp end of this lance of self-ignorance. This immense universe, this infinite diversity, this endless flow of birth and death, this laughter and tears, joy and sorrow, sin and piety, this store of prior tendencies and seeds of future actions are all built on a pillar of this root ignorance of 'I do not know myself.' If by the grace of a *guru*, this root ignorance is destroyed in some fashion, then, like a palace without foundations, this universe will be demolished. Spiritual seekers reach this root ignorance after much effort. Even the Lord has said, 'beings gain knowledge after many births.' Knowledge means the ability to understand what ignorance is. Knowledge from studying the scripture does not make one truly knowledgeable. Truly realizing 'I am ignorant' is knowledge. This root ignorance is discovered by realizing that this tendency of divisiveness is a weapon of a demon, is a torment. The manner in which one nears the temple of liberation by taking refuge at the feet of Mother is especially explained in the principles of *Caṇḍī*. One has to wonder how these bonds are released. Mother kindly finds and tears each of these knots, one after another. Beings do not know where there is ignorance, divisiveness, bondage or where there is liberation. But, nothing is hidden from the eyes of Mother. Like a deft physician, Mother removes the causes of unknown diseases. So, I say, in knowledge or ignorance, surrender yourself to Mother, illnesses of this world will be removed.

Verse 8.

cikṣepa ca tatastattu bhadrakālyāṁ mahāsuraḥ|
jājvalyamānaṁ tejobhī ravibimbamivāmbarāt||

Verse 9.

dṛṣṭvā tadāpatacchūlaṁ devī śūlamamuñcata|
tacchūlaṁ śatadhā tena nītaṁ sa ca mahāsuraḥ||

Translation:

After this, the great demon *Cikṣura* threw a lance at Goddess *Bhadrakāli*. Seeing the lance coming down from the skies like a blazing sun, the Goddess threw her lance towards it. By its blow, the lance of the demon and the demon himself were split into a hundred pieces.

Explanation:

Just as the power of the demons tries to keep us deluded and in bondage, it also releases a strong latch on the door to a temple of salvation. During the monsoons, the waters of the Ganges are muddied, but there are signs that they will become clear in spring. Microbes inside a body are expressed as bodily disease and trouble a person, but they may be needed to free a body from illness. A spiritual seeker has for so long, endured the intolerable oppression of these perceptual demons of divisiveness, but now that demon has brought them to a center of perception. The *asura* has thrown its lance and the spiritual seeker has discovered root ignorance. The moment beings discover this root ignorance 'I do not know myself', it weakens. If one realizes one's faults, one may begin to correct them.

Some may say, who does not know that the reason we are bound is because we do not know our own nature. One does not understand just by saying this. Knowing means realizing it. In the language of *Vedānta*, this is the causal body (*kāraṇa śarira*) or the blissful sheath (*ānanadamaya koṣa*). When one can independently move in the intellectual sheath (*vijñānamaya koṣa*), then one can discover this ignorance. It is not our purpose to bring up all this and complicate our discussion. The focus here is on how children who depend on Mother, who wish to receive Mother, easily arrive at this pure nature of knowledge expounded by *Vedānta*. When worldly persons rely on Mother under all circumstances, in knowledge and ignorance, in joy or sorrow, in sin or piety, then this remarkable state is achieved. By the *asura* throwing its lance towards *Bhadrakāli*, beings discover the root of their true ignorance. The one who is established on the power of supreme time (*mahākāla*), the one who is always gentle, eternally beneficial, that *Bhadrakāli* Mother takes all responsibility for worldly persons, letting them find this root ignorance, giving them the chance to enjoy the pure bliss of reliance.

Whatever it is, the mantra says that seeing the lance coming down like a blazing sun, the Goddess threw her own lance. Both the *asura* and his lance were destroyed. When a spiritual seeker comes near root ignorance, that is, when one understands root ignorance, then its energy appears as impenetrable as a blazing Sun. Coming near this root ignorance, one has to close one's eyes as when looking at the Sun. A blinding knowledge of this material world arises. That this root ignorance is difficult to see cannot be explained by language. When a spiritual seeker silences material vibration and carefully tries to be centered, this root ignorance slowly begins to be experienced. Then, in an instant, one is thrown away from one's target and material vibrations return. This is a final attempt by the power of distraction. But, however impossible it appears, it is destroyed by the lance of Mother. What is the lance of Mother? It is knowledge of Self. At the moment this is realized, all ignorance of worldly persons, and results from it, birth, death, bondage and liberation are destroyed. Realizing that I am pure perception, only knowledge, all tendencies (*saṁskāra*) of mind, intelligence, spirit, senses, and body disappear. Discuss this repeatedly and ignorance will disappear.

Verse 10.

hate tasmin mahāvīrye mahiṣasya camūpatau|
ājagāma gajārūḍhaścāmarastridaśārdanaḥ||

Translation:

When the general of *Mahiṣāsura*, *Cikṣura* was killed, the oppressor of the gods *Cāmara* riding on an elephant, came to battle.

Explanation:

The force of distraction has been destroyed. Now the battle and the destruction of the force of concealment will be described. Now that one principal general has been killed easily by the lance of Mother, that the others will be destroyed soon, is not surprising. The meaning of the demons *Cāmara* and others has been explained in the previous chapter, so there is no need to repeat it here. There are two adjectives used for *Cāmara*. The first, '*tridaśārdan*' means tormentor of the gods. The action of the power of concealment is to provide a perception of non-self. *Ātmā* is divine nectar (*amṛta*) The gods enjoy this divine nectar, they are always centered on Self. By the effect of the force of concealment, they are affected by what is non-self. They are deprived of this divine nectar. This is the torment of the gods by the demon *Cāmara*. The second adjective is '*gajāruḍa*' (riding an elephant). The root '*gaja*' means bondage. Where there is concealment, there is bondage. Bondage is not understanding that Self (*ātmā*), Mother, is the nature of self-expression. By illuminating something other than *ātmā*, the power of concealment covers Self. As long as *ātmā* is covered, beings are in bondage. So '*gaja*' or bondage is the proper carrier for *Cāmara*.

Verse 11.

sohapi śaktiṁ mumocātha devyāstāmambikā drutam|
huṅkārābhihatāṁ bhūmau pātayāmāsa niṣprabhām||

Translation:

Cāmara threw a power weapon aimed at the Goddess. *Amvikā* stopped it with her roaring voice. It was subdued and fell to the ground.

Explanation:

The action of the power of concealment is the perception of the body and other things that are not Self. This is the power weapon of *Cāmara*. My Mother *Amvikā*, quickly with her roaring voice makes it ineffective. This roar (*huṅkāra*) is a loud sound. This sound appears when one is very angry. I am self-expressed nature. Everything is expressed by me. Who will keep me concealed? When such feelings of anger rise, the power of concealment becomes weak. On the other hand, the roar signifies one's individual mantra or *Praṇava* (*Oṁ*). *Tantra* literature calls it *hūṁ*, the '*kūrcca*' or seed mantra. By evoking mantra consciousness in these mantras mentioned in the Tantras, one acquires the power to disempower the forces of concealment. A spiritual seeker can, with the help of these mantras, attract spirit from non-self and attempt to center on Self. As long as one is focused on this self-activity, that is, one feels that 'I will achieve spiritual success by repeating mantras', one usually fails. When one sees that Mother with her roaring voice, appearing as a mantra, is ready to end the state of non-self, the power of concealment is easily destroyed.

Let me explain. Although Self (*ātmā*) is self-expressed and unconcealed, whenever we look at material things, it appears as non-self and appears to be concealed. Even though we repeat that there is nothing else but Self thousands of times, because of prior tendencies (*saṁskāra*) it appears as non-self. The establishment of life force (*prāṇa pratiṣṭhā*) is a way to remove this perception of non-self. First, by belief in Mother, Self is established. This is the establishment of truth (*satya pratiṣṭhā*). Then one has to understand that life force, *prāṇa*, is Mother, Self. One has to establish by repeated practice that it is *prāṇa* that pervades the world, appearing as different material things that we perceive all the time. The seed mantras like *hūṁ* have been used as ancillaries to the establishment of *prāṇa*. When these principles are learned with respect from a *guru*, they yield results within a short time.

Verse 12.

bhagnāṁ śaktiṁ nipatitāṁ dṛṣṭvā krodhasamanvitaḥ|
cikṣepa cāmaraḥ śūlaṁ bāṇaistadapi sācchinat|

Translation:

Seeing his power weapon fail, *Cāmara* in anger, threw his lance. The Goddess split it with her arrows.

Explanation:

Just as a final attempt by the power of distraction is the awakening of root ignorance, a final attempt of the power of concealment is the throwing of a lance to awaken root ignorance. If spiritual seekers holding these powers of distraction and concealment, progress on a path of establishment of truth, they can get close to this root ignorance. Arriving here, by the grace of Mother, one can easily penetrate this ignorance. Mother, with her arrows, by her natural force of attraction, quickly delivers her children from ignorance to knowledge.

How is this possible? Root ignorance, 'I do not know myself', is positioned in pure knowledge. Here is an inexpressible union of knowledge and ignorance. When spiritual seekers, by the grace of a *guru*, move forward to discover the roots of these powers of distraction and concealment, they arrive at this indescribable ignorance. Because of much good fortune and the respect, devotion and faith of many lifetimes, one discovers this root ignorance. Standing here, the nature of pure knowledge is reflected, because this ignorance is set up on pure self-knowledge. Come blind ones, come all of you suffering in this world. Run and come, calling for Mother, *guru*, Self, truth and life force. You will reach beyond ignorance. You will be honored to find divine nectar.

Verse 13.

tataḥ siṁhaḥ samutpatya gajakumbhāntara sthitaḥ|
bāhuyuddhena yuyudhe tenoccaistridaśāriṇā||

Translation:

After this, the lion leaping on top of the elephant, began to wrestle mightily with the demon.

Explanation:

Because of final attempts by the powers of distraction and concealment, beings discover the roots of ignorance and realize the nature of knowledge. The demons clear a path for their own destruction. We see that *Cikṣura* and *Cāmara* both throw their lances at the Goddess and thereby, beings discover right knowledge. The greater the torment by demons, the quicker is the establishment of Self for a spiritual seeker. The demons think that if they bring root ignorance in front of a seeker, the rule of demons will be acknowledged forever. In effect, the result is the opposite. A spiritual seeker, seeing the bright light of self-knowledge, next to the deep darkness of ignorance, begins to fight with the demon *Cāmara* with the strength of a lion.

After all this time, beings have reached the junction of knowledge and ignorance. They are in between bondage and liberation. This is '*gajakumbhāntarasthitaḥ.*' We have mentioned before that the demon *Cāmara* came to battle on an elephant (*gaja*). The point at which bondage ends and freedom begins can be called '*gajakumbhāntar.*' Root ignorance is the last point of bondage. From here on, one can taste freedom. Standing at this juncture of bondage and freedom, the lion, beings, show great valor in fighting the demons.

It has been mentioned, that when one first has a desire for liberation, one thinks that family, children and relatives are bondages. With the growth of knowledge, one understands that body, senses, mind and intelligence are bondages. But, finally, one sees that true bondage is root ignorance, 'I do not know myself.' This ignorance is the true nature of bondage. From some infinite time in the past, we have acknowledged this ignorance. We pass immense time standing on this one bit of ignorance. We flow through many births and deaths. We dream of so much happiness and sorrow. Then again, standing on this bit of ignorance, we try so much to end it. We carry out so many severe austerities and strict religious ceremonies. Seeing this with our own eyes, we cannot but bow our heads at the feet of blissful, playful *Mahāmāyā*.

Mother, blessed is your indescribable play. Even after understanding it a thousand times, we forget. Our poor minds cannot agree that all this birth, death, laughter, tears, bondage and freedom are all wishes of the wishful one. O Mother, it is by your wish that there is ignorance, that there is bondage. It is by your wish that there is liberation. How long will you look at this bondage? Open your eyes and look at these strong chains with which you have tied our hands. For how many lifetimes will we suffer this pain of bondage by ignorance? We cannot bear it anymore. Our hearts are broken. Each wave comes and rips a deep wound on us. Like turbulent waves of an ocean, they keep hitting on us. Mother, when will this pain in our hearts end? Days go by, years go by and we wait with hope in our hearts. You do not come like a loving mother to end our pain, to free us forever from bondage. You do not touch our wounded hearts with the divine ambrosia of true freedom. O Mother, we have nothing more to say. Only, let us understand that you truly love us. Truly you are our life force, our *ātmā*, you are ours. Understanding this, all our pain will end.

Whatever that is, the hand-to-hand battle between *Cāmara* and the lion is described in this mantra. This battle has been explained in Volume One. When beings discover what lies beyond ignorance, standing in between knowledge and ignorance, they hold with both hands acceptance and rejection of material vibrations and try to merge into the heart of knowledge.

Verse 14.

yudhyamānau tatastau tu tasmānnāgānmahīṁ gatau|
yuyudhātehatisaṁrabdhau prahārairatidāruṇaiḥ||

Translation:

Still fighting, both (*Cāmara* and the lion) got down from the elephant, and angrily exchanged mighty blows.

Explanation:

When worldly persons, with their acceptance and rejection, begin to merge vibrations of material things into the heart of great life-formed Mother, when they dissolve feelings of non-self and try to reside in pure Self, they occasionally have to move between bondage and freedom. The purpose is to take all material knowledge into the spirit of perception. This is descent from the back of the elephant and exchanging of mighty blows. To dissolve worldly feelings, that for so long have created material tendencies in the heart of a seeker, one has to repeatedly bring them into perceptual spirit. To firmly establish realizations that whatever we see, water, earth, trees, hills and animals as very material things, their basic nature is but perception or *praṇa*, there is no alternative but to carry out this manual battle.

Spiritual seekers have to see that whatever their desires accept, and whatever they reject, are all life force, their perceptions. You have to take everything from root ignorance to the principle of earth and merge each of them into the spirit of *praṇa*. This is the great battle of beings with the power of concealment. For the demon, for the feeling of inertness, this is a great battle. For so many lifetimes it has taken on an appearance of inertness. Today it is of the nature of consciousness and the nature of perception. What can be a more serious blow for these demons? On the other hand, for worldly persons, this is also a great fight by the demons. By the grace of a *guru*, beings understand that what appears to be this world is nothing but *praṇa*. Yet, a perception of inert things does not go away. This is why the mantra describes a severe conflict.

Verse 15.

tato vegāt khamutpatya nipatya ca mṛgāriṇā|
karaprahāreṇa śiraścāmarasya pṛthak kṛtam||

Translation:

At this, the lion jumped up swiftly and with a blow of its paw severed the head of *Cāmara* from his body.

Explanation:

Here beings have been called *mṛgāri*[4]. The meaning of the word is an enemy of search. The word '*mṛga*' is from the root '*mṛg*' meaning search. When worldly persons become enemies of a search for Mother, they can be called *mṛgāri*. Where is Mother? When feelings for this search end, beings become *mṛgāri*. Spiritual seekers have to shut their eyes to this search. One has to become a *mṛgāri*. Otherwise, *Cāmara* cannot be destroyed. The fault of concealment cannot be removed. What are you searching for? One has to search for things that are hidden. Mother is well expressed everywhere. There is nothing else but Mother. How can one look for her? Whatever you see, whatever you hear, all you think is all Mother. Above, below, to the right, left, front and back, it is Mother everywhere. She resides close, eternally in your heart. What is there that is easier? There is only a lack of asking for her. As long as you see that you are trying to see Mother by meditation and other means, you will understand that you are searching for Mother. Stop searching. See Mother everywhere. Cherish her as Mother, as life force. How much do you love your own life? That life is Mother. It is Mother that enfolds this world. Do not disregard her, do not disbelieve her. In every feeling, in every effort see Mother. You will become *mṛgāri*. Ignorance stored over many lifetimes will disappear.

As long as beings are children, are ignorant and ask 'where is Mother?', they are searching for her. But once they understand, 'inside and out, it is this world', then they do not have to search anymore. Whatever they see, whatever they hold, whatever they

---

4 *mṛg*- deer, *ari*- enemy; implying the lion

know is all *praṇa*, all Mother. If a spiritual seeker cannot touch the earth and say 'Mother', feel water and not understand the sustaining nature of Mother, is not enchanted by a breeze as the touch of Mother, then how can one go forward to find Mother who is beyond all principles, all perceptions? There is a textual saying, 'those who do not remember Self on seeing this universe, how can they reach eternal supreme principle that is beyond it?'

Whatever it is, the mantra says that the lion leaped up and severed the head of *Cāmara*. When a feeling of search is removed from beings, when spiritual seekers can see Mother on opening their eyes, then the lion leaps into the sky and resides in a pure space in the heart. From there it ends the concealment of non-self and attains eternity by tasting *paramātmā.*

In this manner, the demons *Cikṣura* and *Cāmara* are killed and the powers of distraction and concealment end. Pure perception rises. Do not think that if you are saved once from distraction and concealment, your spirit will never again be disturbed in life, or feelings of non-self never return. It is not that. As long as there is a body, there is distraction and concealment. But they can never again obstruct the view of Mother, bring doubts of the existence of Mother, cover any expression of Mother. They will stay headless. They cannot torment us anymore. As long as stored tendencies are not spent, they will remain as corpses. I will speak about this later.

Verse 16.

udagraśca raṇe devyā śilāvṛkṣādibhirhataḥ|
dantamuṣṭitalaiścaiva karālaśca nipātitaḥ||

Translation:

The Goddess felled the demon *Udagra* by hitting him with rocks and trees and the demon *Karāla* with her fists and teeth.

Explanation:

The chief supports for demons are distraction and concealment. When these trunks are destroyed, branches can easily be removed.

The demon *Udagra* is pride, a sense of ego-control. This has been mentioned before. The Goddess killed him by hitting him with rocks and trees. Trees, rocks and earth, all material things are matters of our pride. We collect some of them, keep them as ours and make them substances of our vanity. Sometimes we express this pride with words. When sentient Mother appears, when we are used to seeing life force everywhere, this pride is uprooted. Because, on one hand, due to a lack of knowledge of inertness we do not find anything more to collect, on the other hand, we have nothing to call 'mine.' In this manner, the upright head of the *asura Udagra* is removed. A spiritual seeker has to remember that viewing Mother is the cause of removing ego. As long as we do not see Mother, cannot see true Self, we can be proud of this imagined 'I.' When true 'I' is discovered, there is no trace of pride left. Then, in tune with Ācārya Śankara, we have to say, 'What do we do, where do we go, what do we accept, what reject? *Ātmā* satisfies all great wishes.'

Then the *asura Karāla*; this is a name for fear. It is a hesitation of spirit, because of imaginary thoughts of the destruction of Self. It is natural for those young to imagine a fear of I will not be, I will die. It is because of ignorance that such fears appear. This is the *asura Karāla*. It is this fear of death that does not let persons enjoy happiness independently. It is useful in the young because it prevents unruly behaviour. Without the fear of death, people could act worse than animals. It is the torment by this *asura Karāla* that moves us towards a fear of death. One may not be able to make out that commonly people always harbor a fear of death. They eat, move about, laugh and chatter and join in fun and games. Where is this fear? If you consider it calmly, you will see how they are constricted by a fear of death and how they cannot carry out actions independently with free minds. Even if eating and moving are acceptable, they may give it up with reluctance because it might bring disease. In this manner, one cannot enjoy things independently. Enjoyment is constricted by a fear of death. People are forced towards savings more than enjoyment. It is said in scriptural texts, 'there is fear in everything in this world, except in renunciation.' Renunciation does not come until Mother, the one granting fearlessness is found. If renunciation does not appear, the *asura Karāla* is not killed. Whatever yogic resolutions one may be following, fear of death travels with worldly persons. Because the fearsome cry of death might enter one's ears, people think about material things night and day and are forced to serve wealth and desire. They try to cover that sadness with dry laughter. If you think for a bit, you will see that all our eating, sleeping and thoughts of material things are to save ourselves from the hands of death. Life seems to be a battle with death. Saving ourselves for a few days in this fashion, we have to finally surrender to its hands. There is no other way to be relieved from this but by the grace of Mother. Because you seek the support of Mother, to save you from the hands of fears of death from the demon *Karāla*, she strikes him with teeth, fist and palms. First, Mother opens her mouth to show him her teeth that devour this universe. Second, she takes him in her fist. Third, she bestows fearlessness by showing the raised palm of her hand.

Observe this spiritual mystery. The fear of death appears from knowledge of time. If we focus on the energy of the spirit of *Mahākāli*, where the power of time is stopped, then any feeling of fear of death is removed. One has to understand the term hit by a fist to be the power of receiving. Mother holds thousands of perceptions in her grasp and merges them into her body. Then with her raised palms, she bestows fearlessness in beings. Her palms are knowledge of courage. The *śrutis* say, 'fear appears from the knowledge of a second.' When one arrives at a knowledge of One, when all perceptions of many are dissolved, beings turn fearless. The fear of death vanishes.

Verse 17.

devī kruddhā gadāpātaiścūrṇayāmāsa coddhatam|
bāṣkalaṁ bhindipālena bāṇaistāmraṁ tathāndhakam||

Verse 18.

ugrāsyamugravīryaṁca tathaivaca mahāhanum|
trinetrā ca triśūlena jaghāna parameśvarī||

Verse 19.

biḍālasyāsinā kāyāt pātayāmāsa vai śiraḥ|
durdharaṁ durmukhaṁ cobhau śarairninye yamakṣayam||

Translation:

Angered, the Goddess killed the demon *Uddhata* with a blow of her mace, the demon *Bāskala* with a *bhindipāla* weapon and the demons *Tāmra* and *Andhaka* by arrows. The three-eyed Goddess killed the three demons *Ugrāsya*, *Ugravīrya* and *Mahāhanu* with her trident. She severed the head of the demon *Biḍālākṣya* with a blow of her sword and sent the demons *Durdhara* and *Durmukha* to the land of *Yama* with her arrows.

Explanation:

The deaths of other generals of *Mahiṣāsura* are described in these three mantras. Before this, in explanations of the army of *Mahiṣāsura*, the mysteries of *Bāskala*, *Mahāhanu* and *Biḍālākṣya* have been discussed. Other than those, some more demons are named here. In *Gitā*, the Lord described the natures of demons to *Arjuna* as 'pride, arrogance, ego, anger, harshness.'[5] When one matches the names of these demons with these, they are easy to understand. The names of the demons reveal their meanings. *Uddhata* is pride, *Tāmra* is harshness, *Andhaka* is delusion, *Ugrāsya* is anger, *Ugravīrya* animal force, *Durdhara* unforgiveness and *Durmukha* foul-mouthed. By the grace of Mother, these demons are quickly destroyed. Just by the feeling of seeking refuge, a spiritual seeker is relieved from attack by these demonic natures. It is not necessary to repeat this statement. It is only necessary to observe here that even with the presence of demonic features of ego, pride or anger, beings can receive the grace of Mother. Once the grace of Mother is felt, within a short time, all these attributes become weak.

5 *Bhāgavat Gitā*, 10:4

Using *Arjuna* as a means, the words of encouragement that the Lord imparted to us, are here described in *Caṇḍī* as active principles in the destruction of these demons. *Gitā* says, 'However sinful one may be, one has the right to seek my refuge. You can take me as your sole sanctuary. Your sinful behavior does not remove that ability. When you turn towards me, you will blessed. I will destroy your sinful features. Remember, my devotees are never destroyed'[6]. To show how these words of sanctuary are put into action, Mother carries out her divine play of the demolition of these demons. What is advised in *Gitā* is put into action in *Caṇḍī*. Those who are used to observing the expression of the life force of Mother, have their arrogance, harshness, delusion, anger and unforgiveness, quickly removed.

Verse 20.

evaṁ saṅkṣīyamāṇe tu svasainye mahiṣāsuraḥ|
māhiṣeṇa svarūpeṇa trāsayāmāsa tān gaṇān||

Translation:

Seeing his warriors destroyed, *Mahiṣāsura* took the form of a buffalo and began to terrorize the host of *Gaṇa* soldiers.

Explanation:

One by one, all the leading warriors of *Mahiṣāsura* have been demolished. All material vibrations of active tendency (*rājasa*) have been nearly expended. Now *Mahiṣāsura*, without the support of his warriors, tries to make a final effort. First, taking the form of a buffalo (*mahiṣa*), he terrorized the *Gaṇa* soldiers. One who wishes to adopt *mahi*, or the earth principle, is *mahiṣa*. Active principle, proud of material things, losing support, applies all its energy to hold on to its earthly body. Even when faults like pride and ego arising from *rājasa*, are removed from a spiritual seeker, one cannot discard the delusion of a sense of one's body. The reason is intense addiction to a physical body. This is the final

6 *ibid*, 9:30-31

attack by *Mahiṣāsura*. Until all stored actions are spent, the sense of a physical body does not slacken. Or, as long as the sense of a physical body is not uprooted, stored actions do not end. Remember, one cannot determine the order of cause and effect in this internal kingdom. We see in the world first cause and then results. But here, cause and result appear to reside together. Many will say, first spiritual enterprise (*sādhanā*) and then spiritual achievement (*siddhi*). We however see, first the fruit, then the flower. Like the Sun and its rays, *sādhanā* and *siddhi* reside together.

Whatever it is, until stored tendencies (*sañcita*) do not bear fruit, they are an obstacle to the erosion of prior actions (*prārabdha*). Under pressure from a collected store of actions from behind, the path of dissolution of stored tendencies is blocked. An outer sign of this is intense attachment to a physical body. This is the torment by the buffalo formed *Mahiṣāsura*. His first attack is on the *Gaṇa* warriors. The mystery of the *Gaṇa* warriors has been explained before. Inspiration and expiration are *Gaṇa* soldiers. The sense of a physical body arises from breath. Spiritual seekers can discover this with ease. When they are united with Mother, their breath is stilled. When the sense of a body arises again, signs of breathing appear externally. It is by the breath that the sense of a physical body is revealed. So, the sage says, the buffalo formed *Mahiṣāsura* first terrorized the *Gaṇa* warriors.

Verse 21.

kāṁścittuṇḍaprahāreṇa khurakṣepaistathāparān|
lāṅgūlatāḍitāṁścānyān śṛṅgābhyāṁñca vidāritān||

Verse 22.

vegena kāṁścidaparānnādena bhramaṇena ca|
niḥśvāsapavanenānyān pātayāmāsa bhūtale||

Translation:

Mahiṣāsura attacked some of the *Gaṇa* soldiers with his snout, some with his hooves, some with his tail and others with his horns. He felled some of them to the ground by his speedy movement, some with his roar and others by his breath.

Explanation:

In this mantra, we see that *Mahiṣāsura* used eight methods to attack the *Gaṇa* soldiers. He hit them, with his, 1) snout, 2) hooves, 3) tail, 4) horns, 5) speed, 6) roar, 7) movement and 8) breath. As a spiritual seeker you also will see that the intense attachment to a physical body as the buffalo formed *asura*, that is, desire arising from the active tendency that loves this material world, applies 'recollection, discussion, interaction, observation, secret dialogue, determination, effort and active culmination'[7]. Using these eight means on your breath brings you down to a physical level. It removes you from the affectionate heart of Mother. Come, let us take the name of Mother and try to understand the nature of this eight-fold attack.

First, recollection (*smaraṇaṁ*), memories of desires of form and flavor arrive. This is the first torment by the buffalo-formed *asura*. Remember that the force by which memories of desired objects arise is the active tendency (*rājasa*) or *Mahiṣāsura*. From repeated memories of things, one slowly begins discussions (*kirttaṇaṁ*) about them, that is, one openly begins to converse about them. Then somewhere, one has interactions with them (*keli*). Having interacted, one acquires a taste for the pleasure of material things and begins to look or search for them (*prekṣaṇaṁ*). When one finds what one is looking for, one begins a secret dialogue about them. This may be only with one's mind and intelligence. When one has decided, then there is a strong determination to acquire the object of one's desire. From this comes intense effort and the resulting active culmination. This eight-fold process is not limited to the satisfaction of carnal desires. When desired objects interact with any of the senses, one has to understand that this eight-fold process has been applied.

Let us say that you have found your desired wealth. See how within it, this eight-fold process is carried out. First, we think

---

7 *smaraṇaṁ, kirttanaṁ*. . .eight-fold attachments

about wealth. (This memory comes from what are past tendencies, *saṁskāra*. All of these are modulations of active attribute, *rājasa*. This active attribute is *Mahiṣāsura*. This has been mentioned before.) From the memory of wealth comes talks or discussions about it. Then we may come into contact with some wealthy persons, that is, we associate with the ways and means of the wealthy. This is called interaction or play (*keli*). Then we begin a search to find wealth. After this, secret discussions, to find out how to obtain wealth. In this manner, through resolve and effort, one arrives at culmination, that is, one acquires wealth.

Now, see how *Mahiṣāsura* violates the peace of your inner nature. When we are calm, breath remains within our nostrils. Under this eight-fold attack, breathing becomes unnaturally disturbed. This is the significance of the blows by snout and hoof. The mantra also says that the *Gaṇa* soldiers were thrown to the ground by this eight-fold attack. Here, it is shown very beautifully how spirit is taken from a perceptual plane to the earthly one. The state of the spirit is evident from the breath. The disturbance of the breath of life is an outer sign of disturbance of spirit.

The authors of scriptural texts have called *smaraṇaṁ, kirttaṇaṁ,* etc. eight-fold intercourse or non-celibacy. It appears from the interaction of material things and senses. So, it is called intercourse (*maithuna*). This intercourse takes place whenever any material thing interacts with any of the senses. This is an obstacle to *brahmacārya* or the passage to *Brahmaṇ*. A spiritual seeker should not think that *brahmacārya* is maintained just by celibacy or sexual restraint. Celibacy is just an external sign of *brahmacārya*. You see a flower as a flower with your eyes or hear a sound as sound with your ears, these too are *maithuna*, opposed to *brahmacārya*. True *brahmacārya* is achieved when the senses come into contact with the form and flavor of material things and do not bring any other sensation but that of *Brahmaṇ*. When you 'see everywhere nothing but *Brahmaṇ*'[8], or 'cover everything with

8 *sarvvaṁ khalu idaṁ brahma Chāndogya Upaniṣad, 3.14.1*

God'[9], when you are firmly established in the knowledge that there is 'nothing but *Brahmaṇ*', then will you realize the true nature of *Brahmaṇ*. Alas! Even arriving in this condition, 'the turbulent senses violently steal the mind'[10]. From past habits, senses accept this material world. Without practicing *brahmacārya* with respect, there is no hope of being relieved from the above-mentioned eight-fold intercourse.

Again, look at it from the aspect of spiritual effort. When memory, discussion and the other eight-fold processes are turned towards *ātmā*, then they are the greatest example of *brahmacārya*. Moving in *Brahmaṇ* is *brahmacārya*. *Brahmaṇ* is *ātmā*, my Mother. Let us now look at these one by one. First memory, remembering Mother; if you have received the grace of a *guru*, you have faith in the existence of Mother. This faith is your principal wealth, it is the internal expression of the active attribute or *Puraṇdara*. Just as *Mahiṣāsura* brings a memory of material things, *Puraṇdara* will bring memories of Mother. The degree to which memory will appear begins a similar level of discussion. One will think about the affection, kindness, greatness and nature of Mother. One will enjoy speaking about divine things. *Gitā* says, 'speaking of me, they are satisfied and delighted'[11]. After discussion is interaction by plays, hymns, rosaries, ceremonial worship and so on. Yes, what you call spiritual effort, are games. When we attempt spiritual effort or devotion with one who is supreme energy of creation-maintenance-dissolution of infinite universes, one who is beyond thought and words, what can it be called but a game? Even the texts say 'like the games of children, imaginations of name and form.' Spiritual effort is like games of children. Whatever severe austerity you carry out, whatever yogic mechanism you follow, are to Mother just games of children. Listen. Discovering Mother is the same as becoming one with Mother or becoming Mother. People think that finding God is similar to finding things in this world. It is not so. Finding God means becoming one with God, offering oneself at

---

9 *Īṣāvāsyamidaṁ sarvvaṁ, Īṣā Upaniṣad*

10 *Bhāgavat Gitā,* 2:60

11 *ibid,* 10:9

the feet of God. So, I say, finding Mother, giving oneself and being Mother, are all the same. Can this happen with spiritual effort or from games? It occurs because of her mercy and her wishes. She desires to express herself, so beings give themselves up or lose their selves. The significance of spiritual effort that one can see in this world is different. When Mother expresses herself, when she appears, then before her arrival some events occur in the lives of beings. This is called spiritual effort, *sādhanā*. Just as waters rise before the coming tides, in the same manner, as a sign of the arrival of Mother, beings carry out spiritual effort and worship. Up to this day, no one who has received Mother can say that 'they found Mother by spiritual effort.' Spiritual effort and Mother are as far apart as the Eastern and Western oceans. Until the time one finds Mother, one thinks that 'I am carrying out serious spiritual enterprise.' But, on receiving Mother, one understands well that such a thing cannot be found by spiritual effort. There is no means by which she can be held. All means and ways are activities of mind and intelligence. Mother resides far from all this. However, we have moved far away from our topic, so let us get back to it.

I have said that from discussion one begins to play games. From this begins search or viewing. A spiritual seeker waits for Mother or keeps looking for her. After that, there are secret conversations. Coming close to Mother, one tells her secretly, all one's requests and offerings, tales of joy and sorrow. After this begins serious commitment and attempts to gain Mother. Before this, at the time of play, that is, during a spiritual quest, the attempts that are made are superficial ceremonies. When this new effort appears, (remember that proper effort does not arise before finding Mother), then spiritual seekers by the attraction of their life force, with great longing, try to merge into the great life force. Finally, it is the end of all action, it is inaction. Worldly persons become *Brahmaṇ*. 'a knower of *Brahmaṇ* becomes *Brahmaṇ*'[12].

Look again from the point of view of material objects. You like roses. Instead of seeing these flowers just as flowers, try to

12 *brahmavida brahmaiva vabati*, *Muṇḍaka Upaniṣad*,3.2.9

understand them as life force (*prāṇa*). Then with memory and discussion of a flower, will begin memories and discussions of Mother. In this manner, through eight-fold ceremonies, your actions will end in great life force. Then you will see and truly realize, that it is your life force that comes to satisfy you as a rose. In this manner, when material things are able to take on the form of only life force, only then will you be properly free of likes and dislikes, free of wishes and results, and have rights to the desire-less Yoga of action described in *Gitā*. This may sound severe but is not difficult to carry out. After practicing it for a little time, it becomes one's nature. Then one does not have to understand things to be life force with effort. It occurs by itself.

The love-natured devotion that is described in *Vaiṣṇava* literature appears through this eight-fold performance. Non-dual nature of knowledge, the supreme person, *Śri Kṛṣṇa* has been called *Brahmaṇ, paramātmā* or *bhagabān*. The sense gateways are '*go*', cows. The flows or forces of senses are *gopis*, the cow-herd women. By attraction of *paramātmā*, *gopis* who are of the nature of beings attached to material things, leave everything and float on an ocean of love for *Kṛṣṇa*. When one does not view material things just as themselves but is used to seeing them as *Kṛṣṇa*, eight-fold ceremonies are conferred on *Kṛṣṇa*. Through all worldly actions, only devotion to *Kṛṣṇa*, or the love of *paramātmā* appears. It is expressed outside as the five spirits of devotion, placid, servile, infant, friend and lover[13]. When the formerly mentioned eight-fold processes, that is the connection between material things and the senses, are conferred on the love of *Kṛṣṇa*, then only it takes on the name of *prema*. When it is directed to the satisfaction of one's senses, it is known as *kāma*. This is the difference between *prema* and *kāma*, but that is something else.

---

13 *śānta, dāsya, vātsalya, sakhya* and *madhura*

Verse 23.

nipātya pramathānīkamabhyadhāvata sohasuraḥ|
siṁhaṁ hantuṁ mahādevyāḥ kopaṇcakre tatohambikā||

Translation:

Having felled the *Gaṇa* soldiers, the demon moved on to kill the lion of the great Goddess. At this, *Amvikā* displayed her anger.

Explanation:

In the eight-fold manner mentioned before, *Mahiṣāsura* terrorized the *Gaṇa* soldiers. Once the spirit is attracted to material objects, the *japa* breath of a spiritual seeker becomes like that of a common person. *Mahiṣāsura* achieves his goal. When a spiritual seeker has realized the breath to be that of Mother and is attempting to loosen any sense of body, if the memory of some material object arises in the spirit, then through discussion and play it terminates in action. In this manner, you will see that as soon as you are attracted to material things, your realization of breath as that of Mother is lost. You will be removed from the joy of self-surrender. You are no longer in control of tendencies. Remember that this is the destruction of *Gaṇa* warriors by *Mahiṣāsura*.

The *asura* does not stop here. He attacks the lion. Your aggression towards a state of worldly person is halted. You run after material things like common people. You are removed from that pure, perceptual nature of Mother, where you tried to reside, with so much effort. You are diverted from the sense that you are truly a carrier of the Goddess, a machine for conducting the energy of Mother. Open your eyes of knowledge and see that within moments, the forces of these demons express their power and destroy all your effort and achievement. If you are a spiritual seeker, you will suffer every tinge of this torment. But, do not be afraid. My Mother has appeared in her angry form. She will save you from this *asura*.

Verse 24.

sohapi kopānmahāvīryaḥ khurakṣuṇṇamahītalaḥ|
śṛṅgābhyāṁ parvatānuccāṁścikṣepa ca nināda ca||

Translation:

The powerful *Mahiṣāsura*, (seeing the anger of *Amvikā*), became angry and damaged the earth with his hooves. He tossed tall mountains with his horns and uttered loud grunts.

Explanation:

The *Gaṇa* soldiers having fallen. For a while, spiritual seekers think that they have fallen from the folds of Mother. This is a weakness. Such weakness appears in all seekers. Internal seeds of desire germinate and harass a seeker to no end. Just as a lamp flame sparks before going out, or a patient shows signs of healing before death, so is this attack by *Mahiṣāsura*. When an eye of intellect opens in worldly persons, when concealment and distraction are removed, one thinks that the roots of desire have been eliminated. One is not yet without desire. Even now, seeds of desire are hidden in the heart. It is a divine play by Mother to reveal these hidden seeds. It is a final attack by the form of the active attitude, of *Mahiṣāsura*. When you think that you are without desire, and find satisfaction from it, then look and search, you will see that seeds of desire are hidden in your heart. Or, you may not need to search. Mother will reveal them, holding them up in front of you as confrontations. Then you will see that they are injuring the earth with their hooves. That is, even your earthly body is disturbed. Not only is your mind running after material things, your voice and hands and other organs are running after them too. You will also see that as your body and mind are attracted by material things, your mountainous hopes of 'I will find the Mother' are tossed away. Noises of material disturbances will appear in the spirit. Most spiritual seekers feel hopeless and weak because of this sudden attack. They are filled with angst that they will not be able to progress on a path to liberation.

Verse 25.

vegabhramaṇavikṣuṇṇā mahī tasya vyaśīryata|
lāṅgūlenāhataścābdhiḥ plāvayāmāsa sarvataḥ||

Verse 26.

dhutaśṛṅgavibhinnāśca khaṇḍakhaṇḍaṁ yayurghanāḥ|
śvāsānilāstāḥ śataśo nipeturnabhasohacalāḥ||

Translation:

By the speed of his movement, the earth was injured and took on a tattered look. The oceans struck by his tail were agitated, flooding all over. Clouds were torn to pieces by his horns. Mountains toppled to the ground from their heights by the force of his breath.

Explanation:

What a distressful assault! None of this is exaggeration. When spiritual seekers pursue liberation and try to uproot seeds of desire from the heart, they are repeatedly attacked. The eight-fold torments by *Mahiṣāsura* that have been mentioned, are his only armaments. He applies two, four, six or all eight on different occasions. He has no weapons other than this. In this case, he applies an arsenal of rapid movements, strikes with his tail and horns, and his breath. With them, he disturbs the earth, oceans, clouds and mountains, that is the five elements, earth, water, energy, air and space. Here the word '*ghaṇa*' represents air and energy together. Although clouds are the result of water, because they stay and move in the air, one has to understand them as the element of air. This mantra does not mention the element of energy separately. Because of the connection with lightning, one has to also understand the element of energy with the clouds. All these attacks are on the five elemental principles, five sense organs and five action organs. The nose is the sense organ and the lower bowel is the action organ of earth. The tongue is the sense organ and the genitals action organ of water. The eyes are sense organs and the feet are action organs of energy. Skin is the sense organ and hands the action organ of air, and ears the sense organ and speech action organ of space. In this manner, the five principles, five sense organs and five action organs with the five targets of form, flavor, sound, touch and smell are the arenas of desire. There are no desires beyond this zone. The senses are the result of the right and active tendencies of the five elements. When the arena of desire is mentioned, five elements may be understood in brief. So, in this mantra, we see that attacks by *Mahiṣāsura* disturb the five elements. Here is the difference between spiritual seekers and a common worldly person. Common people do not understand that taking material things as themselves are torments by demons. They cannot understand this even if it is explained a thousand times. They think of it as the ramblings of a mad person. I see a rose with my eyes, where is a torment by demons in that? This is why I have said that only those who have been able to collect their sense of self into the intellectual plane will enjoy ambrosia, the spiritual mystery of *Caṇḍī*.

Whatever that be, when a spiritual seeker moves from the sense that the five principles, five senses and the five elements which appear in the arena of desire are nothing but perceptions, that awareness or life force is their nature, then these take on individual natures and begin a turmoil in the spirit. The acting out of this torment is to bring it to one's attention.

A spiritual seeker should also closely examine these actions by hidden flows of desires in the spirit. One will see that when they appear, the earth is damaged by the force of their movements. My heart trembles, thinking of the many seekers who land in this condition and feel that they have fallen from the folds of Mother. When this flow of desire is strong, then one truly feels oneself small and lowly. Within moments, high enterprise, severe austerities and powers of Yoga, all float away.

Then, the seas struck by the tail, flood over. Understand the word '*avdhi*' to mean not only the oceans of water but also the oceans of nectar. The tail signifies the results of action. The tail is a final form of the demon of desire. Results of action are the final establishment of desire for people. *Upaniṣads* also mention the tail as establishment. Spiritual seekers become engrossed by the results of actions. It could be minor and negligible, but the ocean of nectar in which spiritual seekers thought they would immerse, where they could go beyond all material desire, that ocean becomes turbulent and scatters, because of mere material desires. Not only that, clouds are torn to pieces by strikes of the horns. The horns are the tallest structure, the clouds are the principles of energy and air. Energy and air principles in the body are disturbed by thoughts of material things. They become occupied with everyday materials. As a result, breath loses its parity and moves away from inside the nostrils. It becomes abnormal. One can examine and see that the rhythm of breath turns unnatural when thoughts of material things appear. As long as one knows them as the breath of Mother, they are slow and placid. When thoughts of material things appear, they become disturbed. At the same time, tall mountainous wishes about finding Mother are destroyed. This is the meaning of the mountains falling by the force of the demon's breath.

Whatever torment appears, you are a spiritual seeker, a child desiring Mother, you should not be weak or without hope. Seeing the stain of opposing results of action on your body, do not turn your eyes away from Mother. Do not ponder your gloom, do not think about worldly things. If you have to think, think of Mother. There is nothing to ponder about material things. The actions of the world can be carried out by immediate, general knowledge. One does not have to carry out actions of the world by taxing one's brain with deep thought. We are used to thinking about worldly things for such a long time that we think only of worldly things when we mention 'thought.' In reality, actions of the world can be carried out well even without thought. Just as we eat when hungry and empty ourselves when we feel the need without prior thought, in the same manner, we can earn our living and protect our things without much thinking, if thought is focused on Mother. The Lord has also said, 'those who think of only me, I take care of their needs'[14]. 'There is nothing but me. So, if you have to think, think of me. If you do this, I will carry your burden and needs for you.'

14 *Bhāgavat Gitā,* 9:22

Mother, I understand that if we think of you we would have no other worries. But we cannot do so. Unwanted thoughts come repeatedly and disturb our spirit. We look for breaks to stop thinking of you and engage in thoughts of material things. If for a little time, we sit to think of you, we wait for opportunities to think about material things, just to waste our time.

Mother, such is our externally faced nature. Such is the torment by *Mahiṣāsura*. We know this is not right, yet this is what we prefer. We love material things. Mother, how long will it be before our demonic nature changes? When will we be able to think only of you? When will all our love of material things be given to you? Self-natured Mother, when will all our love center on you? When will our lives be honored by a taste of supreme love? Mother, when will the hopes of your children be fulfilled?

Verse 27.

iti krodhasamādhmātamāpatantaṁ mahāsuram|
dṛṣṭvā sā caṇḍikā kopaṁ tadvadhāya tadākarot||

Translation:

Seeing the *asura* aroused by rage in this manner, *Caṇḍīkā* expressed her anger to destroy him.

Explanation:

Before this, when *Mahiṣa* attacked the lion, Mother had expressed her anger. By that anger, all stored desires of beings had been loosened. We will see later, that the gods are saying, 'when you are angered, then all desires are destroyed' (*ruṣṭā tu kāmān sakalābhīṣtān*). Here the same thing is happening by the anger of Mother. Beings coming into such a condition, do not want to see even the least disturbances of desire. Yet, hidden seeds of desire occasionally appear and disturb them. Mother sees that she can no longer be quiet, cannot just express her anger. She has to destroy this *asura*. Mother expresses anger to destroy the demon. So, the mantra says, '*tadbadhāya kopamkarot.*' Anger needed to destroy the *asura* was expressed. This is the angry form of Mother, that is why the sage has used the word '*caṇḍīkā*' in this mantra.

I have said before when the children are being tormented and when Mother is angered, is the mystery of the angry (*caṇḍīkā*) form of Mother. We do not feel tormented even after thousands of attacks. That is why Mother does not appear in her angry form. The moment we realize that we are being tormented, at that moment a flood of affection will appear in the heart of Mother. She will save us from any terror by demons. This is Motherhood. Otherwise, what is a mother? One does not have to say to Mother, 'save us from terror.' If we are really afraid, she comes and saves us. We say thousands of times, 'save us in this ocean of life.' But in our hearts, do we feel this ocean of life to be sorrowful? No. We say it because others do. When we understand that this life is truly an insurmountable ocean, then we will no longer have to say 'save us.' Mother will pick us up before we can say it. We will cross this difficult ocean with ease. A spiritual seeker has to see if the torment of this world has truly appeared in the heart. Loving Mother is looking at you for that. When will you begin to weep for Mother?

Verse 28.

sā kṣiptvā tasya vai pāśaṁ taṁ babandha mahāsuram|
tatyāja māhiṣaṁ rūpaṁ sohapi baddho mahāmṛdhe||

Verse 29.

tataḥ siṁhohbhavat sadyo yāvattasyāmbikā śiraḥ|
chinatti tāvat puruṣaḥ khaḍgapāṇiradṛśyata||

Verse 30.

tata evāśu puruṣaṁ devī ciccheda sāyakaiḥ|
taṁ khaḍgacarmaṇā sārdhaṁ tataḥ sohabhūnmahāgajaḥ||

Verse 31.

kareṇa ca mahāsiṁhaṁ taṁ cakarṣa jagarja ca|
karṣatastu karaṁ devī khaḍgena nirakṛntata||

Verse 32.

tato mahāsuro bhūyo māhiṣaṁ vapurāsthitaḥ|
tathaiva kṣobhayāmāsa trailokyaṁ sacarācaram||

Translation:

The Goddess bound the demon with a snare. While in that state, the demon left his buffalo form and transformed into a lion. The Goddess cut off its head. He reappeared as a man holding a scimitar in his hand. The Goddess hit him with arrows. The *asura* took the form of a great elephant and with his trunk, while trumpeting loudly, tried to grab the carrier of the Goddess, her lion. With her sword, the Goddess cut off its trunk. Thereafter the great *asura* regained the form of a buffalo and tormented the three worlds.

Explanation:

The explanation of these five mantras is brought together to understand their significance easily. A brief recount of the mantras is that, when *Mahiṣāsura* attacked the lion, the Goddess was angered and bound the *asura* with a snare. The bound *Mahiṣa* then took the form of a lion. When the Goddess cut off the head of that lion, it transformed into a man wielding a scimitar. The Goddess tore into him with arrows. Immediately he took the form of a great elephant and making loud noises tried to grab the lion. The Goddess cut off its trunk. He again took the form of a buffalo and continued on his eight-pronged attack.

This is a beautiful mystery. Come, let us seek the blessing of Mother and immerse ourselves in this. May she arouse our intellect. May we completely know the mystery of *Caṇḍī* and move beyond any doubt.

First, we should understand the changing forms of *Mahiṣāsura*: 1) buffalo, 2) lion, 3) man with a scimitar, 4) great elephant, 5) again a buffalo. As each form was struck, it appeared as the next one. The initial attack by a flow of stored tendencies is by a demon in the form of a buffalo. This has been explained in the previous mantras. The second one is in the form of a lion.

When worldly persons begin to show violence towards their desires, the buffalo transforms into a lion. We need to discuss this clearly. Being repeatedly tormented by a flow of stored desires, and wishing to destroy them, one takes recourse to leaving home, choosing a monastic life and renunciation. Leaving spouse and children, one takes shelter under trees and in caves. This is called the transformation of desire from a buffalo to a lion. Until this time, one was tormented only by desire, now one is tormented by a desire to cease desire. Remember that a wish to cease desire is also a desire. Seeds of desire are piled up inside. From the outside, one attempts with severe austerities and practice to stop their undulations. From the point of view of worldly life, this may be an elevated condition, but in subtle view, this is just a change in costume for desire. Wishes to wear ochre robes or live under trees are also desires. In principle, there is no difference between these two. Someone lying in a soft bed at home, enthralled with the feeling that one is in the lap of Mother is a greater renunciate than a *sannyāsi* lying under a tree, thinking that one has left life. So, I have said, a desire to leave desire is also a torment by demons. To save such a child from torment, Mother cuts off the head of the lion. That is, she makes one understand that nurturing violence to desire is also a transformation of desire. Then, there is no longer any desire for renunciation.

Now, desire takes another form. It is a man wielding a scimitar. A scimitar signifies divisiveness. When by the grace of Mother, one realizes that the wish for renunciation is also a desire, one takes steps to stop all seeds of desire from germinating in the spirit. The method is to stop any natural tendencies. This is a man with a scimitar. One severely tries to stop all tendencies, thinking that if in some way, this flow could be prevented, if good and bad, receiving and avoiding could be stopped, then all obstacles will be removed. The goal is to cut out everything. One appears with a scimitar. But Mother soon removes this one with her arrows. That is, she shows the children that this too is a characteristic of the spirit. Just as arousal or disturbances are characteristics of the spirit, so are practices to prevent them. A commentator of the Yoga *sutras* has also given the same explanation. The goal of beings is to find Self. It is not one's goal to achieve the prevention of tendencies of spirit, though there is an unexpressed pleasure in such prevention. Just as when a great weight is removed from over one's head one feels great relief, so is the pleasure in preventing tendencies. Every moment, one desire after another comes and moves the spirit. Even before a desire is fulfilled, another appears. This goes on for not a day or two, but over lifetimes. If one finds relief from this in some manner, it is a great achievement. Beings engage in controlling tendencies of spirit with this thought. But supreme joy or true peace is not here. Spirit is not an arena of peace. Whether controlled or disturbed, one cannot find true peace here. One has to go above intellect to find true peace. One has to climb to an arena of Self, onto the lap of Mother. One has to go where there is no spirit, no tendencies, no prevention, no disturbance. One does not achieve peace by just laying down one's burdens. One has to sit on a kingly throne. A throne established much above mind, intellect, spirit and ego. One has to reside in the sweet folds of Mother. One has to withdraw into Self, where all errors, doubts and ignorance are removed. One has to reside in that supreme space. When Mother explains this supreme principle, by her grace, the attractions of worldly persons for preventing tendencies of the spirit are removed. This is the destruction of a man with a scimitar by the Goddess.

After this, a great elephant appeared. The root '*gaja*' means bondage. The word '*mahāgaja*' means great bondage. Bondage that is difficult to remove, is great bondage. In this condition, worldly persons realize that whatever they do, preventing tendencies of spirit, discarding their desires or temporarily residing in the folds of Mother, they cannot be relieved of the torments of desire. As long as they can stay in a zero state, as in dreamless sleep, by using various methods, it works. But this prevention does not last forever. They have to awaken again. Or, Mother does not keep her children on her lap forever, she lets them go. Then, desires reappear. As long as one stays in Self they do not rise. Moments later, they reappear as non-self. To beings tormented repeatedly in this manner, it appears impossible to conquer desire. A spiritual seeker is greatly pained. 'Alas! There is no way to be relieved of these irremovable ties of desire.' Thinking in this manner, beings lose hope. This is the attack by a great elephant making loud noises. In the realm of principles, it can be seen that beings are bound when they think that they are bound. In reality, there is no bondage or freedom. Knowledge of bondage by eternally free and independent *paramātmā* is just divine play. Despite that, for worldly persons, such knowledge about bondage is rare. After many lifetimes, much spiritual effort, and by the grace of Mother, beings realize their bondage. Knowledge of bondage is a fruit of spiritual effort. Liberation is not the fruit of spiritual effort. Liberation is eternal. Where is the feeling of bondage? Even if we say a thousand times that we are bound, one does not in the beginning truly understand what bondage is. Knowledge of bondage by common people is an imaginary feeling due to trouble with worldly things. They do not have a true feeling of bondage. But Mother is going to give her children a taste of liberation. So, today she brings in front of them true feelings of bondage. The demon appears as a great elephant. If you have not tasted freedom even for a moment, how can you realize a state of bondage?

There have been cries about bondage in this world for a long time, not only today, but in many philosophical periods. We may see that the idea of bondage has been around for a long time. From the day this land began to think 'we are bound', they have accepted the bondage of *māyā*. Not only that, they have been tormented and weakened by external bondage. But that is something else.

We are sitting under a tree of wish-fulfillment. Whatever we ask from her we will get. It will turn out to be true. Let me tell you a story. A very tired traveler was sitting under a tree to rest. It was a summer afternoon and he was thirsty. He began to think that if he could find a green coconut, its water would save his life, otherwise, he might die of thirst. As he thought like this, he saw a fine green coconut right in front of him. He was very pleased, but not having any sharp instrument to cut it with, without hope, he began to think of one. Immediately, he saw a sharp knife in front of him. He cut the coconut, drank its water and felt much better. Feeling tired, he felt the need for a bed. Immediately he saw a well-laid-out bed next to him. Lying down on it happily, he began to think, 'What is this? Whatever I think of, I find. Good! If at this time a woman would come and massage my legs I could fall asleep easily.' As soon as he thought of this, he saw a beautiful woman sitting near his feet. As she reached out her hands to massage his legs, a different thought entered the mind of the traveler. 'Oh! Are all these ghostly things? All this happening in an empty place, what can they be but ghostly things. These must be spirits. This woman must be a spirit. What will happen if she breaks my neck?' As soon as he thought of this, the woman became a spirit and broke his neck. The traveler did not know that he had taken shelter under a tree of wish fulfillment.

In the same manner, we too are always sitting near a tree of wish fulfillment and thinking 'we are bound.' So, our bondage is never removed. First, we think family and children are bonds. Then we understand the body to be bondage. Those who understand mind and knowledge to be bonds are foremost among men. They are renowned in this world as monastics and great souls. Although the present philosophy of *Vedānta* tries very hard to do away with this bondage as imaginary and untrue, it has not been able to relieve itself of this. They say that once knowledge is reached, that is, when error is removed, results of error continue for a time. Just as when we mistake a rope to be a snake, we express fear, escape and tremble. Even if immediately after that, we recognize it to be a rope, that is, any fear of snakes is removed, for some time, signs of fear linger. In the same manner, even after knowledge of *Brahmaṇ*, an overlay of delusion (*māyā*) remains.

Let those that see *māyā* as bondage, do so. For us, *māyā* is Mother. So, bondage of *māyā* is nothing but an affectionate embrace of Mother. We are forever free. We are unclothed children on the lap of Mother. So, we have no bondage and no freedom. When you see that this universe is the play of Mother, of *māyā*, you will understand that it is the play of Self. Again, when you truly see it as 'my' game, you will see that there are no games. Only 'I' remains. No, even that word is no more. How will I explain what remains? If you can conceive of an 'I' without words, then you may get an idea of it. Oh! It is such a sweet state. It is the nature of bliss! I do not know why some spiritual seekers have said that it is better to taste sugar than be sugar! They may be thinking that a non-alternative state (*nirvikalpa*) is darkness without any sense of 'I', like that of dreamless sleep. It is not so. It is a state of supreme knowledge, supreme bliss and supreme love. No consumer or consumed, only nature of bliss. One cannot taste sugar here without becoming sugar. How can I express this in words?

Whatever it is, when I come down from that state, I engage in a play of this world. That is my game. It is the play of Mother. I wish, so I play. I have wished to enjoy the variety of desires, of spouse and food and drink, I am pleased by that, so I play. When I will not like it anymore, when I do not wish to see this world as a dream anymore, then I will leave everything, naked and go beyond this game. At this time, I see Self and also play the games of this world. Where is bondage or freedom in this? Yoga scriptures say that spirit addicted to material things is bound, spirit not addicted to material things is free. Those who see things of this world as separate from 'I', will have their spirits attracted to things of this world and have an attraction for them. So, they will see bondage and try their best to stay away from things of this world. But, those who see that everything is 'I', all is Mother, have no attraction or repulsion by things of this world. They neither discard nor receive, so they have no bondage or freedom. But, we have moved away from our point of discussion.

From the great elephant or knowledge of great bondage, beings are attracted downwards. Beings go downwards when they think that they are bound. This is the meaning of '*cakarṣa*' in the mantra. Mother, by her kindness, removes this downwards movement of beings. This is described as the Goddess cutting off the elephant's trunk with her sword. Those who have surrendered at the feet of Mother, however close they are to the knowledge of bondage, do not begin to move downwards. They know that they are eternally free. What can attraction do to those who are holding on to the feet of Mother? No, they are not holding on to Mother. Mother is holding them. So, as much as the great elephant tries to attract them, they do not fall. If we try to hold on to Mother with our weak hands, we may fall. But, we are held by the hands of Mother, We cannot fall.

Whatever it is, the great elephant was divided into two by a stroke from the sword of Mother. The nature of imaginary bonds was removed by the pure light of intellect. Then the *asura* again took the form of a buffalo. When seeds of stored desires could not do anything by their various forms, when each of them was caught by the keen sight of Mother, it again took the form of a buffalo. Taking the form of explicit desire, it used its previously mentioned eight-fold weapons. Desire has no other weapons than these, so the mantra says 'tormented again as before.' Before it had terrorized earth and sky, now it attacked the three worlds. The first world is from *Mulādhāra* to the *Maṇipura* center, the next from *Maṇipura* to *Viśuddhā*, and the third from *Viśuddhā* to the *Ājñā cakra*[15]. *Sahasrār* is beyond the three worlds, so attacks by demons cannot reach it. Attack of worldly things (*bhuloka*), reach up to *Maṇipura*. These are the desires for children, wealth and fame. Attacks by divine things, desire for kindness, mercy, respect and devotion, reach up to *Viśuddhā*. Godlike desires of all-power, all-knowledge and all-perception reach up to *Ājñā cakra*. So, the mantra says that *Mahiṣāsura* disturbed all three worlds. Remember that these desires are not visitors, but only the stored tendencies. The demon brings in front of your eyes desires from higher levels. His purpose is to show you unnoticed weaknesses and prevent you from entering the kingdom of Self. But, do not be afraid. When by the grace of Mother, you understand them to be torments by demons, you need not fear anymore. You will soon be relieved from this torment by the grace of Mother.

---

15 centers (*cakra*) in the spinal axis

Verse 33.

tataḥ kruddhā jaganmātā caṇḍikā pānamuttamam|
papau punaḥ punaścaiva jahāsāruṇalocanā||

Translation:

After this, the angered Mother of this universe repeatedly sipped on excellent nectar and with reddened eyes laughed over and over again.

Explanation:

The demon *Mahiṣa* had changed his form and tried to injure the lion, but was repelled by the weapons of Mother. Even after this, when he did not stop, Mother could not be quiet any longer. Before destroying him, she repeatedly sipped some excellent nectar (*madhu*). We will speak about the mystery of sipping nectar a little later. Mother sipped some nectar and with reddened eyes, laughed. This is her appearance before the destruction of *Mahiṣāsura*. Has a spiritual seeker seen the facial expression of this laughing, red-eyed Mother? It is a face where laughter and anger, mercy and cruelty, rescue and destruction, sanctuary and danger, these very opposing natures, arise together. Even thinking of that laughing, angered face of Mother, one's heart feels warm. The facial expression of Mother shows how much affection she has for us. That is why I said, if you have not seen this face of Mother, then you have not understood yourself to be truly tormented. Even now, you think that drinking the syrup of material things is proper effort. That is why Mother has not appeared in her angry form. This love of worldly things is an attack by demons. You are tormented by them. When you see that even after hundreds of attempts, you cannot rid yourself of these attacks, you look at Mother sadly and say 'save me.' You will see Mother appear in her angry form. The three eyes of Mother will be reddened after she drinks the nectar of bliss. An incredible smile will adorn her lips.

We often try to seek the shelter of Mother when we are attacked by illness, sorrow or need. At that time, we do not seek her, we just pray for her mercy. The purpose is to free ourselves from danger. Therefore, Mother only distributes her grace. She does not express her nature. When we understand the state of being to be a great torment, when we realize that this expression through mind, intelligence and the senses are attacks by demons, then Mother is forced to appear in her angry form as *Caṇḍīkā*.

Verse 34.

nanarda cāsuraḥ sohapi balavīryamadoddhataḥ|
viṣāṇābhyāñca cikṣepa caṇḍikāṁ prati bhūdharān||

Translation:

The *asura*, filled with pride and arrogance of his strength, made terrible noises and with his horns tossed mountains and other objects at *Caṇḍikā*.

Explanation:

The spiritual seeker should try to understand this tossing of mountains at Mother. Mountainous, insurmountable piles of desires, our internal store of many lifetimes are being thrown at Mother. Oh! Look. Each of our child-like desires, our infantile demands, give so much trouble to Mother. To give us what we have asked for, knowingly or unknowingly, to uproot those desires, peaceful Mother has to undergo turmoil and disturbance. Do not think that even your tiniest desires will remain unfilled. Each desire is a mountain. It is being thrown at Mother by the horns of the buffalo, by the excitation of active tendency, to hurt her body. Oh! The beautiful body of my Mother is injured by the mountains of my desires. But it is my Mother, not anyone else. She looks at my face, to see if I will call on her, not many times, just once. Can this affection be described by words? Mother! No more. I will not ask for anything. What I have already asked for, gives you so much trouble. Now I understand that as much as blows of desire hurt me, they hurt you more. Under the influence of lust, I have asked for wealth and desire. You, my Mother, have taken the form of wealth and desire and sacrificed yourself in my unquenched fire of want. Not for a day or two, but for uncountable lifetimes, this has been going on. Oh! You who are unreachable by meditations of *Hari*, *Hara* and *Brahmā*, have taken small material forms to satisfy my desires. You have appeared without my knowledge as things that satisfy my senses. I have not looked upon you even once. I have not called on you like a simple-hearted infant. How can I carry this burden of ingratitude? Our hearts are so hard that they are not split by this ungratefulness. Our hearts do not shatter. Mother! Did you build our hearts out of thunder?

Not only that. If ever we stand in front of you as our Mother, if ever we find some sign of your appearance, then immediately we say 'remove our sins, remove our grievances' and so shower all our dirt and impurity on your pure figure. Those who are your children, who call you mother, take flowers of respect, devotion, love and faith to adorn your rosy feet. We are so lowly and inpet, that we call on you and like ingrates tell you 'take all our sins and troubles, take our ills, our nonmanifest pile of desires.' Mother! How much longer will we taint you in this manner? For how many more days will we offer you our control and consumption, our pile of dull tendencies and so taint your pure form?

Verse 35.

sā ca tān prahitāṁstena cūrṇayantī śarotkaraiḥ|
uvāca taṁ madoddhūtamukharāgākulākṣaram||

Translation:

The Goddess shattered the mountains thrown by the demon with her arrows and spoke to him proudly with a reddened face.

Explanation:

When seeds of desire, stored over lifetimes, begin to germinate by the influence of active tendency, Mother collects them together and destroys them with her arrows. Just as one can lay a pile of leaves one on top of the other and pierce them with a needle, Mother expresses our nonmanifest pile of residual tendencies (*saṁskāra*) and demolishes them by arrows of birth and action. Here, if we discuss this mystery of birth and action, this will be clear.

Beings are born with seeds of desires from many lifetimes. Stored tendencies begin to pile up in the lifetime in which one cries for Mother and begins to try to find the kingdom of Self. The results of action that may have taken ten or twenty lifetimes to work out, by the grace of Mother, are finished in one or two. This is a result of calling for Mother. Otherwise, there was no need to call for her. By the natural flow of things, beings will one day find sanctuary in the folds of Mother. However great a sinner or however ignorant one may be, Mother will one day pick one up to her lap. Then, what is the need to call for her? The need is for this volley of arrows. What would have taken many lifetimes to complete, is completed within a few. When beings wish to erode the results of their past actions without consuming them, they begin to cry for Mother. King Suratha, whose story is told to expound *Devī Māhātmya*, avoided births for millions of lifetimes, deaths as millions of animals, and by the grace of Mother completed everything in only one. It is because of this, that those who have turned towards God, have to face much illness, sorrow, disquiet, punishment and reproach in their lives. Seeing this, people may think 'Alas! Even though these people are good and devoted, God directs so much torment towards them.' But, those who can see, know that this is not torment or cruelty from God. It is incredible grace in the cover of cruelty. One needs a physician to operate and heal a serious infection. Although it hurts the patient, applying an instrument to the body, is no doubt for the welfare of the person.

Whatever that is, Mother filled with bliss, in an overwhelming tone, spoke to the demon. This will be expounded in the next mantra. Whatever meaning others may give to the word '*madoddhūta*', we will understand it as overwhelmed by bliss. The root '*mad*' is applied in the sense of 'joy.'

Verse 36.

devyuvāca|
garjja garjja kṣaṇaṁ mūḍha madhu yāvat pibāmyaham|
mayā tvayi hatehatraiva garjjiṣyantyāśu devatāḥ||

Translation:

The Goddess said, "Foolish one, keep shouting as long as I am sipping nectar. When you will be killed by me, the gods will be shouting here soon."

Explanation:

Mother calls *Mahiṣāsura* foolish. That sentient Mother, by whose arrival, all knots of ignorance fall away has appeared. Beings have now found shelter at the feet of Mother. Even then, *Mahiṣāsura* has not stopped tormenting them. So, he is foolish. Mother said I am the form of the great life force, the power of creation-maintenance–dissolution. Beings are my affectionate children. They are tormented and called upon me as their Mother and have understood that I am their only sanctuary. Even now, foolish one, by the delusion of stored tendencies, you are tormenting my favored children. My children carry out dreary acts by remaining small, staying in the heart of desire. They do not discard you and run towards me. Even now, my force of attraction does not bring my children to me, away from your torments. This is why you keep on shouting, you agitate. But, listen. As long as I sipping nectar, so long you may. But soon, you will be killed by me and the gods will be pleased.

The word '*madhu*' means bliss. Bliss is the nature of Mother. 'One who knows bliss-natured *Brahmaṇ*, is not afraid anymore of anything.' When formless *Brahmaṇ*, beyond perception, divides itself into many and carries out a play of bliss between enjoyer and enjoyed, then, even though it is of the nature of bliss, by divine play it imagines an absence of bliss in itself. Imagining itself to be two, it searches for bliss. The one whose nature is bliss is now called enjoyer or viewer of bliss. On the other hand, bringing merchandise of bliss in the form of nature as material things, it plays with the enjoyer of things. It is then called a matter of enjoyment or what is viewed. This meeting and parting of enjoyer and enjoyed, this play of search and discovery of bliss, this is nectar. Spiritual seekers have to carefully open their eyes of knowledge, to see that Mother is continuously sipping this nectar all over this universe. We are nectar for Mother, Mother is nectar for us. We drink nectar in the form of *Mahāmāyā*. Mother sips nectar of divine play with us. From tiny life forms to the greatest of beings, as humans or gods, they are all searching for this nectar. The one whose nature is nectar behaves as if all nectar is missing and plays as if searching for it. This is the fundamental secret of creation. Saying 'where is nectar?' we have moved away from our state as nectar. Sipping this nectar drop by drop, one day we will again land on that eternal state as nectar. This search and discovery of nectar are creation and dissolution. You see that someone who is penniless hopes for a hundred coins. Finding a hundred, one hopes for a thousand. On finding a thousand one hopes for a million. In this fashion, hope is never satisfied. The reason is a lack of proper nectar. Because there is a want of nectar, as long as beings do not find the nectar of Self, they move madly from one object to another. They hold a rose lovingly to their bosom and think they have found nectar. In the next moment, they run for another, not finding nectar in this particular flower. In this manner, many lifetimes are expended. As long as the center of this nectar is not discovered, as long as the hive is not full, so long the work of worldly persons as busy bees, running from material to material will not end.

Where is this nectar? Everywhere and nowhere. When one who is the nature of nectar is left out, there can be no nectar anywhere, only thirst and anxiety. When you see the one who is the nature of nectar, one finds nectar everywhere. There is no dearth of nectar anywhere. The bliss we find in the enjoyment of material things is not in them but inside us, it is nectar of the nectar-formed Mother. This has been discussed in Volume One, but we will speak about it again. Although known well, scriptures may be discussed repeatedly.

Listen carefully and try to understand. Only *paramātmā* is bliss or nectar. Supreme principle (*mahat*) or intellect (*buddhi*) is its first great expression. As long as intellect follows the mind, which is the center of senses searching for materials, that is, is occupied in expressing features of material things brought by the senses, so long worldly persons cannot discover nectar. One after another, the mind brings things found by the senses in front of intellect and they are expressed in the light of intellect. As long as objects of desire are found, so long mind and senses do not rest. So, intellect has no rest. When a desired object is found, for a moment, the mind ceases bringing things, so intellect has a moment of rest. Then, for that instant, intellect realizes the nature of *paramātmā* reflected in itself. This is called by people, sipping nectar of material things. People think that they are finding bliss by enjoying things, by materials of wealth and desire. But bliss is not in these material things, it is inside us. Just as a dog chewing on a dry bone, injures its mouth and tasting its own blood thinks that the bone is succulent, so do people enjoying their internal nectar, paint it as outside and enjoy material things. When spiritual seekers realize this truth by repeated analysis and practice, then the attraction for material things is removed.

Look! There is no bliss in objects of desire, bliss is your inside. The bliss of enjoying things is not in them but inside you. Your acquiringof things, your life and death are for the expression of this hidden nectar inside you. The connection between things and senses is stirred by intellect. Inside us is an ocean of milk, and by churning this, divine ambrosia or nectar appears. On one side a retraction towards Self, on the other attraction towards material things. The churning of this ocean is going on in each being at all times. Who knows from what eternal time this began? Tasting this nectar in the world, a sage loudly sang in the *Bṛhadāraṇyak Upaṇiṣad*, "This earth is nectar of all beings, all beings are nectar of this earth. These waters are nectar of all beings, all beings are nectar of these waters. This air is nectar of all beings, all beings are nectar of this air. This life force (*prāṇa*) is nectar of all beings, all beings are nectar of this life force. *Ātmā* is nectar of all beings, all beings are nectar of the *ātmā*." Look, everything is nectar of everything. Those who find this nectar all over the world, sing joyously, 'the breeze brings nectar, the seas bring nectar'[16].

How much longer will you sip this nectar in ignorance? Now, knowingly drink this nectar. Open your eyes and see, it is not you, a being, sipping nectar. Everything here is only Mother sipping nectar. The eternally blissful, eternally nectar-formed, is eternally drinking this nectar. Mother knows, 'I am everything. Only I exist in every being always, so this universe is my drink of nectar.' So, she says, "Foolish one! You may shout as long as I sip this nectar". Until beings surrender at the feet of Mother, they do not understand the significance of these words. They cannot perceive this universal sipping of nectar by Mother. Mother burns as the fire of desire in the hearts of beings. She offers herself as material things into that fire of desire and carries out this unique play of sipping nectar of Self. To understand this principle, one has to surrender at the feet of Mother. Until this sipping of nectar by Mother is finished, until she desists from this game of multiplicity, until then, the clamor by the demons does not stop.

Oh! Look at Mother sipping nectar. You move untiringly night and day with hopes for wealth. It is but the sipping of nectar by Mother. You suffer pains of hell from disease. It is Mother sipping nectar. You are overwhelmed by the loss of near ones. It is Mother sipping nectar. If you understand this, only then will your life be filled with nectar. No sorrow, pain, life, death, illness or bereavement will remain.

Although we may say, Mother, you do not need to drink this nectar anymore. You are our eternal nectar-formed Mother. Do you have any dearth of nectar that you have to play as materials of the senses, divide yourself into tiny pieces and sip this nectar drop by drop? O our ocean of nectar! Stop these sips of nectar. Take us where one does not have to sip nectar to taste it, where there is nothing but nectar, where there is no enjoyer and enjoyed, only nectar. We cannot stand this wild dance of your drinking

16 *madhu vātā ṛtāyate, madhu kṣaranti sindhava . . . Ṛk Veda* I.90

nectar anymore. Although for you this is the sipping of nectar, it is unbearable for us. This repeated birth and death, this laughter and tears, this mind and intellect, this materials and senses, this meditation and concentration, even though, all of these are your sips of nectar. It is for us like a poisonous drink. Relieve us from this poison. One day, *Viśeśvara*, to save this world drank the poison that came out from the churning of the oceans and became unconscious. At that time, you ran wildly up to him and placed your touch of nectar on his throat which was blue with venom, and removed his burden of destruction. Today, we too are tormented by the poison of worldly matters. Come running to us overwhelmed by love, and save us from this venomous pain. Place your nectar-filled touch on our poisoned bodies. Let us find peace, let us become immortal. O, Mother! Establish this truth that worldly matters are not poison but nectar. Let the world forget the pain of venom. Let them be nectar-formed, sipping nectar. That day let this poor child match his smile with this simple truth of the world, and raising his arms in joy, be honored in praising Mother. But that is something else.

As long as Mother does not finish sipping nectar, the torment by demons will continue. But the hope is that Mother will say 'when I kill you and the gods will be shouting here.' I will end your 'I'-ness and the gods will be shouting in joy. I will destroy the other 'I' that you see separate from me. Then, the gods (consciousness established in the senses), will for the last time, raise shouts of praise and then merge into me. This mystery will emerge in the destruction of *Śumbha*. Until the death of *Śumbha*, 'I'-ness is not dissolved. The destruction of *Mahiṣāsura* is only a preparation for this. The destruction of desires is not the same as the dissolution of the ego. It is true that when the ego is destroyed, desires do not remain. But, Mother first destroys desires and then destroys the ego. This is a mystery of the divine play of Mother.

Verse 37.

ṛṣiruvāca|
evamuktvā samutpatya sārūḍhā taṁ mahāsuram|
pādenākramya kaṇṭhe ca śūlenainamatāḍayat||

Translation:

The sage said, saying this, the Goddess leaped on the great demon and attacking him with her feet, pierced his neck with her lance.

Explanation:

Mother standing on the demon is her stance over desires. Do not understand desires to mean wishes for material results. Those who still wish for offspring and wealth do not yet have the ability to enter into the mystery of *Caṇḍī*. One has to acquire desire-less Yoga of Action of *Bhāgavat Gitā*, be accomplished in spiritual pursuit of the mantra 'forsaking all religions, seek shelter only in me'[17], and only then enter principles of *Caṇḍī*. What happens here is better called a view of the divine play of Mother, rather than spiritual enterprise (*sādhanā*). At the beginning of this divine play, seeds of future actions are destroyed. Then, the roots of stored desires are removed. Here the word 'desire' should be understood as wishes or beginnings. Before this, whenever we have used the word 'desire' (*kāmanā*), we have in most places used it to mean a beginning. One can call actions connected with attraction or wishes to be desires. The author[18] of *Pañcadaśi* has spoken about the tri-fold nature of desire, wishes for oneself, for others and without wishes. Among them, one has to understand the beginning of wishes for oneself as desire or *Mahiṣa*. Spiritual seekers of the principles of *Caṇḍī* do not or cannot carry out actions in the manner that common people driven by desires and wishing for its fruits are involved in actions. The desire formed buffalo of *Caṇḍī* is the natural tendency to act without a specific desire for any results. Common people may think that these persons are

17 *Bhagāvat Gitā,* 18.66

18 Vidyārańya Muni

also slaves of desire, otherwise, why would they engage in action? But that is not true. They just carry out actions. They may not be able to answer why. But, at the root of all actions, there is a fixed principle and that is love for Mother. The actions of a spiritual seeker who has entered the principle of *Caṇḍi* are for the pleasure of the ever-satisfied Mother. Even daily acts of eating, sleeping and movement are carried out for the pleasure of Mother. This is the accomplishment of the state of the mantra in *Gitā*, 'offer everything to me.' Whatever action is started, it is begun by offering it to Mother. This is Mother climbing on the buffalo. In this manner, when Mother appears in the heart of a seeker, as the destroyer of *Mahiṣa* whatever actions may appear from his store of actions, one can see the footsteps of Mother on top of them. The attack by *Mahiṣa* as the beginning of actions is still there, but the spirit of Mother is over them. Mother is established on desires. The buffalo has been attacked by her feet, yet seeing that it does not end its torments, Mother pierces its neck with her lance. The meaning of a lance has been explained in Volume One.[19]

The throat is the location for speech. The Goddess applied her power of destruction to the door by which tendencies are expressed as words. This is the significance of striking the throat with her lance. If the doors of language can be shut off in some manner, then tendencies cannot express their power and appear materially to torment worldly persons. Remember that just by staying silent, the doors of language are not closed. One cannot be truly silent without discovering the nature of that which is beyond perception. Although language is the body of perception (*bhāb*), there can be perception without language. When this is mastered, beings savor a taste of freedom. It is the goal of worldly persons to arrive at this nature where no words are needed to help thought, memory or meditation. Those who have not discovered this nature beyond perception, cannot imagine thought or meditation without words. But, let me say that all spiritual seekers will one day realize the truth of this statement. The awareness that one receives when

19 Chapter One, Verse 54

one arrives at this place that is beyond perception, that is without the three attributes (*guṇas*), from where words return, is the place beyond language. You may call it whatever you wish, *dhyāna*, *samādhi* or memory. It is none of these. How can words reach a place from where mind and language turn back? Whatever that be, so that the door of perception arousing language can be shut off, so that the power of the desire-formed buffalo can be vanquished, the buffalo destroying Mother, strikes at the throat of *Mahiṣa* with her lance. In this condition, because desires are completely of the form of Mother, there are no words or language that can arouse desire. This is the wonderful result of the establishment of *prāṇa*. By the practice of viewing life formed Mother in everything in this universe and every thought, the outside and inside of spiritual seekers become one. They discover a united spirit of *prāṇa* everywhere. They do not have desires for worldly things. They are not bound like worldly persons. Their desires and wealth are Mother, their meditation and concentration are Mother. They do not see anything else but Mother. Because Mother is standing over *Mahiṣa*.

Let me explain. Although a self-surrendered seeker, does not have any self-effort, pride of control does not disappear. As long as the establishment of truth and life force are practiced with this sense of control, there is still a little fault in them. One cannot perceive the true nature of truth and life force. One thinks that what is the truth is amenable to practice. Then, by her grace, Mother appears as the destroyer of *Mahiṣa*. That is, *prāṇa* natured Mother, disguised as all worldly things, expresses herself through all things. A seeker is then honored by seeing this appearance by Mother. These objects of form and flavor are forms of desire or *Mahiṣa*. Understanding them to be *prāṇa*, destroys desires or *Mahiṣa*. Inertness disappears and the nature of consciousness is illuminated. This is the *Mahiṣāsuramardinī* Mother climbing on the back of the buffalo or her appearance as the destroyer of *Mahiṣa*. In this condition, a spiritual seeker tries to be immersed in an ocean of the great life force (*mahāprāṇa*). A seeker has no other language but the life-formed Mother. This is the striking of the neck of the buffalo with her lance.

Verse 38.

tataḥ sohapi padākrāntastayā nijamukhāttadā|
arddhaniṣkrānta evāsī devyā vīryeṇa saṁvṛtah||

Translation:

Under attack by the feet of the Goddess, the demon half emerged from the neck (of the buffalo), where he was stuck because of the great valor of the Goddess. That is, his body could not come out completely.

Explanation:

When *Mahiṣāsura* saw that even after all these transformations, he could not prevent the movement of worldly persons towards Self, he reappeared in his original form, coming half out from the neck of the buffalo. When Mother appears in her buffalo destroying form, that is, when matters of form and flavor are imbued by *prāṇa* or Mother, when external manifestations of active principle are removed, then one lays eyes on *rājasa*. When the power of action is destroyed, then one notices causal power. Until now, one did not pay much attention to the causal force of active principle, because one was preoccupied with torment and action. Now desires have become imbued by Mother. She is upon the buffalo. Torment and power of action are diminished. Now when spiritual seekers move nearer and look at the root of this torment, they see that *rājasa* is its chief cause. This is the original form of *Mahiṣāsura*. When this form tries to come out of the neck of the buffalo, Mother by her power prevents its excursion.

I have mentioned that the beginning of action for self-fulfillment is desire. Even though this beginning is imbued by Mother, one can see next to it, the power of active tendency. When spiritual seekers are so overcome by a love of Mother that they cannot tolerate any other action but those needed to keep the body alive, when all these commencements appear painful, then one's eyes fall on the root cause. Then one understands that if seeds or causes remain, they will always try to express themselves. This is an eternal rule of nature. When actions do not appear, despite causes, one has to understand that there is some severe obstruction. Even with obstruction, the power to generate action by causes does not end. When the action generating power of causes end, they are no longer causal. That which is always trying to generate action is called causal. Imagine that a long strip of steel (a spring) is cleverly wound and constricted and a large boulder placed on top of it. The steel by its static property will at all moments, try to regain its original state, but is unable to do so because of the obstruction of the heavy boulder. In the same manner, because of the pressure of desires imbued by Mother, action forces of *rājasa* are obstructed from turning into material actions. Even though there may not be any outer action, the active tendency remains established. If the obstruction is removed, then its power of action is expressed outwardly. It is expressed as matters of form, flavor and desire, bringing torment by the previously mentioned eight-fold memory, discussion, play and the other methods. By the grace of Mother, the eyes of worldly persons have now fallen on root error. Now, beings have found the lone attacker, without other support, that had gods and demons fight for a thousand years. Even though it is now not complete, only half-emerged. The significance of saying half-out is that because of a strong obstacle, causal force cannot express, cannot apply its power of generating action. More clearly, subtle conditions in things are called causal. Material or expressed conditions are actions. The seed of a banyan tree is a subtle form of the basis for a tree. As long as it is a seed, one may not be able to see a tree, but a huge banyan tree is hidden in that seed. This may be seen by one who has insight. In the same manner, *Mahiṣāsura*, the subtle seed of desire could not express himself fully, only came half-out, appearing as tendencies of stored actions. Because of the valor of Mother, he could not come out completely, remaining inside as a seed. Mother did not allow subtle seeds to emerge as action.

Under these circumstances, seeds of desire remain inside. They do not appear outside as acts of desire, because a spiritual seeker, engrossed by Mother, by the establishment of truth and life force, inside and outside, always sees only the spirit of Mother. This condition is called 'half emerged and stuck because of the valor of Mother.' What Lord *Kṛṣṇa* has called falsehood in *Gitā* is not this condition. There we see that with control over organs of action, going over matters of the world in the mind, is falsehood. But here, whether with organs of action or internal senses, there is no receiving or reminiscing of worldly things. Here material things have become imbued by life force, by Mother. There is no receiving or rejection. Here, the desire for worldly things is prevented 'by the valor of Mother.' Under all circumstances, spiritual seekers see the expression of a great life force. Only future movements of desires are present. This is not falsehood.

Verse 39.

ardhaniṣkrānta evāsau yudhyamāno mahāsuraḥ|
tayā mahāsinā devyā śiraścittvā nipātitaḥ||

Translation:

The great demon continued fighting from that half-emerged condition. By a stroke of her great sword, the Goddess severed his head and it fell to the ground.

Explanation:

Although the form of desire is imbued by Mother, its root movement of active tendency (*rājasa*) wants to remain nonmanifest. At all times, it tries to turn into action, while a spiritual seeker tries to establish life force. As soon as stored tendencies try to leave their form as seeds and get ready to express themselves as actions, the seeker views them as life force. So, they cannot express themselves outwardly as desire. In this manner, repeatedly, active tendency tries to rise and is suppressed by the establishment of life force. This is the battle with the half-emerged *asura*. When eyes of knowledge are opened, spiritual seekers can sense this battle. Remember the example of steel and boulder given before. Here, two forces are fighting each other. Yet, one may not notice from outside. If a scientist is present, the strong battle between steel and boulder may be perceived. But, people in general, will just see a piece of steel under a boulder. In the same manner, this battle with the half-emerged demon can only be perceived by spiritual seekers residing in their intellectual sheath (*vijñanmaya koṣa*). *Saṁskāras* try to raise their heads one by one, and the tendencies of Mother confront and prevent them. Do you want to observe this battle? Sit quietly for a moment. Call on Mother and enter into life force of Self. Then, try to understand it as life force of this universe. You will see inside that worldly tendencies try to creep up and move your spirit away from this great life force. But, you are bemused by the nature of Mother and do not pay any attention to them. The tendencies are unsuccessful and merge into the nonmanifest. But they try to emerge again and again.

When this battle continues for some time, a spiritual seeker finds this to be a great torment. Then, renunciation (*paravairāgya*) becomes the goal. Mother, to satisfy the wishes of her child, by a stroke of her scimitar, cuts off the head of the half emerged *asura*. That is, she removes the power of generation of causal active principle. Cutting off the head means removing the highest segment. Power is in the highest segment. The destruction of this top portion is the removal of power. It has been said that when the ability to generate action is removed, causal parts lose causality. Now, active principle, being without its ability to generate action, cannot appear with its range of desires. This is the destruction of *Mahiṣāsura*.

Vedānta says that by acquiring knowledge, stored actions cannot find fruition. Future actions are destroyed. Only prior actions (*prāravdha*) are left which have to be eroded by undergoing them. We have seen the destruction of future action in Volume One with the destruction of *Madhu* and *Kaiṭabha*.

The destruction of *Mahiṣāsura* is the lack of fruition of stored actions. The first character (*prathama carit*) has taken care of the knowledge 'I do not want anything new.' This second character takes care of 'I will not undergo all that I have wished for.' This is a tighter knot. There is less trouble with 'I do not want anything new.' But it is very difficult to destroy the capability of those seeds that have been already collected. They have yet to germinate. This is the knot of *Viṣṇu*.

By proper actions over many lifetimes, by the grace of Mother, by infallible blessings of *guru*, this difficult knot of *Viṣṇu* is taken apart. *Viṣṇu* is the power of stability or life force. Stored *saṁskāras* do not let individual life force be expressed as supreme life force. One who holds loads of desires of many lifetimes, what is called feelings of tenderness, 'my, mine', what the old texts call *Viṣṇumāyā*, the power of stability or life force, is *Viṣṇu*. This spirit of *Viṣṇu* is present in each individual. This is the knot of *Viṣṇu*. The one who holds eternal resolve of this great universe is the playful *Mahāviṣṇu*. The game of creation-maintenance-dissolution of this universe resides in the power of *Viṣṇu*. He is not engrossed or ego-bound by this power. For him it is not a knot or ignorance, it is play. For worldly persons, this resolution is bondage. It is recurrent birth and death, or evident as dreaming, awake and dreamless states. Beings are engrossed or ego-bound by it, so it is a knot or ignorance. What is a knot of *Viṣṇu* in each individual, is in the Supreme being, the play of *Viṣṇu*.

Let me make this clearer. As long as you do not see what you understand to be your life force, as life force of this universe, so long you cannot pierce this knot of *Viṣṇu*. All your tendencies as a worldly person reside in that life force. Because you keep it narrow and confined, it cannot express itself as great life force. Your knot of life force is still entangled. You are keeping supreme Mother Goddess in the garb of a pauper, painting her face with stains of this world, putting on her torn dresses of our tendencies, seating her in the worn cottage of our bodies. On top of this, seeing that our wants are not satisfied, we rile her for being a pauper. We point out that others are so happy, are applying so much spiritual effort, have got so many special powers, have received such love and devotion, are so full of knowledge and have become such great renunciates, but nothing is happening to us. When you lament in this manner and are disturbed, have you looked at the face of Mother? Have you seen the shadow of pain on her loving face? Although she is the empress of all, at this moment, she cannot remove the needs and grievances of her child. She is pained. My stony heart trembles when I think of how Mother looks at our faces and then remembering in what condition she is, feels that pain. Think. She who was empress of all, is now turned into a pauper. Now her children, not finding proper food and clothing are blaming Mother. How painful is this for her?

When I see people lamenting about disease, sorrow, hunger, want, worries, and torment, spending their days with the shade of sorrow on their faces, a picture of my imperial Mother turned into a pauper floats in front of my eyes. O, Mother! You sit there in sorrow, holding worldly persons on your lap. People have turned you into a beggar. You are now a pauper, trying to satisfy the unbridled desires of beings. You have given away everything. Seeing your sad face, even thunder is ripped apart. But you have built us of such a metal, that far from feeling your sorrow, we rebuke you for being a pauper. When will we grow to be truly human? When will we understand ourselves to be the children of Mother? Forgive us. Forgive the ignorance and faults of your ungrateful children. I have nothing more I can think or say. Forgive us.

Listen. Seeing your imaginary want and poverty, Mother weeps. Overcome by love she tries to rectify all our grievances. Receive these blessings, not blessings, gifts she brings to you today, moving from door to door. All your wants will be fulfilled. You have heard in *Gitā*, 'finding which, nothing else is more worthwhile; residing where the most serious sorrow does not move one'[20]. This is the gift. Come, accept it gladly.

Establish life force (*prāṇa*), cherish *prāṇa* of Self as Mother. Believe, perceive and feel that *prāṇa* is supreme Goddess. It is established in everything. It has taken the form of this universe. View every material in this world as a form of our *prāṇa*.

20 *Bhāgavat Gitā,* 6:22

Realizing that a condensed state of *prāṇa* is perceived as matter, will let your life force express itself as that of this world. The form of Mother as a pauper will disappear. All your shortages and cries of complaint will cease. Mother will appear in her form as an empress worshipped by *Brahmā*, *Viṣṇu*, *Maheśvara* and other gods. Then you will truly understand yourself to be honored and complete. There is no difference in creed as *Śākta* or *Vaiṣṇava* here. There is no difference between Hindu and Muslim. There is no conflict between form and formless. Everyone can stay true to the customs and ceremonies of their sect and be honored to view their chosen deities. It is *prāṇa* that will appear as special forms. Then it will also appear as formless, inner and outer, the nondual nature of existence. The knot of your heart will be pierced. All your doubts will disappear.

But, there is something else to be said. To understand *prāṇa* as Mother, one has to give *prāṇa*. One cannot find *prāṇa* without giving it. You have to surrender at some point. That is why Mother goes from door to door like a mendicant, begging for *prāṇa*. But, you have kept all your doors closed. You do not want to give away life force. That is why Mother appeared in Vṛndāvana in the figure of *Gopāla* and stole butter-cream or *prāṇa*. Today she is begging again from door to door, 'give me *prāṇa*'. My children, give away *prāṇa*, you will find supreme life force. You will discover divine ambrosia. You will reside in eternal bliss. She cries pitifully, 'my child, give away *prāṇa*. Do you not hear? Give away *prāṇa*. If you cannot give up all, give a little. Give me a small place in a corner of your life. Love me a little. I will find you the great life.' Look. Mother who is inaccessible to the meditation of *Brahmā* and *Viṣṇu*, has appeared at your door as a pauper. Call on her once. Give her a little of *prāṇa*.

Verse 40.

tato hāhākṛtaṁ sarvaṁ daityasainyaṁ nanāśa tat|
praharṣñca paraṁ jagmuḥ sakalā devatāgaṇāḥ||

Translation:

Lamenting loudly, the remainder of the defeated demon warriors disappeared. The gods were greatly pleased.

Explanation:

At the dissolution of the principal nature of distraction and concealment and their main refuge of active tendency, associated heaps of *saṁskāras* also disappear. On the other hand, consciousness established in the senses is very pleased by the enjoyment of great life force. When a spiritual seeker is used to viewing the spirit of life force by establishing it everywhere, tendencies of demons are also infused by it. Then, even though forms of multiplicity remain, knowledge of differences goes away. One understands that the same life force or *sadcidānanda*, in the molds of *saṁskāra*, is expressed with different names. Remember the analogy of a sugar doll. When one is aware of sugar, one does not take long to realize that all the elephants, horses and other shapes are sugar too. Then, even though different names and forms are present upfront, their true nature is not hidden. The scriptural language is that of *saṁskāras* which are like scorched seeds. They will not germinate.

When knowledge of differences remains, one receives and discards. When knowledge of difference disappears, so do accepting and discarding. When the knot of life force is untied, stored tendencies become like burnt seeds. They can no longer be the cause of action or sufferance of results. In this way, without suffering the results of stored actions, worldly persons can climb onto the folds of Mother. This is the special result of piercing the knot of *Viṣṇu*. In this condition, a seeker only waits for the erosion of prior actions (*prāravdha*). This mystery will be expounded in the destruction of *Śumbha*.

Verse 41.

tuṣṭuvustāṁ surā devīṁ saha divyairmaharṣibhiḥ|
jagurgandharvapatayo nanṛtuścāpsarogaṇāḥ||

iti śrīmārkaṇḍeyapurāṇe sāvarṇike manvantare devīmāhātmye mahiṣāsuravadha|

Translation:

The gods, together with sages began to sing praises of the Goddess. *Gandharvas* played music and *apsarās*[21] danced.

Here ends this episode of the destruction of *Mahiṣāsura* in *Devī Māhātmya*, in the era of *Sāvarṇi*, in *Mārkeṇḍeya Purāṇa.*

Explanation:

At the death of *Mahiṣāsura*, the power of generation of results of stored tendencies by active principle is lost. The knot of life force in a seeker is untied. Consciousness residing in the senses is freed from the torment of materials. It is natural to wish to show gratitude to the one by whose infallible intent this impossible thing has been achieved. So, gods and sages in chorus, sing praises to Mother. Those verses are explained in the next chapter.

Until this time, because of noise from the rush of tendencies, sounds from *Anāhata* could not be heard. Now that noise has abated. The attractive, heart-warming, sweet sound of *Praṇava* coming from *Anāhata*, can be heard. This is music by the *gandharvas*. This sweet, internal sound of *Anāhata* and recital of praises to Mother, makes signs of excitement, vibrations and movement appear in the body of a spiritual seeker. This is the dance by *apsarās*.

O, the self-merging embrace of Mother! The realization of unthinkable powers of Mother! The perception of incredible greatness of Mother! The enjoyment of endless affection of Mother! How will I describe all this? What signs appear in the mind and body? Nothing is comparable to this happiness> There is no end to this joy. Every atom in the body seems to melt with

21 celestial beings

the nectar of bliss. Not a location remains from the tips of the toe-nails to the ends of one's hair, that is not overwhelmed by joy. The body is no longer felt to be an inert piece of flesh. Only feelings of joy. The body becomes the nature of perception of nectar. There is nothing else but a dense perception of bliss. Even the perception of 'I enjoy bliss' does not remain. Enjoyer and enjoyment become one. There is only a slight separation that cannot be expressed by words.

There is something that has to be said about the dance by *apsarās*, or the movements of the body. The literature of Yoga terms them similar to disturbances of spirit and as obstacles to *samādhi*. In the language of Yoga, they are called *aṅgamejayatva*. When the physical body is seen to move, one is to understand that the mental body is also disturbed. So, there is no doubt that stopping these movements would be good. But, these body movements and the dance by *apsarās* are also indications of the feelings of the gods. These signs of a divine state have to appear in a spiritual seeker before one can enter into the spirit that is beyond perception, in a completely tranquil state.

Here ends this *Sādhan Samar* commentary on the destruction of *Mahiṣāsura*.

Chapter 4
Accolades by the Gods

Verse 1

ṛṣiruvāca|
śakrādayaḥ suragaṇā nihatehatirīrye
tasmin durātmani surāribale ca devyā|
tāṁ tuṣṭuvuḥ praṇatinamraśirodharāṁsā
vāgbhiḥ praharṣapulakodgamacārudehāḥ||

Translation:

The sage said, the very powerful, ill-natured *Mahiṣāsura* and his warriors being destroyed by the Goddess, *Indra* and the other gods, paying their respects, bowed their neck and shoulders and recited praises to her. Animated by joy, their bodies appeared to glow.

Explanation:

In this chapter, the praises by gods are described. *Mahiṣāsura* was ill-natured, of evil spirit. As long as nature is fond of evil, engrossed by divisiveness, satisfied by divided knowledge, it can be called ill-natured. The all-powerful, evil-spirited *Mahiṣāsura* and his warriors have been destroyed. The externally oriented flow of tendencies of active principle (*rājasa*) has been stilled. The gods, expressions of right principle (*sattva*), are now viewing and perceiving Mother undisturbed. When one sees the world-mesmerizing form of Mother, one cannot remain quiet any longer. Knowledge, devotion and action express themselves externally. So, *Indra* and other gods began to sing praises of the greatness of Mother.

Three things have to be given special notice in this hymn, 1) bowed neck and shoulders, 2) beautiful bodies and 3) recitation. These three terms have been used to point to three-fold praises, physical, mental and verbal. We will try to understand this. The gods bowed down in such a way that their necks and shoulders were bent forward. In this posture, the upper body is bowed forward. It is necessary to bend the body forward in this manner, towards her, when one remembers Mother. We are now in front of Mother, the charioteer of birth and death, one for whom we have suffered the toil of million births and deaths. Remembering her love, her great supremacy and her supreme power, the bodies of her children will bow forward, showing signs of joy. Tears, tremors and other *sāttvik* signs will appear. These are signs of mental praise. Together with this, one has to recite about the greatness of Mother. This is the purification of words. Mother is indefinable, not seen by mind or speech. Even then, we praise her with our words. By this, our words will be purified and any awkwardness of voice will disappear. Impurities due to the constant recital of what is not right will be removed.

The scriptures advise silent repetition of *japa* and the loud recital of hymns (*stava*). Silent repetition of a hymn is usually without effect. So, the verse says, 'pleased her with words.' When a spiritual seeker is in front of Mother, (this is easy after the establishment of truth and life force), special attention has to be paid to these three things. At the beginning of a recital, bow your body to the feet of Mother. Your body will be overjoyed. Loudly recite hymns. A loud recital of hymns will prevent external sounds from entering and disturbing the spirit. When the spirit is undisturbed, attention will stay on the meaning of the words. At the same time, feelings and perceptions of this meaning will appear in the field of spirit. In brief, this may be called the consciousness of mantra. (This was explained in Volume One). The external signs that appear when a mantra is recited with consciousness are briefly described here as '*pulakodgamacārudehā*' (bodily delight). Not only recitals, one has to pay attention to this for any action with mantras, rosaries, *pujā*, or ceremony. The performance of prescribed acts with an application of conscious mantra easily provides joy to the spirit, wealth or perception of the greatness of Mother, and food for the sustenance of the five sheaths[1].

1 (Note by Author) These have been explained in Volume One

The author of the *Śrimat Bhāgavat* also said that if one is not a connoisseur and a dreamer, one does not have rights to the *dharma* of the *Bhāgavat*. That is why I say, whatever spiritual seekers do, they should try to be immersed in this feeling. In this manner, actions become successful. Any worship is of the perceptual. Is there worship that is beyond perception? Or can there be? First, the percepts of the world have to be imbued with the spirit of divinity. Then, slowly, by grace, one acquires the ability to enter into the spirit of that which is beyond perception.

Teachers who came before us would recite the *Sāma* and other scriptures and sing praises to fire, water, air, sky and Sun. It was the natural expression of their simplicity. There was no deceit in them. Viewing the spirit of life force everywhere, realizing the spirit of *Brahmaṇ* everywhere, their sense of inertness had disappeared. They behaved with all matter as conscious material. Even now, the people of this country, when plucking leaves of *Tulsi*[2], say with simplicity, 'O *Tulsi*. You are immortal. You are the favorite of *Keśava*. I am picking you for the worship of *Keśava*. Please do not mind. Please forgive me.' Not only in picking *Tulsi* leaves, most daily acts in the home of the devout, which appear to be inert in the eyes of common people, are treated as conscious. Honored are people of a land where applying clay on the body during bathing, say 'O earth, cleanse me of the sins that I commit,' who water a Fig tree saying 'O Lord as a Fig tree, be pleased', who see a boulder or rock as a god. But that is something else.

Here I have to say some words about hymns. The power of hymns created by the sages is greater than those written in recent times. It is unnecessary to say that mantras and hymns, recited by generations of great souls of a lineage, gather much strength. However, it is not being said that hymns or songs written by modern poets cannot arouse feelings or taste. But, it has been tested in many instances that words begun by the sages appear to have more power. When one sees these principles, the music and superficial feelings of modern songs do not have the same

---

2 *Ocimum sanctum* or *tenuiflorum* , holy Basil plant

attraction. Vedic verses appear to be formed of life force. Their pronunciation brings vibrations of pure, right tendency to every molecule of the body. Whatever that is, when reciting hymns, or for that matter carrying out any procedure with mantras, one has to pay special attention to the three things mentioned before. Body, mind and words have to ring with the same tune. Prescribed actions should not become just a recital of sounds. Meaningless repetition of mantras without feeling, or acts towards a spirit far away, are often without results. A spiritual seeker has to be aware of this.

Besides this, if one pays attention to posture, feeling and recital, then knowledge, devotion and action may be practiced together. I have mentioned that knowledge means knowing the divine, devotion is to love it and action is doing something for it. One cannot love something unknown. So, one cannot carry out any action for it. The more a spiritual seeker becomes aware of the nature of Mother and her greatness, the more one's state as a worldly person will diminish. This is a result of knowledge. Its outer sign is bowing down (*praṇām*). Knowing the nature of the loving Mother, a little love appears in one's own heart. This is devotion, and its outer signs are excitement, tears and tremors. As devotion grows, one begins to carry out prescribed actions. They are expressed outwardly as repetitions of name (*japa*), ceremonial worship, recitals and acts for the good of humanity.

Verse 2.

devyā yayā tatamidaṁ jagadātmaśaktyā
niḥśeṣadevagaṇaśaktisamūhamūrtyā|
tāmambikāmakhiladevamaharṣipūjyāṁ
bhaktyā natāḥ sma vidadhātu śubhāni sā naḥ||

Translation:

The Goddess, formed from the energy of all the gods, who pervades everything with the power of her Self, we bow with devotion to this Mother *Amvikā,* who is worshipped by gods and great sages. May she shower us with her blessings.

Explanation:

Mother, you are the Goddess manifest, eternally expressed. Something else is always needed to express all other things in this world. You are self-expressed. Nothing else is needed to express you. Some say that knowledge is expressed with the help of ignorance. Because there is something expressed as ignorance or illusion (*māyā*), *Brahmaṇ* or knowledge is expressible. There cannot be any expression without something expressible. Just as it can be said that without the presence of earth, the expressible nature of the Sun would not exist, similarly, if expressible objects or ignorance did not reside next to it, one could not perceive the existence of knowledge.

Mother, those who try to determine your indefinable self-expressed nature, try to reach it by winding ropes of logic around themselves. They do not understand that you cannot be captured by logic and inference. Withdrawing all expressed materials, only you exist, residing in your nature. Or, you are expressed to that extent in them, what they cannot reach beyond proof. Then, one day, when you appear as the *guru*, they also will say, 'that alone shines, everything else shines by it. By that light, all shine with various forms'[3].

Mother, you pervade this universe with the power of your Self. When Self (*ātmā*) is expressed as power (*śakti*) then this universe is expressed. There is so much difference of opinion about the power of your Self. Different opinions and schools are saying, Self and power, power of Self, Self with power, Self that is power. To establish their view and oppose that of others, so many arguments are raised. As long as you are not seen, as long as you are far away, so long there are arguments about *ātmā* and *śakti*. O, Mother! Great is your divine play (*lilā*). In expressing yourself, in putting away your disguise of ignorance, you play such games. Here you have begun another *lilā*. What is the outcome of this?

3 '*tameva bhāntam anubhāti…*' *Kaṭha Upaniṣad*, 2.2.15

Only you know the answer. Whatever it is, when one lays eyes on you, it can be seen that *ātmā* and *śakti* are different words, without any differences between them.

Mother! You are *ātmā*, only you are the true nature of 'I'. That single 'I' is always echoing in every atom of every being. That single 'I' pretends to be many in various containers of various beings. The name of that 'I' is *ātmā* and the expression within many is *śakti*. This *ātmā* and *śakti*, whatever they be called, one, two or a specific One, basically does not change your real nature. Dissecting them in this manner, one day, beings will realize your proper nature. Ignorance stored over many lifetimes will disappear.

What is the harm in trying to understand the nature of your Self-power (*ātmaśakti*)? In 'I see' we find two things, 'I' and the power to see. The conclusion as to whether these are one or two can be arrived at by anyone with their individual intelligence. With the words, *Brahmaṇ* and *māyā*, *puruṣa* and *prakṛti*, *Śiva* and *Durgā* , *Kṛṣṇa* and *Rādhā*, the difference (even though they are one) between power and the one with power, are continued. As long as there is a spiritual enterprise, as long as there is a body, as long as there is a world, so long, even though they are nondual, the perception of duality appears to remain. This perception of duality is expressed in trying to explain and understand through language. As long as there is language, thought and spiritual effort, so long the duel between *Śuk* and *Śāri*[4] will remain. *Śuk* says "My *Kṛṣṇa* held up the mountain". *Śāri* says "My *Rādhā* gave him the power, how could he otherwise". My Mother is the spirit of divine play. As long as she plays, so long the difference in the non-different will continue.

Whatever it be, Mother, this universe is pervaded by the power of your Self, '*tatamidaṁ jagadātmaśaktyā*.' Everywhere we see, the one 'I' is expressed in many forms. In every being, in every animalcule, the power of that Self, this form of *Hara* and *Gouri*, the dual form of *Rādhā* and *Kṛṣṇa*. This is your world-pervading universal power of Self. Mother, tell these many forms of yours,

4 mythical birds in *Vaiṣṇava* literature

these children, "Feel the presence of 'I' in yourselves, that feeling is *ātmā*, and whatever action or effect of that 'I' can be seen is *śakti*." If one pays close attention in this manner, one's birth and life become worthwhile, fear, death and controversy disappear forever.

'*niḥśeṣadevagaṇaśaktisamūhamūrtyā*': Mother, you pervade this universe with the power of Self, which is your general form. We do not notice this form even though we see it, we do not want to understand it. That is why, overcome by affection for your children, sometimes you appear in a special form and are forced to appear in the form of cherished deities. Those are formed by the combined power of all the gods. You have appeared in such a special form to destroy the demon *Mahiṣāsura*.

Mother! As long as there is a perception of power in worldly persons, there is ignorance. When perception of the gods appears, it is called knowledge. Then, when the sense of the power of Self appears, it is indefinable, beyond ignorance and knowledge. Perception roams on these three levels. First, there is the perception of the power of worldly persons. All power appears to be overcome by the feeling as a worldly person that attainment, saving, expenditure, enjoyment, sin, virtue, fame and establishment, all are carried out by the sense of ego as 'I carry them out.' Then, after repeated divine obstacles, this ego or ignorance is crushed. Slowly belief in divine power appears. One understands that powers are gods. This is knowledge. It is the second level of perception. Finally, when divine power is unified and expressed as united, then seeing oneself completely in it, one discovers the power of Self. O! What bliss it is! What satisfaction! When spiritual seekers are engrossed by Mother, they see that they are expressed as this universe. Sun and Moon and stars are always worshipping 'I.' The planets do not veer even a little from their path and keep going for eternity because of 'I.' This air keeps flowing for me. This flow of water washes my body for all time. These flowers appear for my worship. What can I say? All this is 'I.' There is nothing else but 'I.' All is Self. All is power. All is Mother.

This is my 'I', Mother worshipped by gods and sages. That is my you, my that. That I, me, is what we all pay homage to. We bow with devotion. Mother! Where will we find devotion? Even that is you. If we do not understand you to be Self, do not offer you Self, do not cherish you as life force, then you do not appear as devotion. Those who can bow down with devotion (*bhaktyā natāḥ*), can climb onto your folds by force. We bow down without devotion, we do not know what devotion is. We do not know how to love you, how to pour our hearts at your feet. Mother, will you not pick us up? You are our hope, our reliance. We suffer the blows of so many lives and deaths looking up at your face. Mother, when will you rise as devotion in our stony hearts? When will we bow down with devotion and go beyond our state as a worldly person? Owner, father, mother, companion, supporter, friend, spouse, *guru*, all are you. You sit by, having stolen all our love and attraction. My relatives in this world, look at my face and then give me love. If I can follow their intentions, then I have the rights to the love of my worldly relatives. But you love me because of the attraction in your heart. You are Self (*ātmā*). You are life force (*prāṇa*). When will we understand this supernatural love? When will we be honored to see your appearance in the form of devotion?

O, Mother! We have no devotion, yet we bow down to you. 'Without devotion, we bow down to you. We bow down to you a thousand times. We bow down to you again and again. We bow to you before and after, we bow to you everywhere.' Mother, accept the obeisance of your poor, devotion-less children.

Prescribe what is good for us. Not only for me but for all of us. Mother, shower beneficence on all this world. May all who live in this world find your blessings. May what is inauspicious for the world disappear. My Mother who gives rise to the world, bless us, give us the gift that all your children may find the right blessing of truth and love and be relieved of all that is inauspicious. O Mother, my Mother!

Verse 3.

yasyāḥ prabhāvamatulaṁ bhagavānananto
brahmā haraśca na hi vaktumalaṁ balañca|
sā caṇḍikākhilajagatparipālanāya
nāśāya cāśubhabhaysya matiṁ karotu||

Translation:

Even the gods, *Anantadeva*[5], *Brahmā* and *Maheśvara* are unable to describe her incomparable influence and power. May this Goddess *Caṇḍikā* set the direction for the welfare of this world and the destruction of all inauspicious fear.

Explanation:

Mother, even the infinite-headed *Anantadeva*, four-faced *Brahmā* and five-faced *Hara* cannot describe with words your incomparable influence and power. Even though they are all-knowing, all-powerful gods, even then, why are they unable to express your power? Mother, to know your influence and power completely, one has to merge with you. As long as one does not merge with you, one cannot realize your greatness. But one cannot merge with you as long as one has words and thoughts. Or, in merging with you, words and thoughts cease. When one again returns to the land of words and mind, one moves away from your incomparable greatness. So, no one can know your influence, or determine your nature. Mother, you are beyond thoughts and words.

Mother! *Brahmā*, *Viṣṇu* and *Maheśvara* are your older children. They are the ones who realize your influence and greatness. That is why perceiving your unthinkable greatness, they have turned away from words. They remain silent. We, your younger children are rather immature. The slight reflection of your greatness that falls on us, whether we understand it or not, we sing about it to everyone. A young child does not know much about the greatness of Mother, yet it speaks about the glory of Mother to everyone. In

5 *Viṣṇu*

the same way, we will sing your praises everywhere. If nothing else, our mouths tainted by speaking untruth will be purified.

Listen to the influence of my Mother. This Sun that you see, is one hundred and forty thousand times larger than the earth we live on. Other planets (Mercury, Venus, Mars, etc.), larger and smaller than the earth, are attracted by it and go around it constantly. These planets have satellites. All these together form this solar system. The innumerable stars that you see at night form larger systems. For eternity, these innumerable systems are going around some unknown center. There is so much more in this great space where they move that remains unknown. This great space, this immense universe is held in the heart of my Mother. This infinite universe has been moving for eternity in the heart of my Mother. For once, look at my Mother.

Then, even with the power of this unthinkable, great influence, she takes care to see how even an atom in the far corner of this earth can be properly placed so as to merge into her. She keeps her steady eyes on even the tiniest beings, in whose heart a perception of Mother rises, or who sheds a sigh. With great alacrity, she does what is necessary. She is our Mother. Again, when she wishes, at that moment, this immense, unthinkable creation, like magic, can disappear into the nonmanifest arena. Creation-maintenance-dissolution of this huge universe occurs in a blink of her eyes. This is our Mother. There is another great influence. One who is today wicked and ignorant, can after some time become holy and knowledgeable. Creation - maintenance- dissolution of this universe is simple for the one who can do this.

Mother, whatever it be, you are *Caṇḍīkā*. By your influence, in the blink of an eye, the nature of *Brahmā*, *Viṣṇu* and *Śiva* disappear into depths of dissolution. You are that Mother *Caṇḍikā*. You inspire intelligence to maintain this great universe and destroy all inauspicious fear. To maintain this universe, inauspicious fears have to be destroyed. The word '*aśuva*' means death. The fear of it is '*aśuva bhaya*.' Look, Mother! This world is always afraid of death. See how in the heart of all living things, death rules. How a great demon, fear of death, at each moment sucks blood from one's heart. All the noise that you hear in this world is to prevent the shouts of this demon from reaching our ears. Acquirement, savings, eating, sleeping and enjoyment, are all to momentarily cover this fear of death, with a contrived smile. Mother, inspire intelligence so that it can remove this terrifying shadow of death that covers this world. My Mother who brings fearlessness, remove the fear of death from this world. My Mother, who is of the nature of divine nectar, take away this fear of death. Mother, you are fearless, divine nectar, truth, *paramātmā.* Death and immortality are toys in your hands. So, you are truth, you are courage. Mother, stand forth in your form as fearless truth. Take care of this world. May the fear of death disappear in a flow of ambrosia. May the world of beings become fearless on seeing your form as truth. May they drink the nectar of knowledge and become immortal. May everyone in this world forget that there is such a thing as fear of death. Speak into every heart, 'There is no death. You are the children of divine nectar. You reside in the nectar of the heart of Mother. Your fear of death is from ignorance. It is false. I am you Mother bringing courage, you are my all-dependent children.' Mother, sound this in the heart of all beings. May all understand that we are fearless, we are immortal. Mother, the painful cries of sorrow and hurt of this world, cannot be tolerated any longer.

Our intelligence is always vibrating with multiplicity, tormented by sorrow and sadness we are fearful of death all the time. Because we view multiplicity, we sacrifice ourselves from death to death. Because we do not understand that only you, the nature of immortality is reflected in intelligence, we do not look at you but run after multiplicity. We suffer pangs of death over and over again. But now, may our intentions be always engrossed by you.

Verse 4.

yā śrīḥ svayaṁ sukṛtināṁ bhavaneṣvalakṣmīḥ
pāpātmanāṁ kṛtadhiyāṁ hṛdayeṣu buddhiḥ|
śraddhā satāṁ kulajanaprabhavasya lajjā
tāṁ tvāṁ natāḥ sma paripālaya devi vīśvam||

Translation:

We bow down to the one who is bounty (*śrī*) in the homes of those who do good, is scarcity (*alakṣmī*) in the home of sinners, intelligence (*dhi*) in the hearts of the conscientious, respect (*śraddhā*) in the well-mannered, and modesty (*lajjā*) in those of good birth. O, Goddess! Take care of this world.

Explanation:

You reside as bounty or wealth in the homes of those who are good. Only money and jewels are not wealth. A lack of obstacles to desire is proper wealth. It is an outer sign of purity of the spirit of intelligence (*buddhi*). In this land, during *Tantra* ceremonies, it is prescribed to worship eight deities of wealth, poverty, renunciation, attachment, *dharma*, *adharma*, knowledge and ignorance. These eight are characteristics of intelligence. Intelligence is rightly a location for Mother. Mother resides in the principle of intelligence. Ceremonies, worship, service and meditation are all for this intelligence. So, the previous mantra says 'direct our intent' (*matiṁ karatu*). When intelligence is pure, beings carry out good actions. With it, they find wealth or riches. There are no obstacles to their wishes. Because of it, they receive renunciation, *dharma* and knowledge. They earn a title of liberation. Mother! In this manner, your form as *śrī* is seen in the homes of those who carry out good deeds.

You reside as ill-fated (*alakmṣī*) in the homes of those who are sinful, whose intelligence is sinful. *Alakṣmī* is the lack of wealth and obstacles to one's wishes. As long as the desires of beings are unfulfilled, we have to understand that intelligence is sinful. The meaning of the word sin (*pāpa*) is contraction or hesitancy. As long as intelligence is satisfied by the expression of matters of form and flavor, it is soiled by active and inert tendencies, it contracts and it is sinful. When intelligence is dim, it is an inauspicious kingdom or a lack of wealth. From this comes, *adharma*, attachment and ignorance.

Sins and virtue are in the realm of intelligence. Beyond it, there is no sin or virtue. Knowledge, ignorance, *dharma*, *adharma*, renunciation, enjoyment, realization and failure are all at the level of intelligence. What is known as sins and virtues in this world, are all relative. What is a sin for one may be a virtue for another. What is sinful under one condition may be virtuous in another. In the judgment of sin and virtue in this world, the aim is the health and stability of society. On a spiritual path, analysis of sin and virtue aims to remove obstacles. Whatever that is, one day by this analysis, beings arrive at the nature of intelligence. The knowledge of sin and virtue that is found in it is not relative, but applicable to all places, at all times, to all conditions.

Two-fold expression resides in intelligence. One is the expression of things acquired by the senses, the other is the expression of *paramātmā.* The first is sin, the second is piety. Intelligence contracts by the expression of worldly things, but expands with the expression of *paramātmā.* So, I said, sin is contraction, piety is expansion. If you accept a flower as a flower, intelligence contracts. But, if you accept it as Mother, as life force, intelligence expands. Transactional sins and virtues are mostly arranged by this contraction and expansion of intelligence. Contraction of intelligence is ignorance. From ignorance comes a lack of wealth and unfulfilled desires. When desires are unfulfilled, renunciation cannot develop. So, we see that on one side of intelligence is wealth (*śrī*) and on the other is the lack of it (*alakṣmī*). On one side are knowledge, *dharma*, wealth and renunciation, on the other ignorance, *adharma*, lack of wealth and attachment.

Mother! Those who understand that you reside as both, are successful (*kṛtadhi*). You are 'intelligence in the hearts of the conscientious.' That is why the twice-born in their triurnal worship, pray for expression as pure intelligence (*dhio yo naḥ pracodayāt*). Mother, arriving at intelligence, one finds everything. All wants are banished. So, the entire world of beings prays at your rosy feet for the arousal of intelligence with '*dhio yo naḥ pracodayāt*'.

You reside eternally as respect, as a firm conviction of the words of a *guru*, in the hearts of those who have discovered the truth. Those who have found an undivided, unending, eternal spirit in this ever-changing, temporary world are truly honorable. When one is conscientious, one finds existence (*sat*). It is found by respect, by unmoving mountain-like faith, in the words of gurus and scriptural texts. Mother, you reside in the heart as respect in those you make truthful, take them away from untruth. This is your motherhood.

'*kulajanaprabhavasya lajjā*' In the hearts of those of good birth, you reside as modesty. Modesty or shame is avoidance of undesired acts. You always reside as shame in the hearts of those who are ashamed of carrying out proscribed acts in this world. On the other hand, those who have found existence (*sat*), those who have discovered that which is beyond these shores, while roaming the shores of material things, have realized undivided spirit, are always reluctant to confer control on you, who is ever-detached. This is their shame of avoidance of undesired acts.

'*tāṁ tvāṁ natāḥ sma*': we bow down to that Mother. You appear always in our hearts as wealth, lack of it, intelligence and modesty. Even though you are invisible, intangible and untouchable, you appear in all these forms in our hearts, at all times. Mother, we bow down at your feet. Not only with words, we bow at your feet with body and mind.

'*paripālaya devi vīśvam*': you take care of this world. Arouse this faith, this firm belief in the hearts of all beings that truly you take care of this world, that all beings in this world reside in you. Your children are tormented by the pains of three worlds. Their hearts are torn by severe scourges of famine, plague and untimely death. Even though they are nurtured in the folds of the eternally blissful, they are dulled by fear and pain. Remove them. Appear as a *guru* in the hearts of all and remove ignorance. Let beings be relieved of the pressure of this long-drawn pain, imagined due to ignorance. This is rightly your caring for this universe. Otherwise, what is the justification of caring for it? You are in the form of this universe, you are creator-maintainer-destroyer of this universe. So, saying that you take care of the world is redundant.

Mother! Let us understand that we are not homeless. Remove this feeling from us that we think ourselves to be homeless and tired, because of sorrow and fear of the torment by the powerful. Give us the strength to realize in our hearts that you, who is the controller of this universe, hold us in your heart.

Verse 5.

kiṁ varṇayāma tava rūpamacintyametat
kiñcātivīryamasurakṣayakāri bhūri|
kiñcāhaveṣu caritāni tavāti yāni
sarveṣu devyasuradevagaṇādikeṣu||

Translation:

O, Goddess! How will we describe your unimaginable beauty? Your great valor (*vīrya*) in destroying demons and your incredible character reflected on the battlefield have surpassed those of any demons and gods.

Explanation:

Mother, your beauty (*rupa*) is beyond description and thought. Truly, your form cannot be described by words or understood by the mind. We can understand that all visible things have *rupa*. But what that form is, we cannot express by words or think in our minds. What we understand as form is not truly form but an aspect of it. We try to express it with words such as spherical, cubic, triangular, red, blue, white, hard, soft, fluid, high or low. In reality, nothing of a form is expressed. Nothing of form is expressed by words, only some of its shape and construction are revealed. When we apply the words beautiful or ugly to form, they too are aimed at the outer aspect. Really, form is form. It is neither beautiful nor ugly. It is one, not two. This world floats in a sea of form. How will I express by words, what the nature of this form is? It cannot be expressed by words. It is beyond thought. Yet we cannot say that there is no form. It seems that we are always looking at form. But what we see is not form but only outer aspects. Names and shapes float in an undivided ocean of form. We do not seem to understand that these shapes are nothing but form. These shapes are the names and forms described by *Vedānta*. When we pay attention to form, we arrive at a great field of truth unreached by our senses. It is beyond words and thought.

Mother! On the other hand, if we say that what we understand as beauty is your *rupa*, then it becomes beyond our thought. A drop from an ocean of beauty is what we see in the Moon, a lotus, in a beautiful woman, in the faces of our babbling children, and we are engrossed by it. Who knows how mesmerizing you are, one who is an ocean of beauty. Mother, forms of these divided, transient things can keep us blind to your *rupa*. It is not surprising that those who are engrossed by your unified form feel forms of this world to be inconsequential. Mother, you are the one who 'enchants the enchanter.' Those who have immersed in your incredible ocean of form, engrossed by it, know that there is nothing ugly, nothing profane. Everything is beautiful. Mother! What an enviable condition!

Here it is hinted as to how one can immerse in an ocean of your *rupa*. Form has five natures, first, physical, or shape, second, visual or visible. A subtle expression of form is in the eye. Third, is the subtler expression of form (*tanmātra*). Fourth, *asmitā*, the nature of perception; this is an even subtler expression of form. Arriving here, one understands that form is nothing but perception. Other than this, there is another condition of *rupa*, which is the objective of man (*puruṣārtha*), because it satisfies the wishes of *puruṣa*. It is *paramātmā* as pure perception, it is called *puruṣārtha*. This is the fifth and most subtle nature of form.

In the beginning, in the perception of truth, when the physical form, that is the outer aspect of any object is taken to be Mother, a second nature of form, visible power, is expressed. One perceives that all over this world, visible power is a nature of form. Then, by the establishment of truth in it, and moving forward towards its center as Mother, one arrives at a subtler expression of its extent. This is very subtle, but a discernable form in perception, attractive and very satisfying. Then if one calls for Mother and goes forward, she brings one to a place where one perceives 'I' as the nature of form. Words cannot express what becomes of this 'I.' It is a formless nature of form. There, if one weeps for Mother, one gets a glimpse of the proper viewer of this form, one in whose vision this 'I' resides. What happens when a spiritual seeker returns to a physical state? Their thirst for form and expectations of beauty are gone forever. They no longer pray to Mother saying 'show us your form.' This is the achievement of the mantra '*rupaṁ dehi.*'

Mother, let your dear children know that when one goes forward on a path of establishment of truth in physical form, saying '*rupaṁ dehi*', one can easily immerse in an ocean of form and discover the nature of the formless. [The meaning of the word '*rupa*' was given in the explanation of the *Argalā stotra* in Volume One. It was also hinted there, about levels of form to be passed to arrive at the nature of *paramātmā.*]

'*kiñcātivīryam*': Mother, your incomparable valor that destroys innumerable demons is beyond our imagination. You are valor of the demons and you are valor that destroys them. The word '*kṣaya*' has two meanings, destruction and residence. The root '*kṣi*' is also used in the sense of residing. So, the valor of destruction of demons means both. Valor that appears as demons is you. That which destroys their valor is also you. Such opposites residing together are only possible in you. The demons and gods are both your expressions. So, we see the mantra say '*asura deva gaṇādikeṣu.*'

Even before the expression of your great valor of creation-maintenance–dissolution of this universe, we see an expression of valor in the demons. We are astounded by this great valor. We see you appear as demons of desire, anger, greed and delusion, then as the valor of the gods, lack of desire, anger, and greed. When the valor of the gods becomes strong, that of the demons weakens. In this manner, we always see the effect of your valor in our hearts. Again, incredible valor appears in the conflict of the expression of this opposing valor. When torments of the valor by demons begin, an unearthly divine play proceeds in spirit. Then again, as valor of the demons diminish and that of the gods becomes strong, it brings heavenly peace to the spirit.

Besides this, a different effect of your valor can be seen that is beyond gods and demons. Where all valor is defeated, is your divine immortal valor. It is that, in fear of which, the Sun rises, winds flow, clouds bring rain, that which even death fears. We bow a million times at the feet of that valorous Mother, who is beyond all valor.

Verse 6.

hetuḥ samastajagatāṁ triguṇāpi doṣai
rna jñāyase hariharādibhirapyapārā|
sarvāśrayākhilamidaṁ jagadaṁśabhūta
mavyākṛtā hi paramā prakṛtistvamādyā||

Translation:

You are the cause of all this universe. Even being the nature of the three *guṇas*, you are the cause of error, you are not knowable. Therefore, you are inaccessible even by meditations of *Hari*, *Hara* and other gods. You are a sanctuary for all. All this universe is but a portion of you. You are unaltered, primal, supreme nature.

Explanation:

Mother, you are the cause for all this universe. Not only this universe we live in, not only this one universe, all universes, millions of them. All changeable material in the eternal cycle of creation, you are the cause for all of it. Cause is twofold, instrumental (*nimitta*) and material. Both these causes are you.

We may understand this somewhat by the example of dreams. Just as the instrument or controller and the matter viewed in dreams, are both caused by nothing but the mind, in the same manner, both the instrumental and material cause of this visible and perceptible world in the waking state, is nothing but you. My Mother, Self, has divided into many and is reflected as viewer and viewed.

Mother, maybe some of your learned children will say, 'No. Self is not the cause of this universe. Self is without attributes, inactive, there cannot be anything causal in it. The material cause of this universe is inert Nature (*prakṛti*). Because of the proximity to conscious Self, inert nature is transformed. It is this universe. Even instrumental cause is not in Self, because even viewing the result of the transformation of nature as this universe is not a characteristic of Self. There is no intent in Self. Because of proximity to the self-expressed nature of Self, characteristics of consciousness are seen in Nature. The result is this universe.'

We have no conflict with those who say this. We accept their conclusion by the knowledge of truth. But, Mother, you have not only appeared to us in this manner, appearing as the *guru*, you have shown us that inert forms of nature are also you, *ātmā*, my Mother. So, the mantra says 'of the three attributes (*guṇas*).' You are ingredients of this universe as three attributes.

My Mother, *paramātmā*, you are the spirit of consciousness. How can we accept that your form as Nature is inert, unconscious? Conscious *ātmā* cannot be inert. It can be said to be a manifestation of the conscious as unconscious. If we saw that you could reside somewhere else other than as Nature with its three attributes, then we might have accepted inert Nature. When like its rays and the Sun, Nature and Self are together, how can we call it inert? As long as there is discussion, as long as there is an 'I', so long you are Nature with three attributes. We say 'my nature.' In reality 'I am nature.' Just as when we say '*Rāhu*'s head', we speak as if the head is separate from *Rāhu*. Similarly, when we use dual words like *puruṣa* and *prakṛti*, *Brahmaṇ* and *māyā*, *ātmā* and *śakti*, they are nondifferent. When Self appears as Nature *māyā* or *prakṛti*, then it is so named.

It may be of concern to some as to how a pure perception or knowledge (*jña*) natured *ātmā* could become shaped as inert Nature, that is in the form of three attributes. In answer to that, it has to be said that the 'knowledge' substance, expresses three percepts of knowledge, knower and known. In an attribute-less condition (*nirguṇa*), this is not manifest, so another name for *prakṛti* is 'nonmanifest.' It is from '*jña*' that characteristics of knower-knowing-known are expressed. These are the three attributes. Knowledge with right attribute (*sattva guṇa*), knower with active attribute (*rājasa*) and known with static attribute (*tāmasa*). These three things do not come from somewhere else. They are expressed from '*jña*.' So, we can see that in the three conditions as worldly person, *Isvara* and *Brahmaṇ*, '*jña*' or *ātmā* remain intact. The characteristics of knower-known as expressed in Self and the world of name and form is thus reflected. Mother, this is why, wherever I look, I am engrossed by the beauty of your variety. That is why wherever I call, I hear your answer. I am proud of your affection. That is why the gods, in singing your praises, saying 'You are the reason for all this universe, even beings with the three natures' bow down at your rosy feet.

O, Mother! If it is so true that you are reflected as this universe in the form of the three attributes, then like the gods, why do we not see it when we look at this universe? Just as we see clay when we look at a vessel and see gold when we look at ornaments, why do we not see you when we look at this world? O sentient one! If you are this universe, if you are form and name, then why can we not see you?

'*doṣai ma jñāyase*': we do not know because of error. The first error, we do not want to see. The second error is uncertainty and doubt. We only want to see name and form. We only wish to see them as an ever-changing universe. So, we do not see you. Then, when like a flash of lightning, a ray of desire to see Mother appears, doubts and lack of faith come before the eyes. They say, 'Can it be? Can this inert material be Mother? Can this inert earth and water be sentient Mother, be your universal form?' As a result, the faint rays of desire quickly vanish.

Alas, Mother! How much longer will you deceive worldly beings tormented by three sorrows in this manner? You create error. You cover your figure with error. That is why you cannot be found. Our eyes are used to seeing your figure of errors, so we do not see your figure of good traits. If we could understand error also to be Mother, if we could concede *māyā* to be Mother, if we accepted *prakṛti* to be *puruṣa*, if we embraced mind as *prāṇa*, if we enjoyed material things as enjoyer, if we viewed the visible as the nature of the viewer, if we realized the inert to be sentient, then your cover of error would be removed. Oh! Everything else but you are mistakes. Other than consciousness, other than Self, all else is error. If one understands that it is you as all forms, where would there be error? As long as there is something called error separate from you, so long you will it be 'not known' (*na jñāyase*). Those who call these faults, false, error, inconsequential or imaginary, even they have a taint of error on them. They see fault as they call it false or error. So, I say, as long as error is seen to be separate from you, as a cover for you, so long will you be 'not known.' So long you are concealed.

You have said in the *Gitā*, that just as smoke covers a fire, dirt covers a mirror, amnion covers a fetus, so does ignorance cover knowledge[6]. Ignorance is the fault. It is true that as long as ignorance remains, there is no knowledge. But, just as smoke is the natural fault of fire, dirt the attendant fault of a mirror, the amnion the protective fault of the fetus, so ignorance is the attending fault of knowledge. If one knows that ignorance is also knowledge, then faults vanish and knowledge appears. Then you are no longer 'not known' but 'known.' Or, then you again appear as knowledge.

'*hariharādibhirapyapārā*': Mother, how will we know you? Not only are you unfathomable to us, but you are also inaccessible to the meditations of *Hari*, *Hara* and other gods. As long as meditator, meditation and objects of meditation remain, so long your true nature is not revealed. As long as a special perception

6 *Bhāgavat Gitā,* 3:38

as *Hari* and *Hara* remain, how can your nature as *paramātmā* be revealed. Oh! As long as I remain, you will not appear. You will come when this 'I' goes away. Until this specific 'I' is not immersed in an infinite ocean of spirit, you do not appear as Self. So, you are inaccessible to *Hari* and *Hara*.

O Mother, even though you are unfathomable, you are a sanctuary for all. There is no reason for us to be without hope because you are a sanctuary for all of us. You give shelter to everyone. We are protected by you. In simpler words, you keep us in your folds. Even though we do not know or understand you, we are on your lap, sheltered by you. If we understand this, we are greatly benefited. We are not homeless orphans. You are with us. Whatever calamity appears, birth, death, sorrow, pain or torment, Mother, who is a sanctuary for all, holds us. Even for a moment, we are not without you. What other words of assurance can there be? We are honored to be your children, naked infants in your folds.

'*akhilamidaṁ jagadaṁśabhūta*': How will we know that you are a sanctuary for all? This infinite universe is a part of you. Just as one knows one's limbs in all manners, just as a dweller is the occupier of a form, a tree the sanctuary of a fruit, a fire that of smoke, because this universe is a part of you, you are a sanctuary for all. A part of you is expressed as this universe. *Śrutis* say that 'only a portion is expressed as this world and worldly persons' (*pādohasya visvābhūtāni*[7]). Mother, one part of you is this world, the other three parts are self-expressed, there is no universe there. So that we, with little comprehension, understand, beneficent *śrutis* have imagined, you who is undivided and the nature of completeness (*purṇa*); to have parts. In case there is any concern, that by calling you a sanctuary of this universe, you are limited by the extent of it, they said that this universe is expressed by only a small portion of you. The rest is self-expressed, always complete, of undivided nature. You have said, 'I support this world with only

7 *Puruṣa Sukta. Ṛk Veda*

a portion of myself'[8]. As this universe is a part of you, then it is superfluous to say that you are a sanctuary for it. So, you are the sanctuary for all.

'*avyākṛtā hi paramā prakṛtistvamādyā*': Seeing disturbances and constant apprehensions in this world, we may have anxiety that you too are disturbed and ever-changing. So, in their praises, the gods call you undistorted, supreme and primal Nature. Mother, even though you are transformed into many forms (take special forms), you keep your unchanging nature intact. Molecules of water do not change when they appear as a piece of ice. Transformed into a piece of cloth, cotton remains unchanged. Appearing as a circle of light, the nature of a rotating flame does not change. In whatever fashion matters of perception may be transformed, there is no change in the nature of the percept. So, even though you transform into this universe, your nature remains unchanged. You are unperturbed, eternally still. There is no perturbation or outcome in you. The six changes of beginning, remaining, increasing and others move across you, but you remain eternally unchanged. Because you are the nature of the power of existence, all these opposite events can take place in you. You are supreme primal Nature[9]. What *Sānkhya* calls *puruṣa*, *Vedānta* terms *Brahmaṇ*, *Upaniṣad* calls *ātmā*, devotional scriptures call *Bhagavān*, is this primal supreme Nature. Nature with three attributes that finds outcomes is non-primal. When you, pure spirit of perception, supreme Nature are reflected as knower- knowing-known, right-active-inert attributed non-primal universe, you remain unchanged. So, your influence is inconceivable. Truly you are sentient Mother who carries out incredible deeds.

---

8 *viṣṭabhyahamidaṁ kṛtsnam*, *Bhāgavat Gītā,* 10:42

9 *ādyā prakṛti*

Verse 7.

yasyāḥ samastasuratā samudīraṇena
tṛptiṁ prayāti sakaleṣu makheṣu devī|
svāhāsi vai pitṛgaṇasya ca tṛptihetu
ruccāryase tvamata eva janaiḥ svadhā ca||

Translation:

O Goddess! You are the mantra *svāhā*, which is pronounced in oblations to satisfy the gods. As the mantra *svadhā*, you are recited for the satisfaction of our ancestors.

[Commentary on *svāhā* and *svadhā* is in Volume One.]

Explanation:

O, Mother! Those who are in this world, carrying out actions for gods and ancestors according to the scriptures, even though they living in a world full of sorrow, they can pass their time in peace and happiness and reach their final sanctuary. So, you have said in *Bhāgavat Gitā*, 'worldly persons should nourish the gods with oblations and gods will nourish them by sustenance. Thus, engaged in thinking of the good of each other, they will be fit to reach the supreme sanctuary. Those who do not present a portion of offerings to the gods and enjoy it are thieves'[10] and so on. Truly Mother, if the array of things of form and flavor acquired by the senses are not offered to the residing deities of the senses, then because of a lack of it, gods become frail. The expressive power of individual special senses grows weak and as a result, sickness, sorrow and untimely deaths occur. The veil of ignorance is not removed. Even some modern investigators agree that there are deep mysteries in actions carried out for gods and ancestors. That we cannot grasp any concept of you even after so much discussion is because of the weaknesses of the residing deities. We do not offer any of our worldly materials to the gods by whose power we acquire them through our senses every day and enjoy internally. So, our senses are slack, powers of our mind, intellect and spirit are weak. We do not have the power to think or grasp anything

10 *Bhāgavat Gitā,* 3:11-13

subtle. Our spirit and intellect show weakness whenever we try to think of anything beyond our senses. The reason is that we do not give them proper sustenance.

By *svāhā*, that is actions for the gods, and by *svadhā*, that is actions for the ancestors, funeral services and offerings (*tarpaṇa*), our internal and external residing deities are sustained and pleased. As a result, Mother is revealed and may be known. Other than this there is one more principle. If instead of trying to satisfy each deity, all acts of *svāhā* and *svadhā* are offered to life-natured Mother, if materials acquired by the senses are offered in the fire of the supreme life-natured Mother, then all gods are greatly pleased, and as a result, consciousness residing in the senses is sustained. If the base of a tree is watered, it nurtures all the branches, leaves and flowers. When water is poured on the top of the head, the whole body is cooled. Mother, when you are satisfied, all are satisfied. When you are pleased, the three worlds, divine and ancestral are all pleased.

Mother! You are eternally satisfied. What is all this about satisfying you? Because we are never content, we imagine discontent in you. We move to satisfy one who is eternally content. Then, you come at our door as if unsatisfied and say 'leaves, flowers, food or water, whatever my devotees offer, I accept those gifts of the pure hearted'[11]. It is as if, you are begging for our fruits and flowers. As if you are not satisfied without them. So, you say, 'O my engrossed children, offer whatever you can. Even if it is a little water, I will take it with pleasure. Do not look at the quantity, only offer it with devotion. It will give me complete satisfaction.' It makes my heart tremble to think that one day, you were satisfied by the offering of a grain of rice by the devoted Draupadi. There is so much compassion in your heart. You have to appear dissatisfied to remove the discontent filling my heart. You, who is my all-complete, eternally content Mother to remove our discontent, you appear in your discontented form, begging at the door of worldly persons. We are honored.

---

11 *Bhāgavat Gitā,* 9:26

You engage people in prescribed acts for gods and ancestors. The purpose is that after trying to find satisfaction in acts of *svāhā* and *svadhā* for some period, at a fortunate moment, we will look up at your face. Then we will realize that you are the ever satisfied, eternally still Mother, without an alternate. Then we will acquire rights to renunciation. Worldly persons will learn non-action. This is the nature of your actions for the gods and ancestors.

Verse 8.

yā muktiheturavicintyamahāvratā ca
abhyasyase suniyatendriyatattvasāraiḥ|
mokṣārthibhirmunibhirastasamastadoṣai
rvidyāsi sā bhagavatī paramā hi devī||

Translation:

Those whose senses are well controlled, who have understood that only the supreme principle is of any worth, whose faults have all been removed, such sages seek freedom and practice or meditate upon the unthinkable cause of liberation and nature of great enterprise. O Goddess, that supreme knowledge formed divinity is you.

Explanation:

Mother! When one is satisfied with the practice of before mentioned acts to gods and ancestors, that is, when satisfaction of Mother is achieved, then the senses of worldly persons are well controlled. They do not harbor greed for material things. In that condition, it is felt that only Self is the supreme principle. So, beings are excited by the hope of discovering Self or finding liberation. As the focus is only on Self, voice turns off. One becomes silent (*mouna*) and becomes a sage (*muni*). When one becomes a sage, all stains, disturbances and coverings of faults are cleaned. At this time, what these meditating sages practice, is you. It is all you.

What is the nature of this practice (*abhāsya*)? '*abhi asyase*': forward throw, the root '*as*' means 'to throw.' *Upaniṣad* says, 'attaching the arrow of being in the bow of *Praṇava*, one has to throw it repeatedly, aimed at *Brahmaṇ*.' This is the significance of the word '*abhyasyase*.' Carrying out some action repeatedly is practice. In this case, repeatedly throwing the arrow of Self at *Brahmaṇ* has been called practice. There is no error in calling it spiritual enterprise or meditation.

Mother! When beings are engaged in practice, you appear in your nature as unthinkable supreme enterprise. Because practice-natured supreme enterprise is really beyond thought. Only when worldly persons begin to get a hint of the nature of *paramātmā* beyond words and thought, can they begin to aim an arrow of Self at it. So, even though we try to describe this enterprise with words, it really cannot be imagined. One cannot realize its true nature by writing, speaking or thinking. Because, what the arrows are aimed at is 'beyond thought, pure.' But it is definite, that this practice is the supreme one. Because this is the final exercise. Beyond this, there is nothing that can be practice or is function. This results in liberation.

Mother! This nature of yours as the reason for liberation, an unimaginable supreme vow, has another name. It is 'knowledge' (*vidyā*). It is by which, the unalterable nature of *paramātmā* can be found. All actions, all ceremonies, are secondary reasons for discovering *paramātmā*. So, they can be called minor expressions of knowledge and ignorance. But, because this great vow of practice is a direct reason for liberation, it may be called supreme knowledge. O, Mother Goddess! For worldly persons, you appear as the power of divinity to remove forever any fear of bondage from ignorance. You are knowledge and lesser knowledge (*avidyā*). You are bondage and liberation. You are also beyond freedom from bondage.

Mother! When will you appear in your nature as supreme knowledge and remove all darkness of ignorance? When will you take us on your lap in your form as *vidyā* and make us taste this flow of knowledge? How long will we be seated on your form as *avidyā* and without seeing you, keep looking at material things? Because we are seated on your form as *avidyā*, our senses are not well organized and we do not even get a glimpse of your form as great promise. Mother, when will our pitiful cries reach your ears?

Verse 9.

śabdātmikā suvimalarg yajuṣāṁ nidhāna
mudgītharamyapadapāṭhavatāñca sāmnām|
devi trayī bhagavatī bhavabhāvanāya
vārtā ca sarvvajagatāṁ paramārttihantrī||

Translation:

Mother, you are in the form of sound. So, you are the only receptacle of pure *Ṛk*, *Yajuḥ* and the beautiful verses of *Sāma Veda* sung loudly. To maintain the stability of this world, you *Bhāgavati* exist in three forms. Again, as the message (*vārtā*), that is as profession, you remove all distress from this universe. So, you are the supreme one, the greatest.

Explanation:

Mother. Before, when singing your praises, the gods had viewed you as the reason for the vision of superior knowledge. Now, they say that other knowledge (*aparā*) derived from superior ones, that is, knowledge of *Vedas*, *Ṛk*, *Yajur* and *Sāma* are also expressed by you. They say that you are the nature of sound, and you, Mother are the spirit of sound. It is you who is expressed in all beings as transcendental, intellectual, mental and physical sound (*parā*, *paśyanti*, *madhyamā* and *vaikhari*). *Praṇava* is the primal message or root sound. In connection with different times and places, this may be heard as various appearances. *Vedas* are special expressions of *Praṇava*. The sage *Jaimini* has said, that by which one can easily understand the meaning, and where verses of a mantra are well arranged is named *Ṛk*. That which can be recited loudly, with beautiful music, rhythm and beat is called the *Udgitha* or *Sāma*. Other than this, what remains, that which is neither sung nor in verse, that is recited like prose, is called *Yajuḥ*. Mother, these are the forms of your triad. The other parts, *Atharva Vedas*, education and grammar, are included in this triad. Because *Vedas* have three attributes (*guṇas*), they are called a triad. Superior knowledge can be called threefold because it expresses percepts of knowledge, devotion and action. The Lord has also said that the *Vedas* entail the three attributes [12]. Although the *Upaniṣads* advice about nature beyond attributes, even then, they are included within this triad, because as long as there is advice about *Brahmaṇ*, description of the greatness of Self, and determination of its nature, they are included in this triad.

Whatever that be, it is for '*bhavabhāvanāya*', that is for the stability of beings, that your forms as this triad are expressed. So that worldly persons do not fall, that they do not take on irresponsible activity but remain controlled, you exist as advice of scriptures, as prescriptions of *Vedas* in your triadic form. Mother, your greatness is beyond imagination. Your triadic form is supreme, of infinite wealth. The power of God that can keep in check unbridled movement in this world, what else can it be but Goddess *Bhagabati*?

In a spiritual view, it may be seen that as long as one needs the help of mantra (sound) to find the perception of Self, it is called *Ṛk*. In *śrutis*, speech (*vāk*) has been named *Ṛk*. Then, when this perception is particularly expressed and flows as a blissful sensation all over the body, *Ṛk* is transformed into *Yajur*. In this condition, mantras are not recited as verses, that is, one does not pay attention to rhythm. Only sounds are pronounced, without tune or beat. This is *Yajur*. Then, as control of a kingdom of feeling is acquired, exuberance recedes, feelings are expressed peacefully and sounds are pronounced with tune and rhythm, they are called *Sāma*. If one watches closely, one can observe this triad during worship ceremonies. The expression of this triad may be especially seen during occasions like chanting (*kirtana*). Not only that, in the eyes of those who have the vision, an incredible

---

12 *traiguṇyaviṣayā vedāḥ, Bhāgavat Gitā*, 2:45

expression of this great force of primal sound in triadic form can be seen in all countries and all communities.

Ṛk, *Yajur* and *Sāma* are *Vedas* . The name for sensation (*vedan*) or perception is *veda*. When a perception of Self that is discovered inside is expressed outside as sound, it is called *Veda*. Because it appears from perceptions of truth-natured Self, it is called *Veda*. They are not an arrangement of sounds created by the brains of some individuals. They appear from a perception of truth or some infallible sensation. That is why the *Vedas* are said to have no authors. *Vedas* exist in all lands in some form or other.

Mother! Not only in this triadic form as prescription of scriptures do you protect stability as knowledge, but in the form of *vārtā*, you remove entreaties of this world and all its sorrows. *Vārtā* is profession. As an appropriate profession to protect the material body, as sustenance, for all beings, you exist in all places and at all times. Because we are moved from the truth that you are our *vārtā*, our profession, we have reached a crisis in our lives. Our countrymen are worried as to how they will carry out their professions. Mother, when will people of this land realize in their hearts that, those who see your form as an expression of their profession, never suffer from a lack of it? When will the people of this land desist from lies, falsehood and flattery for their profession and learn to cherish you as their profession and be relieved of their worry about survival? But, all that is something else.

In the *Mahābhārata*, we see another meaning of the word '*vārtā*.' In one incident, *Dharma* in disguise, asked king *Yudhiṣṭira*, "What is the message (*vārtā*)?" In reply, *Yudhiṣṭira* said, "With imaginary divisions of time, month and season as ladles, with the Sun as fire and night and day as fuel, great enchantment of this world as the cauldron, Time is simmering all worldly persons. This is the message."[13] Mother, you as time, at all times, are preparing the host of worldly persons. Birth, growth and destruction, as all six changes, you appear in beings as a message. Professions are part of these six changes. Mother, those who keep their attention on your form as *vārtā*, and offer their flowers of devotion, are never

---

13 *Mahābhārata, Vana Parba*, 313:118

enchanted by your changing form. Then they have no worries about their profession. You appear in a loving maternal form and take care of their needs and wants. Their vision is directed at your supreme, undivided, loving form. So, all changes pass them by unnoticed.

Mother, your love is admirable. As long as we think of stability in the world as our greatest goal, so long will you keep your imperishable nature unexpressed and appear to us as *vārtā*. We will until that time, appear at the door of material things as beggars. When we understand this stability in the world to be painful, when we realize that it is you in the form of *vārtā*, then our worries will disappear, and you in a destructive form, will remove all our percepts, and appear in your unique form as the remover of all yearnings. Mother, then will your name as 'supreme' be appropriate. We will then understand that you are truly the greatest. You are mother of even the great, *Brahmā* and all the others. As long as you do not appear in your form as the remover of yearnings, we will not escape from its hands. Mother, we pray to you pitifully, appear in the form of remover of sorrows in the hearts of your children. Cool these hearts which are rent by sorrow. You are Mother, the supreme one who removes sorrows, supreme Mother who removes all yearnings.

Verse 10.

medhāsi devi viditākhilaśāstrasārā
durgāsi durgabhavasāgaranaurasaṅgā|
śrīḥ kaiṭabhārihṛdayaikakṛtādhivāsā
gaurī tvameva śaśimaulikṛtapratiṣṭhā||

Translation:

O Goddess! You are intellect that holds all the scriptures. You are *Durgā.* You are a ship on this arduous ocean of life. You are *Kamalā* (*Lakṣmī*) who resides in the heart of *Kaitabhāri*[14] (*Viṣṇu*), and who is seated in the heart of *Chandraśekhara* (*Śiva*).

14 the enemy of *Kaiṭava*

Explanation:

Mother. It has been said that you are in the form of the *Vedas*. Now we see that you are also intellect that holds the knowledge of the *Vedas*. You hold knowledge of all scriptural texts (*śāstra*) in the form of intellect, so we can hope that someday, we will discover and understand you. If whatever we learn, all that we receive by the senses, are all forgotten at death, then our bondages would never end. But Mother, you as intellect hold those drops of knowledge, so at each birth, they increase. The knowledge that we collect in one lifetime, we do not have to exert much in the next to recollect. The energy by which this flow of knowledge is held over lifetimes is intellect (*medhā*).

The final condition or the greatest nature of this intellect is the memory 'I am *Brahmaṇ*.' Ācārya Śankara has also said that 'the memory of I am *Brahmaṇ* is *medhā*'[15]. One day, you will arise in our hearts as this intellect, and being aroused by the memory 'I am *Brahmaṇ*', we will throw away inexorable bonds as worldly persons and be established in the nature of Self. Because you appear as intellect, we do not recognize you or our Self. This is the essence of all scriptures, the basic message of all *śāstras*, to know Self. Who am I? Once this is understood, the need for all scriptures end. Mother, this is your form as what is known (*viditā*). When worldly persons understand their Self, then you appear in your form as *viditā*. All mysteries of scriptures are explained, aimed at this form of you as *viditā*. At first glance, words of scriptures may appear to be contradictory. But, when you appear in your form as *viditā*, then the words of *śāstras* do not have conflicting natures. It can be clearly understood that all scriptures echo the same One.

It has been said in the *Mahābhārata*, 'scriptures are different, opinions of the sages differ, the principles of *dharma* are hidden in the depths of caves; where the great ones have traveled, that is the path' [16]. Although this verse is taken to prove that there are differences between the scriptural texts and opinions, it may not

15 *brahāhasmi iti smṛtireva medhā*

16 *Vana Parba, Mahābhārata,* 313:117

be out of the way here to mention what we have understood by it. If the '*na*' in the second half of the verse is evaluated with the first verse, the meaning is different. It then says that the scriptures are not different, they are aimed at the same thing. He is rightly a sage (*muni*), whose views do not differ. That is, one can be called *muni* if one is not divisive. The principle of *dharma* is hidden in the heart (cave). (*Upaniṣads* use the word cave to signify the heart.) The path that the sages traveled, by which they reached the grotto of their heart and discovered knowledge of Self, that is the path. Traveling on this path, one can discover the principles of *dharma*.

Whatever it is, I was saying, Mother, that knowable (*viditā*) nature of yours is the fundamental of all scriptures. All scriptures are prepared to express you. But, as long as you, by your grace, do not appear in your 'knowable' form, no scripture can express you. Again, when you are known, then a spiritual seeker does not need *śāstras*. Mother, you express yourself in your knowable form, as nature of perception in all beings, yet no one is able to know you. So, you are *Durgā*, incomprehensible, difficult to reach.

On the other hand, we see that because you hold our stores of knowledge over many lifetimes as intellect, in this difficult ocean of life you are the only vessel. Beings can cross this arduous ocean of life by getting on this ship of intellect, saying 'I am *Brahmaṇ*.' Our ships need captains. They cannot move without captains. But, Mother, you are our unaccompanied vessel. No one else is needed. You are the ship and you are the captain. My intellect formed Mother is truly alone, without accompaniment, uninvolved. Although you hold our drops of knowledge as intellect, although all good and evil is associated with you in your intellectual form, you are not divided or dimmed by this contact. You are our eternal, pure, freedom-natured, solitary Mother. Even though you carry multiplicity in you, it does not touch you. So, the gods praise you as the 'vessel on this difficult ocean of life.'

Mother! You are *Śrī* in the heart of *Viṣṇu*, destroyer of multiplicity as *Kaitabhāri*. You are *Gourī*, the other half of *Śiva* as

Candraśekhara, wearing the Moon in his hair. Their natures are expressions of you. We see, that on one hand, even though you give rise to them, you also express yourself as their feminine form, *Vaiṣṇavī* and *Śivānī*. The energy of *Vaiṣṇavī* or *Śrī* is the nature of this universe, this multiplicity, this nature of worldly person. Again, when this solitary energy is expressed, without expressing any other percept, it appears as the destroyer of all percepts. So, your nature as intellect and *viditā* appears to us as *Śrī* or *Gourī.*

Verse 11.

īṣatsahāsamamalaṁ paripūrṇacandra-
bimbānukāri kanakottamakāntikāntam|
atyadbhutaṁ prahṛtamāptaruṣā tathāpi
vaktraṁ vilokya sahasā mahiṣāsureṇa||

Translation:

O Mother! *Mahiṣāsura* saw your face which held a slight smile, beautiful as a pure full Moon, like superior gold. Still, he was ruled by anger and attacked you. This is very strange.

Explanation:

It is strange that even after seeing your face, the beauty of which enchants the three worlds, active attribute (*rājasa*) is still disturbed externally and desires to have inconsequential things of form and flavor. 'Finding that, for which one does not desire anything else.'[17] One cannot understand how after this the spirit is keen to find material things. Is this not strange?

Mother! Even if all the beauty in this world is brought together, it is not equal to a drop of your other-worldly beauty. Despite this, we do not notice and are attracted to the beauty of worldly things that are mixed with sorrow. We forget your ethereal beauty. We cover it with momentary desires for inconsequential things. What is stranger than this?

Even though the nature of Self is experienced once in a while,

---

17 *Bhāgavat Gitā,* 6:22

actions of active attribute do not stop. Repeatedly, disturbances of material things cover the incredible beauty. This is the attack by *Mahiṣāsura*, despite seeing the beauty of Mother. Just as the beauty of the full Moon cannot be seen when reflected on disturbed waters, just as dark clouds moved by the wind prevent a view of the Sun, in the same manner, disturbances of spirit due to active attribute, are obstacles to a view of the incredible beauty of Mother. This is the attack by *Mahiṣāsura*.

Mother! When will we understand in our hearts, that the material beauty that makes us neglect your ethereal splendor is also your eternal expression? Whatever is in this world, is all covered by your beauty. Your form is reflected in every object. Until our hearts are filled with this simple truth, can we ever discover your ethereal beauty?

Verse 12.

dṛṣṭvā tu devī kupitaṁ bhrukuṭīkarāla-
mudyacchaśāṅkasadṛśacchavi yanna sadyaḥ|
prāṇān mumoca mahiṣastadatīva citraṁ
kairjīvyate hi kupitāntakadarśanena||

Translation:

O Goddess! Seeing your face frowning in anger, yet beautiful as the rising full Moon, it is strange that *Mahiṣāsura* did not immediately lose his life. Who can still be alive after seeing the ruler of death?

Explanation:

Mother, it is surprising that even after seeing your frowning, angry face, *Mahiṣāsura* did not immediately lose his life. When your anger is expressed, when you stand in your destructive form, even *Brahmā*, *Viṣṇu* and *Maheśvara* disappear, let alone *Mahiṣāsura*. Mother, the gods describing your frowning, angry face compared it to the 'rising full Moon.' Just as when the full Moon appears, darkness goes away, in seeing your frightening, destructive face, darkness of ignorance, percepts of duality vanish. This is the inevitable rule. But here we see something different. Even after seeing your frightening face, *Mahiṣāsura* remains alive, he fights with you, taking the bodies of a lion, elephant, half-emerged man. He attacks you. This is surprising. How did this happen?

Mother, you expressed anger in your form as *Amvikā*. Your form as *Amvikā* is that of a mother. The frowning, terrible face of a mother may frighten a child, but will not destroy it. Mother, you took time to sip nectar and gave *Mahiṣāsura* a chance to roar. So, he did not die at once but died fighting. What we think to be nearly impossible, takes place because your wish can carry out the unattainable. We can see this if we pay attention to our daily lives. Even then, we cannot believe in your all-powerful, all-pervading control and surrender to you. We do not offer all our false ego at your feet and be relieved of all worry. This is our ill-fortune.

Mother. Seeing this difference from the general rule, the gods asked, 'Who can remain living, even after seeing the ruler of death?' It is true that no one remains alive after seeing the ruler of death (*Yama*), but why will a child not live after seeing Mother? As long as you do not appear as the ruler of death, the glory of affectionate and kindly motherhood appears on your frowning, angry face. That is why *Mahiṣāsura* did not die at once and gave you time to sip nectar and fight with you. Great is your incredible divine play. When you wait to hear us call you Mother, when your heart fills with glory to hear us call you Mother, then our sorrowful hearts fill with pride. Mother, give us the chance to feel this pride.

Verse 13.

devi prasīda paramā bhavatī bhavāya
sadyo vināśayasi kopavatī kulāni|
vijñātametadadhunaiva yadastameta-
nnītaṁ balaṁ suvipulaṁ mahiṣāsurasya||

Translation:

Oh Goddess, be pleased. You are the greatest, to be worshipped. Your pleasure brings us good. When you are angry our lineage is destroyed. This we understood, as the whole army of *Mahiṣāsura* was destroyed.

Explanation:

Mother! You are the supreme one, the greatest. You are the mother of the superior (*para*), Mother of the greatest gods. *Brahmā*, *Viṣṇu* and *Maheśvara* who are known as superior, appear from you and reside in you, so you are the supreme one. If you are pleased, then we will be blessed (*bhaba*). From another aspect, we see that your satisfaction and anger are both greatly beneficial for worldly persons. When you are pleased, they find good fortune here and hereafter. When you are angry, their whole lineage (*kula*[18]) is destroyed. Even this is beneficial for them. If *kula* is not destroyed, one cannot find that which is shoreless. Mother! For so many lifetimes have we moved from shore to shore, enjoying form and flavor, spending life as worldly persons. We cannot give up our shores. We leave one shore and reach another. Who will say, not for a day or two, but for what eternal times, we have been doing so? Mother, when you are angry, all our shores disappear. Then we bathe in the shoreless ocean and lose ourselves in it. We are forever freed from this divisive happiness mixed with sorrow. Our travel from shore to shore ends. So, I say, Mother, both your pleasure and your anger are beneficial to us.

O, Mother! We have to understand that those who only pray for your pleasure, only want to see your smiling face, have not yet recognized you as Mother. Those who have understood that you are Mother, are your children, are not afraid of your angry, frowning face. Those who are your children, equally see the love of Mother in her pleasure and her anger. Those engrossed by the love of Mother, do not see any sign of misfortune in her angry figure, in the travails of life. Like fearless beings, like unclothed children, they stand in front of your devastating figure and leap onto your lap, calling on you.

18 *kula*, means lineage or dynasty, also sea shore or river bank

If we understood that there was some sanctuary other than you, then, seeing your angry form, being frightened, we might have run towards that other refuge. But we have understood that the only refuge is you. Whatever comes, birth or death, laughter or tears, happiness or sorrow, anger or satisfaction, under all conditions, you are our only sanctuary. Then, why will we back out on seeing your angry form? We know that when you are angry, we have to suffer much torment, disease, sorrow, humiliation and assault. Poverty and torment come from all sides. Despite this, we remember your kind face. Then, O *Caṇḍī*, within moments, all our misfortunes are removed. We are honored to know how fortunate we are.

Mother, in this manner, you appear in the hearts of all beings and destroy the great army of *Mahiṣāsura*. You remove the legacy of inconsequential things of form and flavor. We leave the shores of material things and leap onto your loving form, our Mother, you who is a ship on this shoreless ocean. One day, you stood by the shores of the Yamunā, and with enchanting notes of your flute, made the *gopis* leave their *kula* and attracted them. You justified your name as *Kṛṣṇa* (one who attracts). Appear again, at this junction of times, and with your sweet, attractive sound of truth, remove our errors, move us from our lineage (*kula*) and let us float on shoreless oceans (*akula*). For long, we have floated from shore to shore, beaten by endless waves, our ribs broken by so many blows, our hearts torn apart. We cannot take it anymore. Now, give these children, who are unable to move, a place in your heart.

Verse 14.

te sammatā janapadeṣu dhanāni teṣāṁ
teṣāṁ yaśāṁsi na ca sīdati dharmmavargaḥ|
dhanyāstaeva nibhṛtātmajabhṛtyadārā
yeṣāṁ sadābhyudayadā bhavatī prasannā||

Translation:

Mother! When pleased, those that you allow to rise are

honored in this world. Their wealth, fame and *dharma* are not weakened. Their children, spouses and servers are well behaved and healthy. In this world, their lives are worthy.

Explanation:

Mother, in your contented form, those that you hold on your lap, that is, those that have realized you to be the eternally satisfied, eternally happy Mother, in this world, receive honor like gods. Although they may not think much of worldly happiness, wealth, desire, honor and fame, even then, you appear to them in your form as the donor of prosperity. Those that are not used to seeing you in all perceptions, those who do not believe or agree that you appear as the donor of worldly prosperity, only have a hint of your angry form when they are in danger. They have no idea of what your peaceful form is like. So, such people can never find prosperity and be truly happy.

Those who under all conditions, in joy or sorrow, in rising or falling, realize that they are children on the lap of Mother, their *dharma*, wealth, desires and liberation are never diminished (*na ca sīdati dharmavargaḥ*). While in this world, they receive these four-fold results. Mother, those that do not serve your form as *dharma*, and only service wealth and desire, are repeatedly distressed by pain and sorrow. Mother, see how many of your loved children are now without *dharma*, serving only wealth and desire, suffering terrible circumstances. There is a conflagration of want everywhere. Tormented by famine, plague, untimely death, sickness and sorrow, they are forgetting that there is such a thing as peace and joy in this world. Tormented by such sorrow, they declare this world of bliss to be sorrowful.

Mother! Speak to them. Let them understand in their heart that there can be no happiness without *dharma*. To understand that this world is blissful, to enjoy that bliss, one has to first serve *dharma*. Beings receive satisfaction of spirit to the degree that they are aligned to *dharma*. When the spirit is satisfied, there is no want. When there is no want, there is no dearth of wealth. There is no obstacle to fulfilling rightful desires. When desires are fulfilled, beings become desire-less (*niṣkāma*). Mother, then you appear in the form of a liberator and rend all imaginary bonds and give worldly persons a taste of divine nectar.

Even though there is such an easy, liberal path, why most beings are lost and with uncontrolled movements, suffer untold miseries, is only known by you, my Mother, in your form as error. Come and stand in front of us in your form as error, and let our errors of eternities vanish. Let us understand that it is you who appears as error and let us travel beyond it.

Mother! Those that you hold on your lap in your form as the donor of prosperity, their servers, children and spouses are all loyal, well behaved, healthy and of good character. So, they do not have to leave their homes and take shelter in mountain caves in the hope of finding *dharma* or liberation. They can conquer both this life and the hereafter. *Gitā* has also said, 'those whose minds are fixed in evenness, while in this world, conquer heaven'[19]. Those whose spirits are seated in constancy, that is, always established in the even nature of Mother, while living in this world conquer heaven. Their lives are worthy. Even the gods while singing your praises say that these persons are honorable (*dhanyāstaeva*) and thank them.

To easily understand the mystery of this mantra at a spiritual level, children, servants and spouse, may be taken to mean respectively, conscience, conquered senses and tendency towards Self.

Verse 15.

dharmyāṇi devī sakalāni sadaiva karmmā
ṇyatyādṛtaḥ pratidinaṁ sukṛtī karoti|
svargaṁ prayāti ca tato bhavatī prasādā-
llokatrayehapi phaladā nanu devī tena||

19 *Bhāgavat Gitā,* 5:19

Translation:

O Goddess! By your favor, right-acting people, respectfully carry out all actions imbued with *dharma*. As a result, they acquire both heaven and liberation. O Goddess, in these three worlds you are the donor of results.

Explanation:

It has been said in the previous mantra that '*dharma* is not weakened.' Only by serving *dharma*, can one acquire rights to wealth, desire and liberation. This mantra advocates how *dharma* is to be served. Every day, all actions need to be carried out with great affection, imbued with *dharma*. By this, persons are right-acting and acquire both heaven and liberation. Let us clarify this.

Generally, people think that actions are of three kinds. Some are acts of *dharma*, such as evening worship, penances, rules, fasts and others prescribed by scripture. Some are not *dharma* (*adharma*), such as violence, resentment, lies, theft and other proscribed acts. Others are general actions like eating, sleeping, traveling and earning money. There is neither *dharma* nor *adharma* in them. Although actions are so stratified, we see them as only one kind. When material things interact with senses, actions are performed. The classification of action, inaction and opposed actions[20] in the *Bhāgavat Gitā* are only variations of action because of the interaction of material things with senses. That root actions are targeted in this mantra is evident by the use of the word 'all' (*sakalāni*). All actions have to be carried out with respect, not with disrespect. They have to be done with great affection (*atyādṛtaḥ*). How can all acts become part of *dharma*? By viewing control by Mother. Worldly persons while performing action united with Mother, carry out acts of *dharma*. This is the condition of spiritual enterprise in the mantra in *Gitā* of 'offer all that to me'[21]. Carrying out acts with a sense of ego, and then offering them to God are actions of a lower capacity. Acts have to be performed imbued by union with Mother. So, the mantra uses

20 *karma*, *akarma* and *vikarma*

21 *Bhāgavat Gitā*, 9:27

the present tense of 'to do' (*karoti*). From beginning to end it is the present. Viewing control of Mother from beginning to end of any action is a proper act of *dharma*.

There is an immense influence over all this world. This influence or power of action is expressed at all times through the interaction of material things with the senses. Practicing this for some time, it becomes second nature. Then one does not have to try to see the rule of Mother in all actions. In this manner, all actions of an accomplished spiritual seeker are imbued with *dharma*. On the other hand, vows, penances, fasts and other acts not viewed to be by the rule of Mother, although they appear to be acts of *dharma,* are not so. When daily acts of eating and traveling are performed in union with Mother, they become acts of *dharma*. Those that carry out all activities in this manner, all the time, are properly right-acting. Their actions are all good (*su*) that is, bearing auspicious results.

Those that carry out desired acts with the hope of reaching heaven and other such aims, move into that arena in the afterlife. Those that carry out acts without desire, only for the pleasure of Mother, find liberation. All of this is by 'her favor' (*bhabatiprasādat*). Mother, they are all acquired by your blessings. You make people 'right-acting' on this earth, you give worldly persons the right to heaven in the afterlife, and it is you who offer fruits of liberation beyond here and hereafter and so honor beings. You are the one who determines the results in three fashions in these three worlds (*lokatryyehapi phaladā*).

The word '*phaladā*' has a deeper meaning. The word can be formed from the root '*do*' meaning divisive. That makes the meaning of the word 'that which destroys results.' That which can destroy the results of action is also '*phaladā*.'

Mother! On one hand, you grant results of joy, sorrow, birth, death, heaven and hell, so you are 'the granter of results.' On the other hand, with a fire of knowledge, you turn all results of action to ashes, so you are the one who 'destroys results.' O Mother, even though you are the grantor of results, you are also their destroyer.

Because you appear in this form as the destroyer of results, we have hope that one day we will find a place in your immortal heart. We will go beyond all results of action.

As long as worldly persons carry out general acts by their ego, you appear as the grantor of results and give them fruits of joy and sorrow. When beings offer their ego at your rosy feet and as machines, carry out the acts of your universal, immense, supreme form, you appear as 'destroyer of results' and removing all results of actions, give them the right to liberation.

Verse 16.

durge smṛtā harasi bhītimaśeṣajantoḥ
svasthaiḥ smṛtā matimatīva śubhāṁ dadāsi|
dāridraduḥkhabhayahāriṇi kā tvadanyā
sarvvopakārakaraṇāya sadādrarcittā||

Translation:

Mother! When people remember you falling into danger, you remove fear from all living things. When they remember you in times of contentment, you give them great, beneficial intent. O remover of poverty and sorrow, who else is there, who is so merciful, a beneficiary of all worldly persons?

Explanation:

Mother! When your dear children fall into difficult times, when in trouble or struggling, they see no other means of relief. When all their attempts fail, when their vision is covered by deep, dense clouds of danger, when worldly persons are weakened by fear and terror, under those conditions, in those days of deep distress, they sorrowfully cast their sight at unknown, supreme powers. They are in dark times when there is no one able to help. In those difficult days, they remember you and seek your refuge. So, the mantra says 'remember in difficulty' (*durge smṛtā*).

Even if it be difficult times in the eyes of others, for a worldly person, they are really good ones. As a result of much virtuous action, one gets an opportunity to remember you. When one remembers you, properly remembers you, all dangers immediately pass. When a child cries for you as Mother, can you remain calm for very long? You are forced to come running from the realms of truth when the cries of your poor children reach you. O, Mother! We are overcome just thinking of that figure, my Mother with ruffled hair, clothes disheveled, moving wildly, her heart filled with affection.

Whatever it is, when worldly persons have practice in calling you during danger, they learn to call you when they are calm. Slowly they acquire belief in your existence. When their hearts fill with the belief that 'under all conditions, my propitious, affectionate Mother, always keeps her eyes on me', then there is no more doubt about the existence of Mother. Then beings become free of anxiety. Then there is no more danger. One does not remember anything that can be sorrowful or difficult. As long as one does not acquire faith in the existence of Mother, one cannot be free of anxiety. Without serenity, one has to suffer anxiety. Again, how can one be serene (*svastha*) without finding Self (*sva*)? That Self is Mother.

Mother! Beings learn to call you when in danger, then get used to calling you all the time. Dangers pass and they acquire belief in your existence, they become *svastha*. Even in that condition, calling you continues. There is no more danger, no more desire, yet they call. They remember you because of the attraction in their heart. What do you do then?

'*svasthaiḥ smṛtā matimatīva śubhāṁ dadāsi.*' When one calls on you when they are not anxious, you give them great, good intent. The purity of nature of intelligence is good intent. The intelligence with which we generally move in this world and carry out our daily lives is marred by active and inert tendencies (*rājasa* and *tāmasa*), so it is impure or inauspicious. But Mother, when children without desire, repeatedly call on you, then by your grace, that poverty of intelligence is removed, it becomes pure. When they acquire great, good intent, then your image as Mother who is awareness and bliss, is reflected in it. Beings are honored to discover your nature. Birth, death and delusion are removed forever. Who is there other than you, who is so kind-hearted for her children, other than you? You are our Mother who removes all our poverty, sorrow and fear (*dāridra duḥkha bhaya hāriṇi*). Expressing yourself in this manner, in all worldly persons, you show your immense mercy. Their poverty is removed forever.

We will try to understand more clearly 'one who removes all our poverty, sorrow and fear.' Poverty is the feeling of need or want. If there is want, sorrow is inevitable. Fear comes from sorrow. So, poverty, sorrow and fear are companions. Poverty is a characteristic of spirit. Spirit always seems to hold on to one want or another. All the noise and turmoil in this world is to remove this feeling of want or poverty. However much one can save or enjoy, feelings of new needs always arise in the realm of spirit. The reason that there rises a great sense of poverty is because of this feeling of need. There is not a dearth of things or consumption as much as there is an increase in this feeling of need. It is intelligence that will let one know what will remove this poverty. As long as intelligence is inauspicious, is dull, so long, one cannot know the nature of that which removes want. So, the feeling of want never goes away. This is why we require good intent.

Who will give us that by which, nothing else would be of greater value, residing in which, no amount of sorrow would be able to disturb us anymore? The eternal item of supreme bliss, by which all poverty, sorrow and fear are removed forever, is right intent, a pure spirit of intelligence. In the language of *Upaniṣads,* it may be called intellect (*prajña*). When intellect is illuminated, beings can realize the nature of the spirit of *paramātmā.* Then, poverty, sorrow and fear are removed. Come. Let us tune in with the gods and say, 'Mother! When people remember you, falling into danger, you remove fear from all living things. When persons remember you in time of contentment, you give them great beneficial intent.' Mother! Who else is there but you who is always filled with kindness and affection for our good? You are our all-loving, kind Mother, your heart filled with maternal love and kindness. But Mother, when will we learn to feel your incredible maternity and truly become your children?

Verse 17.

ebhirhatairjagadupaiti sukhaṁ tathaite
kurvantu nāma narakāya cirāya pāpam|
saṁgrāmamṛtyumadhigamya divaṁ prayāntu
matveti nūnamahitānvinihaṁsi devī||

Translation:

O Goddess! When these demons are destroyed, this world will find happiness and the demons will not ever be able to carry out sinful action. On the other hand, being killed in battle by you, they will reach heaven. Thinking of all this, you destroyed the demons.

Explanation:

Mother! If you do good to all, if your spirit is filled with kindness for all, if you do not judge friend or foe, sinner or devout, learned or ignorant, then why did you destroy this host of demons? There are three things to say about this. First, if they are destroyed, the world will be peaceful. Second, these demons will no longer carry out sinful acts and turmoil. Third, being killed in a frontal battle, they will reach heaven. Because of these reasons, you destroyed the demons.

If there was truly something called destruction, if there was properly something called cruelty, then we would see assistance and hindrance, kindness and cruelty as two different characteristics. When all your wishes are auspicious, every action noble, then there can be nothing inauspicious or cruel. As long as we do not understand this, so long, in the view of a material world, do we see assistance and hindrance, kindness and cruelty as two different things in you. This duality will remain with any, differentiating sight. But Mother, from those that you kindly remove this sense of difference, those who understand that there is nothing but you, those who know that creation and destruction are both your divine play, how can they say that you are kind to some and cruel to others?

But even if we look at you with eyes of differentiation, we see that you are Mother, and worldly persons are your children. A mother can never be cruel to her children. But those things that we think to be cruelty, harm, sorrow, poverty and death, what we think to be hindrances or malice, to understand them to be the affection of Mother, we have to especially notice the three intentions in them mentioned before.

The first intent (*jagadupaiti sukhaṁ*) is that when demons are destroyed, this world will find peace. In the physical sense, one can understand that when demons are destroyed, all torment is removed from this world. With a subtle sense, it may be seen that when desires are not allowed to increase and are taken towards dissolution, worldly persons can find true peace, because happiness derived from the satisfaction of desire is less than the disturbances of desire. Happiness from the enjoyment of material things with a disturbed spirit is less than that of happiness from a steady spirit, because of the absence of agitations of desire. Disturbance of the spirit is sorrow and calmness of the spirit is happiness. To be truly happy in this world, the demons, the horde of desires have to be destroyed.

The second intent (*narakāya cirāya pāpam*) is that the host of demons, trying to satisfy their desires all the time, do not suffer torments of hell (*naraka*) forever. The place where humans (*nara*) are very narrow, is called '*naraka*.' People are so involved with tiny things, tiny desires, that they never find proper happiness. So, these need to be destroyed in a frontal battle. This is the third intent for the destruction of the demons. Holding in front, what is true happiness, collecting all tiny desires together and confronting them, destroys impious tendencies.

This is the mystery of the destruction of the demons in frontal battle. Worldly persons are able to discard temporary happiness mixed with sorrow of desires by getting a hint of the joy of immensity (*bhumā*). When my Mother appears in her blissful, supreme form of joy, then all demonic tendencies disappear. That is why the gods say that 'all that is inauspicious is destroyed.' That which is '*ahita*', not for our good, such senses are destroyed and a path for our good is opened. This is the reason for Mother to take the trouble to be involved in a battle.

Verse 18.

dṛṣṭvaiva kinna bhavatī prakaroti bhasma
sarvvāsurānariṣu yatḥ prahiṇoṣi śastram|
lokān prayāntu ripavohapi hi śastrapūtā
itthaṁ matirbhavati teṣvapi tehatisādhvī||

Translation:

Mother! You could have turned the demons into ashes just by looking at them. But instead of doing that, you threw weapons at them. Purified by your weapons, your enemies proceed to superior lands. Oh! Even for your enemies, you have such noble intent.

Explanation:

You are the great power of creation-maintenance-dissolution. By your wish, any host of desires of demons could vanish in a moment. Even then, why did you take the trouble to fight them in battle? Even in this, there is your virtuous intent, your wish for good fortunes. Pierced by weapons thrown by your hand, they will be sanctified, sinless, and will travel to excellent lands. They will merge into your blessed figure. It is with this liberal, virtuous intent that you play these war games. It is surprising how even for your enemies you have such supreme kindness. What we think to be cruelty, is not so. It is mercy in disguise.

O, Mother! When you bless demonic tendencies of worldly persons with your weapons, when you attract masses of tiny desires towards you, when tendencies of spirit lose their delusion of inertness and find a spirit of perception, then they begin to enjoy the pleasure of heaven. This is what the gods are saying respectfully, 'stricken by your weapons and purified, even your enemies travel to superior lands.' Mother, by letting our outward-facing tendencies taste these drops of bliss, you merge them into yourself. Then you exist in your nature as the 'one without second.' Blessed is the discipline of your manner of action.

Verse 19.

khaḍgaprabhānikaravisphuraṇaistathograiḥ
śūlāgrakāntinivahena dṛśohasurāṇām|
yannāgatā vilayamaṁśumadindukhaṇḍa
yogyānanaṁ tava vilokayatāṁ tadetat||

Translation:

Mother! The reason that the sparkle of your scimitar and the rays from the tips of your lance did not blind the demons is because they had seen your incredibly adorned face, like a bright Moon.

Explanation:

Mother! We see that the sparkle of your scimitar and the rays from the tip of your lance did not blind the demons. With subtle vision, we see that the brightness of your scimitar of intellect and the beauty of your lance of knowledge cannot remove demonic sight. Why does this take place? Even by seeing sharpened weapons of pure perception, by whose influence, the host of demons of duality are uprooted, why is demonic view not blinded? In answer to this question, the gods said that 'because they had seen your incredibly adorned face, like a bright Moon.' Because they had looked at your bright face, the sight of the demons was not damaged. Can there be any danger of losing one's sight when one looks at the beauty of the smiling, loving face of Mother? If one realizes the mystery, that the spirit of demons is also that of awareness-bliss-filled Mother and nothing else, then these doubts are removed. Those who want to destroy all demonic percepts and only find your nature of pure perception may look at this mystery with eyes of disdain. Let them do it. But if they look at this calmly, they will also clearly declare that after seeing the face of Mother, the sight of the demons remains, and only with time it disappears slowly. Mother, let your dear children understand that even when demonic sight remains, one may be fortunate to see the beauty of your merciful face. Even evil persons can show one-minded adoration for you. Can one adore you with one mind without ever seeing you? But that is something else.

Mother! From the example of the Moon, we may arrive at the same truth. In the common view, it is seen as rays of the Moon, but in principle, it is seen that the rays are not of the Moon, but of the Sun. It is the rays of the Sun, reflected by the Moon that are seen as rays of the Moon. In the same manner, that which we think to be the viewpoint of demons or demonic perception is also empowered by your nature. They are expressed by your expression, they have no separate nature. For those who can perceive this properly, the disappearance of demonic vision is equal to its presence. Only you as life force is expressed as gods and demons. We are cheated because we are engrossed by outer form and do not see you. O blessed Mother, remove our delusion, arouse our beneficent sight, establish us in life force.

Verse 20.

durvṛttavṛttaśamanaṁ tava devī śīlaṁ
rūpaṁ tathaitadavicintyamatulyamanyaiḥ|
vīryañca hantṛ hṛtadevaparākramāṇāṁ
vairiṣvapi prakaṭitaiva dayā tvayettham||

Translation:

O Goddess! Your nature is to suppress the propensity of the wicked. Your beauty is beyond thought. Your valor in destroying the demons who defeated the gods, and your kindness even to enemies, can only be compared to you and no one else.

Explanation:

O, Mother! As long as inclinations (*vṛtti*) of spirit are present or engrossed in all that is transient, so long they are wicked (*durvṛtta*). As long as you who is the nature of existence is forsaken and vibrations of material things appear in the spirit, so long inclinations are wicked. But your nature is to completely suppress the wicked. Your action is to destroy all evil (*vināśāya ca duṣkṛtaṁ*[22]). How is this accomplished? Seeing your beauty, the wicked are suppressed; '*rūpaṁ tathaitadavicintyam*' your beauty cannot be imagined. Thinking is a characteristic of the spirit. When your beauty is expressed, there is no such thing as spirit, cannot be. So, there is no thought. The wicked are easily suppressed. This is your nature.

Spiritual seeker, have you ever seen that form beyond form? You may not be engrossed by forms that are divided and bounded, but if you dive into the ocean of form which is beyond form, you will surely be mesmerized. Being enchanted by some mere material form, people throw away relatives, heritage and honor. Standing in front of this undivided form that is the nature of sweetness, life and love, how can one not be mesmerized? Come, let us all leap into this incredible ocean of form of Mother. Our thirst will be quenched forever. All evil will be suppressed. But that is something else.

Mother, reveal this mystery to those who do not believe that just by seeing you, tendencies of spirit are calmed. They try to suppress them using various methods. When one calls on you as Mother, as life force, as Self, then your incredible form is expressed. That form is so appealing, so limitless and beyond language, that when it is expressed, spirit is charmed by it and evil is removed. My formless Mother is with no alternate, beyond thought! When you appear, all perceptions, all material matters disappear.

Not only your beauty, but your valor can suppress the inclinations of the wicked. Only you can destroy demonic tendencies that turn divine percepts powerless. By focusing on your immense valor, supreme power that accomplishes creation-

---

22 *Bhāgavat Gitā,* 4:8

maintenance-dissolution of the world, one can without effort, stop inclinations of spirit.

Mother! Those who cannot imagine your formless form, that is, those who cannot stand in front of you holding on to the nature of 'truth, knowledge and blissful *Brahmaṇ*' [23], this advice about your immense valor is for them. They will hold on to your characteristic as 'from which birth, living and dissolution take place' [24] and stand in front of this playful supreme power. With this, inclinations of spirit are easily stopped. Those who are unable to do even this, are reminded of your incomparable kindness. She who is not reluctant to shower kindness even on her enemies, she is Mother, we are her children. We can never be defrauded of your kindness. Mother, if one stands with simplicity and knowledge of the truth, in front of your immense kindness that is strewn all over this world, this always perceived, clearly expressed compassion, then inclinations of spirit are stopped. Demons are destroyed.

Mother, in this manner, if one takes shelter in your form, your power or your kindness, then disturbed spirit is shut down, wicked inclinations easily calmed. So, the gods said, 'Mother, your nature is to quieten the inclinations of the wicked.' All these are incomparable. No other spiritual effort, no other method can be compared to it. So, the mantra says 'without comparison' (*atulyamanyaiḥ*).

O, Mother! We are your younger children. For us, this third piece of advice is most appropriate. We are begging for your grace. We will try to be engrossed by the universal form of your kindness. We will sit down, calling you Mother and looking at your face, that one day you will show yourself, one day we will feel your kindness. Then, our wickedness will be calmed. Then, without effort, we will reach your valor or your intrinsic characteristic. Finally, you will appear in your formless form, as Self, as truth-knowledge-bliss natured *Brahmaṇ*. Our calling you Mother will be worthwhile. We will happily cry 'hail to Mother'

---

23 *satyaṁ jñānam ānandaṁ brahma*, *Taittiriya Upaniṣad*, 2.1.1

24 *janmadāsya yataḥ*, *Brahmaṇ Sutra*, 1.1

and go beyond birth and death, happiness and sorrow. Mother, when will that day come?

Verse 21.

kenopamā bhavatu tehasya parākramasya
rūpañca śatrubhayakāryatihāri kutra|
citte kṛpā samaraniṣṭhuratā ca dṛṣṭā
tvayyeva devī varade bhuvanatrayehapi||

Translation:

O Goddess! What is comparable to your valor? This immensely beautiful form appears fearsome to enemies. There is grace in your heart, yet cruelty in battle. In all three worlds, this can be seen only in you.

Explanation:

Mother, you are the great power of creation-maintenance-dissolution of infinite universes. It is superfluous to say that there is nothing comparable to your valor. On the other hand, in this world, what is known as strength is applied on the weak. If the weak do not shed tears, then strength is not meaningful. But, Mother, your strength is the opposite of this. The result of your valor is the showering of your infinite grace, even on enemies. So, there is no comparison of the valor in this world to yours.

Then, your form is incomparable. Fearsome and attractive, these two opposing characteristics are present in you together. Nowhere in the world are such opposing characteristics able to be present together. Only in you, is it possible to be at the same time, frightening for enemies and joyful for your children.

The enemies, disturbances of spirit due to active principle, trying to immerse in your formless ocean of form, fearfully merge into it. On the other hand, the hearts of spiritual seekers, seeing the emergence of this unimaginable form, are filled with incredible joy. Mother, your spirit is filled with supreme grace, but outside there is the cruelty of battle. You wield sharp weapons to destroy enemies. Such opposing characteristics are present only in you. Your younger children see only cruelty in illness, sorrow, torture, torment, grief and poverty that are in this world. But those who have been nurtured at your affectionate breast, are honored to see both grace and harshness in your spirit. They see that you hide yourself in a severe cloak of cruelty in battle but shower infinite grace on all your children. Under all conditions, they are happy to imbibe the unending bliss of your grace.

Verse 22.

trailokyametadakhilaṁ ripunāśanena
trātaṁ tvayā samaramūrdhani tehapi hatvā|
nītā divaṁ ripugaṇā bhayamapyapāstam
asmākamunmadasurāribhavaṁ namaste||

Translation:

Mother, you saved all this world by destroying its enemies. You sent the enemies to heaven by killing them in battle, while removing our fears. Mother, we bow down to you.

Explanation:

Mother! By completing these actions for all who are in this world, your name as the nature of kindness becomes meaningful. Peace in all three worlds, heaven for the demons and removal of our fears, these are your three actions. These are the outer effects of your kindness. For many lifetimes, we have been attacked by desire and anger, tormented by demons of stored tendencies. You appeared sword in hand, on the battlefield of the heart and destroyed these demons. Strong tendencies of dread of these demons that were in our hearts, the fear that contracted us, prevented us from calling on you. We used to think that while there was desire and anger, while the spirit was gloomy, while we were within a family, we would be unable to call you. Today, forced by affection for your children, you have removed our anxieties. Limitations of life have been removed. Demonic disturbances of spirit due to stored tendencies are gone. Those that were inimical to union with

Mother, those who we nurtured as enemies, we see, that showered by your affection, they are purified and are merging into you. By your unending kindness, they reach heaven. We see that those that were one day creating trouble in the three worlds with their torment, have now become your ornaments and the disturbances of the three worlds have been removed. (The torment of the three worlds has been explained before.) You are ready to liberate this universe, that preparation is on all around. You are beyond thought and language, undivided, yet you have to appear as a tiny form, in the heart of each being. Your kindness is beyond words and thought. What else do we have Mother? We bow down to you, '*namaste, namaste, namaste.*'

Verse 23.

śūlena pāhi no devi pāhi khaḍgena cāmbike|
ghaṇṭāsvanena naḥ pāhi cāpajyāniḥsvanena ca||

Verse 24.

prācyāṁ rakṣa pratīcyāñca caṇḍike rakṣa dakṣiṇe|
bhrāmaṇenātmaśūlasya uttarasyāṁ tatheśvari||

Translation:

O Goddess! Protect us with your lance, scimitar, the sound of your bell and the twang of your bowstring. O *Caṇḍika*! O, Goddess! Wave that lance of Self and protect us in the East, West, North and South.

Explanation:

Mysteries of lance, scimitar, bell and bow have been explained in detail before. There is no need to mention them again.

A spiritual seeker should look and see that East, West, North, South, the power of Mother and her call are present everywhere. Specific knowledge and primal sound (*nāda*) exist everywhere as material things. Come, like *Indra* and the other gods, let us also pray to Mother pitifully, with simplicity. Mother, protect us with your lance, scimitar, the sound of your bell, the twang of your bowstring and all your other weapons. Wherever we lay our eyes, we see impenetrable dense forms of inertness. Protect us from these demons of inertness. In thousands of discussions, we forget that it is only you who resides on all sides as life force. We are repeatedly tormented by inertness and so suffer the burden of millions of births and deaths. Mother! Protect us from this danger. Where ever we lay our eyes, may we see the form of Mother. May we no longer be burnt by the triple poison of percepts and desire for material things. Mother! Use all your power to remove our perceptions of this inertness.

Verse 25.

saumyāni yāni rūpāṇi trailokye vicaranti te|
yāni cātyarthaghorāṇi tai rakṣāsmāṁstathā bhuvam||

Verse 26.

khaḍgaśūlagadādīni yāni cāstrāni tehambike|
karapallavasaṅgīni tairasmān rakṣa sarvataḥ||

Translation:

Mother! Protect us in your tranquil and terrible forms that exist in these three worlds. O *Amvikā*! Protect us with your scimitar, lance, mace and the other weapons that adorn your hands.

Explanation:

Mother! Your presence can be seen in this world in two forms, one tranquil, the other terrible. When you sit with us on your lap, with all earthly and other worldly riches, may we not forget this touch of kindness. May we not be engrossed by the enjoyment of worldly desires, other-worldly powers or joys of heaven. Mother! In your tranquil form, you must protect us from this engrossment. May it not disappear from our hearts even momentarily, that it is you who appear as all pleasure. Again, when sorrow, misfortune and darkness come, when we are tormented by illness, grief, poverty, maltreatment and fear of death, may we understand that it is you holding us in your fearsome form. At that time, may we not be afraid of seeing your terrifying form, not be exhausted and not have doubts about your existence, about your motherhood. However hostile nature may appear to be, may we not have a shred of doubt that you are truly our Mother. O, Mother. This cycle of life is ever-changing. It is always undergoing changes of happiness and sorrow and always will. These are expressions of your tranquil and terrible forms. Protect us with both these forms. Not only us, protect all beings in this world. Protect them all, '*tathā bhuvam*.' Paint in the hearts of every worldly person that it is you who appears as happiness and sorrow. This is called protection. Under no condition should we think that we are motherless. Apply whatever weapons you need to get this done. O Mother, who holds all weapons, apply all your weapons to protect us. Protect us from everything, '*rakśa sarvvataḥ*.' Protect us from the multiplicity of percepts. Establish us in truth that there is no multiplicity of percepts, it is you, existence-awareness-bliss, who appears as all percepts. Be established in the hearts of beings, as great knowledge, that under all conditions we have refuge in truth, we are established in truth. Establish this. May all fear be removed from this world forever.

Verse 27.

ṛṣiruvāca|
evaṁ stutā surairddivyaiḥ kusumairnandanodbhavaiḥ|
arcitā jagatāṁ dhātrī tathā gandhānulepanaiḥ||

Verse 28.

bhaktyā samastaistridaśairddivyairdhū paistu dhūpitā|
prāha prasādasumukhī samastān praṇatān surān||

Translation:

The sage said, "In this manner, singing the praises of Mother who holds the world, the gods worshipped her with flowers from a heavenly garden, perfume and unguents. With devotion, they all offered the Goddess divine incense. Pleased the Goddess began to speak to the host of gods."

Explanation:

Indra and the other gods, with their praises, perfumes, flowers and incense, worshipped the supreme power of the one who holds this universe. With spiritual sight, one can see that consciousness seated in the senses worships the Mother of this universe, with flowers of blissful, pure percept, burning incense of knowledge and action, in a fire of conscience, and unguents of respect, renunciation and purity. Pleased with such worship, the Goddess is ready to bestow her blessings. Here it may not be inappropriate to say a few words about ceremonial worship (*pujā*).

Bhāgavat Gitā says, 'leaves, flowers, fruits, water, whatever my devotee offers'.[25] In *Devī Māhātmya* there is mention of worship with leaves and flowers in many places. Other than this, all histories, *saṁhitās* and ancient texts mention ceremonial worship. However, elsewhere it has been said that 'external worship is worse than the worst.' Some, under the influence of such advice, discard all ceremonial action and try to meet Supreme Self only by meditation. What should we understand about this?

We should understand that as long as there is eating and sleeping, as long as there is a sense of support and disruption, knowledge of important and unimportant, so long, external worship will continue. One cannot just discard it by getting rid of flowers and leaves. But one has also to be attentive that it is not conducted just as an external ritual. It is true that external worship is worse than the worst. *Śrutis* say, 'those who worship gods with a divisive knowledge that the worshipped is one and worshipper another, are but sacrificial animals for the gods.' The Lord has said, 'it is not legitimate when one worships other gods.' Worship with knowledge of divisiveness is external worship. As long as there is a strong sense of 'external', one does not acquire rights to worship. When one is established in the knowledge that there is nothing external, 'all is inside', then there is no external worship. Just repeating these words, does not work. One has to perceive this world as internal. Spiritual effort and adoration are

25 *Bhāgavat Gitā,* 9:26

to remove this divisive knowledge of internal and external. By carrying out ceremonial worship to a physical form, a divisive sense of external-internal may be removed. There does not seem to be easier methods than this for the simultaneous practice of knowledge, devotion and action. If there were, the sages would not have introduced the worship of form (*murtti*) in this land. But that is another matter.

As long as this divisive knowledge of internal and external is not removed, one does not even know the gods, so who will one worship? 'One cannot conduct worship without having acquaintance with the gods.' On the other hand, 'when one is acquainted with the gods, one does not desire to conduct formal worship.' So, from both sides, it is not possible to carry out formal worship (*pujā*). By conducting worship with a divisive knowledge of worshipper and worshipped, it becomes ignorant worship by the lowly. When one worships with the feeling that the one worshipped is life force, it is me, such worship never fails. Beginning to worship with a sense of division in the undivided, slowly weakens senses of division. There are interruptions, rules are ignored and prescribed sequences are forgotten. One offers flowers in place of incense, yet there appear results of complete worship. The *śāstras* say, 'perception of the gods can make one forget sequences of worship. Even with such obstructions, the results of worship are complete.'

Even today, millions of people in this land carry out ceremonial worship. I am not saying that these are without any results. But it can be seen that after doing this for a long time, many do not feel that they are making any progress. They conduct worship like any other daily activity. Those who are carrying out such a performance for greed or wealth, are a separate issue. Why does this happen? Why can one not find knowledge and devotion by carrying out worship? It is because of a lack of acquaintance. One is not acquainted with the one for whom *pujā* is performed. 'Who is that one? I do not know. Where and how does it exist? That also I do not know. Because it has to be done, to keep up the practice, I perform *pujā*.' Because one has feelings of this sort, worship does not bring proper results. These things have been discussed in a book called 'Principles of worship' (*pujā tattva*).

Daily acts of worship, fire ceremonies and others have been turned into a lifeless set of actions. It appears that in this land, if these actions are established on bright knowledge and superior devotion (*parābhakti*), so that they acquire life, then laments, poverty and torment would be removed. Once one tastes the pure nectar of *dharma*, people cannot continue without it. When one is not without *dharma*, happiness is easily found. This responsibility is mainly dependent on *brahmiṇs*, because, they directly or indirectly have kept alive all these special acts. It is they who will establish life in the lifeless skeleton of acts and turn them lively and successful. They will again stand in an ideal immensity (*bhumā*) and holding all people of this earth, turn them all towards *dharma*, filling all with action. All acts will turn towards knowledge. Knowledge will be revived in a stream of superior devotion. The kingdom of this earth will turn into a kingdom of *dharma*. Untruth will vanish and truth will be established. It is with this hope that our Mother stands in front of us with her hand held in a posture of assurance.

A spiritual aspirant can see that Mother, pleased by this worship is ready to grant our desires. If one worships in this fashion and is ready to bow down, my Mother is pleased. Do not think that she is only pleased by the worship of the gods. She accepts with great affection even worship and obeisance of children like us who are without devotion, respect, or knowledge, who are weak and unbelieving. Even in this age of disbelief, she appears and caresses her children with assurances of courage. Come all, come spiritual seekers, let all of us who are without mantra, without action, fall at the feet of Mother, calling on her. Our Mother will be pleased.

Verse 29.

devyuvāca|
vriyatāṁ tridaśāḥ sarvve yadasmattohabhivāñcitam||

Verse 30.

devā ūcuḥ
bhagavatyā kṛtaṁ sarvvaṁ na kiñcidavaśiṣyate|
yadayaṁ nihataḥ śatrurasmākaṁ mahiṣāsuraḥ||

Translation:

The Goddess said, "O gods, ask from me whatever you wish for." The gods replied, "Everything has been accomplished by Goddess *Bhagabati*, there is nothing that remains, because our enemy Mahiṣasura has been destroyed."

Explanation:

This is what happens. When Mother appears and is ready to grant our wishes, then the children say, "Mother, there is nothing that we want. There is nothing left for us to want. We have no more needs. The one who is complete has appeared. We have nothing more to ask for. Only you remain. Stay in front of us forever. We have nothing more to ask for, our hearts are full. Searching the depths of our insides, we find no needs." '*na kiñcidavaśiṣyate*', nothing more remains.

All spiritual seekers reach this state. Whatever desires and wishes they may have when beginning worship, once they see Mother, they remember nothing. Then they think that they have got everything, what else could they ask for? The same thing happened to the young *yogi Dhruba*. He began *sādhanā* with the desire for a kingdom, but when he saw the lotus-eyed one, he said, "Looking for glass, I have found divine nectar, I have nothing more to ask for."

Do not think that this happens only rarely to some lucky individuals. Not so. Everyone, every day can find proximity with the divine and enjoy totality. There is nothing unnatural or impossible in this. God is manifest everywhere. One can see this just by wishing to do so. You hear that seeing God, takes spiritual effort for a long time. The significance of that is different. To raise the desire 'I want to see God', takes spiritual effort for a long time, not only a long time, but many lifetimes. If anyone even has a tinge of such desire, then it is achieved very soon. But that is something else.

There is another hidden meaning in this mantra. If the '*na*' in the first line is moved to the beginning, then the meaning is different. Mother, you have done much for us, but not everything is finished, a little bit remains. The state of worldly person does not end with the demise of *Mahiṣāsura*. It is necessary to destroy the demon *Śumbha*. So, the gods say that 'a little is bit is left.'

Verse 31.

yadi cāpi varo deyastvayāsmākaṁ maheśvari|
saṁsmṛtā saṁsmṛtā tvaṁ no hiṁsethāḥ paramāpadaḥ||

Verse 32.

yaśca martyaḥ stavairebhistvāṁ stoṣyatyamalānane|
tasya vittarddhirvibhavairdhanadārādisampadām|
vṛddhayehasmat prasannā tvaṁ bhavethāḥ sarvvadāmbike||

Translation:

O, *Maheśvari*! If you want to grant us our wishes, then do this, may we be able to call on you always and as a result may all our great dangers be removed. O beautiful-eyed one! O, *Amvikā*! May you be always pleased and grant knowledge, wealth, property and children to those who praise you with such hymns.

Explanation:

When her children see Mother, they become overwhelmed with joy and surprise. They do not find anything they need to ask for. But Mother knows all their wants and grievances. There is nothing that can be hidden from her all-seeing eyes. So, Mother arouses in the hearts of her children their forgotten needs. This is exactly what occurs. At their first meeting, spiritual seekers forget all wants and needs, because Mother is the nature of completeness. Then, as this feeling slowly fades, as Mother becomes nonmanifest, needs reappear. This is the asking for favors. One has to understand that standing in front of Mother, when thoughts of any needs arise, they will be fulfilled quickly. Mother is so engrossed by affection for her children, that even without voicing anything, their hidden needs in their hearts are fulfilled. She honors them by granting them their wishes indiscriminately. We are such ungrateful children, that finding the one who is inaccessible to the meditation of *Brahmā*, *Viṣṇu* and *Maheśvara*, we bring to her inconsequential wants and grievances. Mother, when will this narrowness of our hearts be removed? Come, like the gods, let us say, 'may we always be able to remember you, and may you always remove our great obstacles.'

We should understand the word '*paramāpada*' to mean great danger. Whatever is an obstacle to our realization of the supreme is *parmāpada*. Whatever is an obstacle to the state of supreme realization, 'I will reside in the nature of *paramātmā*' is *paramāpada*. In other words, forgetting Mother is *paramāpada*. There is no other greater misfortune for us than this. Mother is close to us, yet forgetting her, we are happy with the grime of this world. What greater danger can there be but this? So, we pray, may we remember you always, and as a result, may all our obstacles be removed.

Another thing, Mother, if you are truly pleased with us, may the results of that pleasure spread all over this world. May everyone in the world be honored to see your smiling face, your form as affectionate *Amvikā*. Let those who are considered by common people to be wicked, also be able to realize your eternal pleasure by singing such praises and hymns. As a result, let them enjoy worldly wealth, family and knowledge. Even though the world of beings is mortal, have the property of death, let them enjoy by your grace, a taste of immortality. Appear in this manner in the hearts of all, in the form of one who bestows desires and liberation, the ever pleased *Amvikā*. Let the cries of sorrow of this world end forever.

Look, your children do not know how to fulfill their desires, let alone find liberation. Just with hopes of satisfying their desires and acquiring things, they are tormented with fears of destruction and want. From a beggar in a shanty who is always hungry, to wealthy ones in palaces feeding on delicacies, all are needy. No one enjoys the satisfaction of their desires. When they consume a portion of it, they only get some satisfaction. They collect materials of their desires by intense effort but do not know how to enjoy them. Mother, so I say, stand before us in your form as satisfaction. For once, let the children fill their hearts enjoying the satisfaction of the affection of Mother. With true knowledge, may the intense hunger of this world be satisfied. Then, you can easily appear in your form for bestowing other-worldly desires and grant immortality to worldly persons.

Mother! Our tiny hearts do not have much to ask for. You have not left out anything that we have asked for. We bow at your feet and pray for the good fortune for all this world.

Verse 33.

ṛṣiruvāca|
iti prasāditā devairjagatoharthe tathātmanaḥ|
tathetyuktvā bhadrakālī babhūvāntarhitā nṛpa||

Verse 34.

ityetat kathitaṁ bhūpa sambhūtā sā yathā purā|
devī devaśarīrebhyo jagattrayahitaiṣiṇī||

Translation:

The sage said "O, king Suratha! In this manner, the gods pleased the Goddess for the world and you. Goddess *Bhadrakāli* saying 'so be it' disappeared. O, king! The manner in which the Goddess, who brought good fortune to the three worlds, appeared from the bodies of gods has been described for you."

Explanation:

From times eternal, the gods have sung such praises to the Goddess, to please her and for the benefit of this world. What is beneficial to the world is also good for the gods. It is Self that is expressed as this world and acts out the play of suffering triple sorrows. It is necessary to please *ātmā* to remove this sorrow; *ātmā*, Mother is eternally complete, eternally pleased. Understanding that there is no sorrow in it, is the attainment of pleasure of Self. This brings benefits to the world. We see that because of the gods, the Goddess is pleased. The gods ask for the good fortune of this world, and Mother saying 'so be it' vanishes.

This is not imaginary, not fiction. This is completely true. Just as it takes place in the heart of each individual being, in the assemblage, the gods try to please Mother for the benefit of this world. If it has not taken place in your heart, but you are keen to see it happen, seek it with simplicity. Pray to Mother. You will find this place of great union. What is the harm in purifying the heart by becoming a part of this divine play of the gods?

The intellectual formed *guru* Medhasa now said to king Suratha, "O king, you were interested in knowing about the origin, actions and nature of *Mahāmāyā*. In that connection, you have seen her appear as *Mahākālī* in her dark form to destroy *Madhu* and *Kaiṭabha*. Now you have seen how *Mahāmāyā* appeared from the bodies of the gods, in her active form as *Mahālakṣmī*, for the benefit of the three worlds and rips apart the bonds of action of worldly persons. But this is not yet finished.

Verse 35.

punaśca gaurīdehā sā samudbhūtā yathābhavat|
vadhāya duṣṭadaityānāṁ tathā śumbhaniśumbhayoḥ||

Verse 36.

rakṣaṇāya ca lokānāṁ devānāmupakāriṇī|
tacchṛṇuṣva mayākhyātaṁ yathāvat kathayāmi te||
*iti mārkaṇḍeyapurāṇe sāvarṇike man*vantare *devīmāhātmye śakrādistuti|*

Translation:

In time, I will tell you how *Mahāmāyā* appeared again as *Gourī* to destroy the wicked demons *Śumbha*, *Niśumbha* and others, to protect all people and help the gods. You should listen to that with great attention.

Here ends this episode of praise by the gods in *Devī Māhātmya*, in the era of *Sāvarṇi*, in *Mārkeṇḍeya Purāṇa.*

Explanation:

Mahāmāyā will have to appear again in the form of *Gourī*, the fair one. Even now, the knot of *Rudra* in worldly persons has not been pierced. Even now, the evil demons *Śumbha* and *Niśumbha* and their companions are alive. The gods are not free from danger. People are not safe and a kingdom of *dharma* has not been established. So, Mother has to appear again. She will have to appear as *Gourī*, the calm, peaceful form, residing in the heart of *Maheśvara*. Come Suratha, come all, prepare to see this fair form of Mother. Purify and clean the seat of your heart. Mother is coming, see that she does not have to sit on a dusty seat. Do not try to put on torn apparel of past tendencies on her pure body. Calmly, with a patient heart, wait for that auspicious day. Truly, Mother will reappear.

The knot of the mental body (*manomaya koṣa*) has been pierced. Delusion in the shape of names has been shed. That the forms of name are nothing but Mother has been perceived and understood. The constant torment of new desires has been removed. One is established in truth. Now the knot of life force (*prāṇa*) is also torn. One has understood that it is *prāṇa* that appears in the shape of names. life force is no longer felt to be narrow, unexpressed awareness. One has perceived that everywhere, one's life force is that of Mother, of *guru*. The knot of *Viṣṇu* or *prāṇa* has been torn. One sees that all material things are forms of *prāṇa*. Now one feels *prāṇa* to be a universal existence. So, the special affection or liking for forms with names is removed. Like burnt seeds, the stored tendencies of actions are unable to germinate and produce new fruit. A spiritual seeker is now established in *prāṇa*, in consciousness.

Now we will approach the knot formed by knowledge. This is the last bond in a state as a worldly person. If by the grace of Mother, it is torn, then the darkness of ignorance will be removed. The wide nature of beings will be illuminated. Suratha, you have called on Mother and with the yoga of surrender leaped into the ocean of liberation. Two waves have passed over you. The prides of the physical and subtle bodies have been removed. Only one more is left. By the grace of Mother, you will cross this with ease. You will be established in bliss.

Come spiritual seeker, come all worldly persons, let us go forward together calling on Mother. Let us bow down at the feet of the one, who holding us to her loving heart, saves us from the torment of the terrible demons and is taking us to a temple of bliss. What else do we have but our obeisance? Let us lower our high head of arrogance and say, 'we bow down to you a thousand times, we bow down to you, again and again.'

❍ ❍ ❍

Here ends the piercing of the knot of *Viṣṇu* in *Sādhan Samar*, a commentary on *Devī Māhātmya*.

Brahmarṣi Satyadeva

Brahmarṣi Satyadeva (Saratcandra Bandhopdhyāyā), was born in 1883, in the village of Navagrām in Bariṣāl district in what is presently Bāngladesh. He was given the honorific Brahmarṣi for his exalted spiritual attainment. Brahmarṣi passed away in 1932. Sādhan Samar is an enlightened and much-admired spiritual interpretation of Devī Māhātmyain Bengali. It was written by Satyadeva in the early 1900s and first published from Calcutta in 1920.